GLOBALIZATION FROM BELOW

D1554851

"The word globalization summons up images of transnational corporations and internet-savvy human rights campaigners. This important book brings to our attention a wholly different and quite fascinating phenomenon – vast webs of traders, travelers, and marketers, crossing borders and transforming economies and societies from the bottom up."

Josiah Heyman, *University of Texas at El Paso, USA*

This book explores globalization as actually experienced by most of the world's people, buying goods from street vendors brought by traders moving past borders and across continents under the radar of the law. The dimensions and practices of "globalization from below" are depicted and analyzed in detail by a team of international scholars. The chapters provide intimate portrayals of routes, markets and people in locations across the globe and explore theories that can help make sense of these complex and fascinating case studies. The book will be invaluable for students of globalization, economic anthropology and developing-world economics.

Gordon Mathews is Professor in the Department of Anthropology at the Chinese University of Hong Kong. His books include *Global Culture / Individual Identity: Searching for Home in the Cultural Supermarket* (2000) and *Ghetto at the Center of the World: Chungking Mansions, Hong Kong* (2011).

Gustavo Lins Ribeiro is Professor of Anthropology at the University of Brasilia and Research Fellow of Brazil's National Council of Scientific and Technological Development. His books include *Transnational Capitalism and Hydropolitics in Argentina* (1994) and *World Anthropologies* (2006, edited with Arturo Escobar).

Carlos Alba Vega is Professor and Researcher at El Colegio de Mexico. He has been a Visiting Fellow at universities in Mexico, France, Germany and the United States.

GLOBALIZATION FROM BELOW

The World's Other Economy

Edited by
Gordon Mathews, Gustavo Lins Ribeiro and
Carlos Alba Vega

LONDON AND NEW YORK

First published in 2012
by Routledge
2 Park Square, Milton Park, Abingdon, Oxon OX14 4RN

Simultaneously published in the USA and Canada
by Routledge
711 Third Avenue, New York, NY 10017

Routledge is an imprint of the Taylor & Francis Group, an informa business

British Library Cataloguing in Publication Data
A catalogue record for this book is available from the British Library

Library of Congress Cataloging in Publication Data
Globalization from below : the world's other economy / edited by Gordon
Mathews, Gustavo Lins Ribeiro, and Carlos Alba Vega.
p. cm.
Includes bibliographical references and index.
(ebk) 1. Small business. 2. Globalization. I. Mathews, Gordon. II. Ribeiro,
Gustavo Lins. III. Alba Vega, Carlos.
HD2340.8.G56 2012
337–dc23
2012003472

ISBN: 978-0-415-53508-3 (hbk)
ISBN: 978-0-415-53509-0 (pbk)
ISBN: 978-0-203-10600-6 (ebk)

Typeset in Bembo
by Taylor & Francis Books

MIX
Paper from
responsible sources
FSC
www.fsc.org   FSC® C004839

Printed and bound in Great Britain by
CPI Group (UK) Ltd, Croydon, CR0 4YY

CONTENTS

Illustrations

Figures

Tables

NOTES ON CONTRIBUTORS

José Carlos G. Aguiar (PhD University of Amsterdam 2007) is an anthropologist specializing in cultures of illegality, security policies, borders, and minority issues. He has conducted extensive fieldwork in Latin America, and is an assistant professor in the Department of Latin American Studies at Leiden University.

Ritajyoti Bandyopadhyay is a Postdoctoral Fellow at the National Institute of Advanced Studies, Indian Institute of Science, Bangalore. He works on poverty, informality and globalization in contemporary Indian cities.

Mélissa Gauthier is a Visiting Assistant Professor in the Department of Anthropology at Binghamton University. Her publications include a chapter in Brunet-Jailly's (2007) edited collection *Borderlands: Comparing Border Security in North America and Europe* and a chapter in Donnan and Wilson's edited book (2010) *Borderlands: Ethnographic Approaches to Security, Power and Identity.*

Gordon Mathews is a Professor of Anthropology at the Chinese University of Hong Kong. He has written *Ghetto at the Center of the World: Chungking Mansions, Hong Kong* (2011) and *Global Culture / Individual Identity: Searching for Home in the Cultural Supermarket* (2000), among other books.

B. Lynne Milgram is Professor of Anthropology at OCAD University, Toronto, Canada. Her research on gender, development and globalization in the Philippines analyzes the cultural politics of social change with regard to microfinance and to women's work in crafts and in the secondhand clothing trade between the Philippines and Hong Kong.

Olivier Pliez (PhD University of Provence 2000) is a Senior Researcher of Geography at the CNRS research centre LISST (Toulouse, France). He works on transnational trade and migration networks and their relations with urban spaces in the Arab world, especially Algeria, Egypt and Libya.

Fernando Rabossi is Associate Professor of the Cultural Anthropology Department at the Federal University of Rio de Janeiro (UFRJ). He coordinates – with Federico Neiburg – the Culture and Economy Research Group (www.cultura-economia.org).

Gustavo Lins Ribeiro (PhD in Anthropology, City University of New York, 1988) is Professor of Anthropology, University of Brasilia, and Research Fellow of Brazil's National Council of Scientific and Technological Develoment (CNPq). He has been engaged in research on globalization since the 1980s.

Robert Shepherd is an Assistant Professor of Anthropology and International Affairs at the George Washington University in Washington DC, where he teaches courses on international development and human rights. His research focuses on tourism theory, heritage in China, and marketplace behavior.

Alan Smart (PhD University of Toronto, 1986) is Professor, Department of Anthropology, University of Calgary. He is the author of *The Shek Kip Mei Myth: Squatters, Fires and Colonial Rule in Hong Kong, 1950–1963* (2006), and numerous articles.

Josephine Smart (PhD University of Toronto, 1987) is Professor, Department of Anthropology, University of Calgary. She is the co-editor of *Petty Capitalists and Globalization* (2005), and has written numerous articles.

Vera da Silva Telles is Professor of Sociology at the University of São Paulo. She has recently written *A cidade nas fronteiras do legal e illegal* [The city on the borders of the legal and illegal] (2011). Her research deals with urban illegalities, in particular informal markets and markets for illicit drugs, in partnership with researchers at the University of Toulouse, France.

Carlos Alba Vega earned a PhD in Social Sciences from the Ecole des Hautes Etudes en Sciences Sociales, Paris, France, and is Professor and Researcher as well as Member of the Board of El Colegio de Mexico. He has taught and been visiting fellow in universities in Mexico, France, Germany and the United States.

Yang Yang carried out research among African traders in southern China during her Master of Philosophy studies in the Department of Anthropology at the Chinese University of Hong Kong. She currently works as a Field Archaeologist at AECOM.

INTRODUCTION

What is globalization from below?

Gordon Mathews and Carlos Alba Vega

What this book is about

"Globalization from below" is globalization as experienced by most of the world's people. It can be defined as the transnational flow of people and goods involving relatively small amounts of capital and informal, often semi-legal or illegal transactions, often associated with "the developing world" but in fact apparent across the globe. Throughout much of the world today, we don't see the high-end globalization of transnational corporations with their billion-dollar budgets and batteries of lawyers. We instead see the low-end globalization of traders buying used or copy merchandise under the radar of the law, and transporting these goods by container or in their luggage across continents and past borders, to be sold by street vendors at minimal prices with no questions asked. This is business without lawyers and copyrights, run through skeins of personal connections and wads of cash. If we hope to develop an adequate approach to the study of the current world-system, then we need to take globalization from below as seriously as we take globalization from above. This is what this book seeks to do: to map out and depict the dimensions and practices of globalization from below.

There are opposing visions about the activities carried out in globalization from below (Naím 2006). Consider, for example, the copying of goods, or piracy as it is often labeled. On the one hand, we find anti-piracy organizations in various countries responding to the interests of the largest global companies, who are increasingly lobbying their governments for harsher penalties against pirated goods, and engaging in campaigns to delegitimate and criminalize those activities. These organizations may promote the idea that the consumption of these copy products is financing contraband, theft, and even narcotics trafficking. They claim that people who buy pirated goods are causing legally constituted businesses to disappear, job openings to vanish, workers to lose their jobs, and technology to stagnate; they are also holding back the discovery of new talent, and causing "informal commerce" to spread.

On the other hand, it also may be argued, as do most of the authors in this book, that globalization from below exists because it solves problems that globalization from above cannot, in providing employment and sufficient income to acquire goods trumpeted by the media (see Ribeiro 2006). A street peddler said to Alba Vega in Mexico City:

> There are those who come to study this kind of commerce as if it were a problem. It is not a problem, it is a solution. The problem was created elsewhere; we are solving it. These goods get to a lot of people who would not be able to afford them otherwise. Beyond this, we create pressure for prices of the original products to go down.

A Kenyan trader in Hong Kong buying China-made goods told Mathews:

> Nobody in my country can buy an original brand of suit, or an original phone by a famous company. It's too expensive. But […] copies can show them good things. The traders are bringing the world to Africa. They are bringing home goodness!
>
> *(Mathews 2011: 149)*

This kind of analysis supports the idea that globalization from below not only offers cheap merchandise otherwise inaccessible: it also provides employment for millions of people who wouldn't find it anywhere else. From this perspective, globalization from below allows an improvement in the quality of life for millions of consumers and providers, both those working in the formal and in the informal economies of societies across the world (see Karaganis 2011).

Many analysts over the past several decades have discussed the informal economy. Keith Hart (1973), for instance, distinguishes the formal economy, typically involving wage-earning employment, from the informal economy, often involving self-employment. Many analysts and institutions have elaborated on the informal economy, outlining its other attributes: ease of access, support from local resources, family property of businesses, small-scale operation, labor intensivity, adapted technology, skills obtained outside the formal educational system, and unregulated markets (International Labor Office 1972). Hernando de Soto (1987, 2002) has been one of the more noted scholars writing on the informal economy, although his work seems to find more favor among policy makers than among scholars. There has also been Portes, Castells, and Benton's 1989 collection, as well as books by scholars such as Lomnitz (1977) and Tokman (2007) and journalists such as Neuwirth (2011) on workings of the informal economy. Scholars such as Lautier (2007) have set forth criticisms of terms such as "the informal economy" and "the informal sector" as theoretical and analytical concepts.

The chapters in this book do not much use the term "informal economy"; instead we prefer the broader rubric "globalization from below," reflecting the fact that it is not fully possible to distinguish between formal and informal sectors of the economies in different societies. Beyond this, the term "informal economy" is often used in such a way as to implicitly assume separate national economies, each with their own formal and informal sectors. But today, in a world of ever-increasing globalization, this is no longer the case. There are no autonomous national economies but a single global economy (see Arrighi 2005); thus we must speak not of "the informal economy" in this society or that one, but rather of "globalization from below" encompassing all societies. While we who edit this book owe much in our thinking to these earlier treatments mentioned above, we believe that in our contemporary era, a new, more globalized treatment of the topic is required.

This book examines globalization from below on two levels. Part One offers large-scale ethnographic depictions of the routes, nodes, and channels of globalization from below. Part Two then offers more intimate portrayals of the entrepreneurs, traders, and peddlers who participate in and constitute this world.

In this introduction, we first describe briefly what this book is about. We then analyze how globalization from below may best be studied: not through economic statistics, but rather through ethnography. Then we discuss how globalization from below differs from globalization from above, and find parallels as well as contrasts. We then turn to China, the source of so many of the goods of low-end globalization discussed in the chapters of the book, and finally we consider the future of globalization from below.

This book's first chapter, by Olivier Pliez, depicts the transnational trading route, today celebrated as the revival of the Silk Road, between North Africa and China. The logic of this trading route is barely perceptible on a local level, but remains fundamental to the functioning of a global network of trade: the movement of garments and small commodities, bought in Yiwu, China, and transported to Egypt directly or via the Libyan port of Tripoli. This chapter explores this global trade through the anchoring points in these flows—Cairo, Salloum, Tripoli, and Yiwu.

Chapter 2, by José Carlos G. Aguiar uses the concept of "global commodity chains" to consider the 400 million blank CDs that are smuggled into Mexico every year from China, recorded with pirated music and films and sold across the country. Based on ethnographic material gathered in the San Juan de Dios market in Guadalajara, a pivotal Mexican point in the commodity chain of pirate CDs, this chapter unravels the complex strands of this chain.

Chapter 3, by Fernando Rabossi, considers the Paraguayan city of Ciudad del Este, a major center of informal trade in recent decades. The city became by the 1990s the major supply center of imported goods for Brazilian informal traders known as *sacoleiros*, who in turn spread these goods throughout Brazil and the South American continent. This chapter presents a historical account of Ciudad del Este's development as a center of globalization from below, examining and explicating the multiple actors involved in its shaping.

Chapter 4, by Gordon Mathews, turns to Chungking Mansions, a dilapidated building in downtown Hong Kong where African and South Asian traders buy China-made mobile phones and clothing. Chungking Mansions exists because of Hong Kong's ideology of neoliberalism, with its lenient immigration rules. But neoliberalism today is neoliberalism of capital rather than labor. Perhaps a somewhat more just version of neoliberalism may eventually emerge, involving the abolition of borders and a merger of globalization from below with globalization from above, the chapter speculates.

Chapter 5, the final chapter of Part One, by Vera da Silva Telles, examines illegality in the city of São Paulo. The chapter begins with the depiction of a worker struggling to get by on the margins of the law, and then uses her story as a launching pad for exploring the traffic of people, goods, commodities, and wealth across the porous frontiers of what is formal/informal, legal/illegal and licit/illicit. The chapter examines the informal trade circuits of downtown São Paulo in the folds of the legal and the illegal: distinctions which in São Paulo, as elsewhere, no longer have a clear meaning.

Part Two begins with Alan and Josephine Smart in chapter 6, depicting Hong Kong petty capitalists investing in China. Hong Kong small investors who established factories in China in the 1980s played an important role in generating the export-oriented manufacturing miracle that has since transformed the world. Recently, however, they have become marginalized, a decline that has had a significant impact on the processes through which China-made goods are distributed throughout the world.

Chapter 7, by Lynne Milgram, examines how Filipina entrepreneurs travel to Hong Kong to purchase used clothing. Because importing used clothing into the Philippines for resale is illegal, and because these Filipina entrepreneurs are not Hong Kong residents, their trade is continually threatened. These cross-border Filipina entrepreneurs, small-scale actors working under the radar between Hong Kong and the Philippines, engender the fabric of globalization from below.

Mélissa Gauthier, in chapter 8, looks at Mexican traders on the El Paso/Ciudad Juarez border. Around all of Mexico's border-crossing points, there is a system of smuggling from the United States called *fayuca* or *comercio hormiga*, the "ant trade." This chapter examines the working lives of Mexican "ant traders," who regularly smuggle small amounts of goods across the Mexican border for resale on the other side. It follows their journey across the Rio Grande, and discusses Mexico's new border inspection system, and its implications for the livelihoods of these traders.

Chapter 9, by Yang Yang, examines how Nigerian traders have flooded into Guangzhou, China's "world factory." These traders purchase counterfeit Nike shoes, Adidas T-shirts, Sony audio sets, and brand-name mobile phones in bulk and ship or carry the products back to their home countries. Some have become wealthy, while others, less successful, overstay and become illegal. This chapter looks at the economic activities of individual African traders in Guangzhou and how they are related to the larger picture of China–Africa trade.

Chapter 10, by Ritajyoti Bandyopadhyay, examines the relation between street hawkers and the new malls springing up in Calcutta (Kolkata). Hawkers are often portrayed as representing the "premodern" past, as opposed to the consumer-paradise modernity of shopping malls, but this chapter shows how the relationship between hawkers and malls is more complicated. Hawkers criticize but also utilize the malls, and their own business may increase because of malls—consumers often marvel at the expensive goods in malls and then buy the cheaper, copy goods that hawkers offer.

Robert Shepherd's chapter 11 analyzes how, in Washington DC's Eastern Market, local vendors and community leaders seek to counter the presence of a diverse array of immigrant vendors. Far from celebrating marketplace diversity, they instead have sought to restrict the presence of immigrant vendors and imported goods by emphasizing authenticity and localism over the "cheap" and "foreign." Globalization from below is countered by globalization from above not through legal or economic pressure but through an ideological smokescreen proclaiming "you don't belong here."

Chapter 12, by Carlos Alba Vega examines the street peddlers of Mexico City's center in their economic practices and political organization. Street peddling expanded after the opening of Mexico to foreign merchandise since the mid-1980s, and today is practiced by some 400,000 people in the city, 20,000 in its center, selling copy, genuine, and smuggled goods. The political leaders of these groups, often women who grew up in poverty, bring together the worlds of formality and informality, legality and illegality, in creating a place for the vulnerable denizens of globalization from below at the table of the politically powerful.

The book's conclusion, by Gustavo Lins Ribeiro, offers, on the basis of the chapters in this book and of his previous works on the subject (Ribeiro 2006, 2009, 2010) a fuller analysis of what globalization from below consists of. He begins by discussing copies and their pivotal position in the relation between globalization from below and globalization from above, and then turns to "the non-hegemonic world-system." He then examines street markets and transfrontier border areas as pivotal sites through which to comprehend and theorize globalization from below, before returning again to the issue of copies and "superlogos."

This, then, is what this book is about. But before proceeding to its different chapters, let us offer a more detailed analysis of some of the themes apparent in the chapters that follow.

Investigating globalization from below

Globalization from below is difficult to fully comprehend. Globalization from above can be grasped through statistics: corporate sales figures and national economic indicators of various sorts. Globalization from below, by definition, provides no such data; it can't be measured through economic statistics because there are no such reliable statistics, only rough estimates. Because globalization from below is below the radar of the state, and of multinational institutions, it is also beyond the reach of their apparatuses of economic measurement. Formal economists cannot know globalization from below from their figures; they can only guess.

This leaves other social scientists, those who typically work closer to the ground: those anthropologists, sociologists, and geographers who engage in ethnography, the detailed examination of people in their daily lives and livings. This is what the chapters of this book offer. Ethnography is absolutely essential to grasp globalization from below because only through looking at the particulars of how its different parts work in different areas can it be made sense of. This book's chapter writers depict parts of what Ribeiro calls "the non-hegemonic world-system." This is a concept that allows us to understand globalization from below as part of a larger and complex whole that has its own systemic dynamics and characteristics. It does not exist in a vacuum but in complementary and contradictory relations with the powerful agencies and agents of globalization from above: those formal agencies (nation-states, global governance organizations, and corporations) that control national and global economies. The chapters of this book do not provide a fully comprehensive view of the non-hegemonic world-system, an abstraction that to be fully described would require hundreds of chapters, but they do provide a broad panorama of some of the different ways in which this system may be understood and studied.

Globalization from below can be studied in terms of global trading routes, although this type of investigation is comparatively unusual. One way this can be done is to follow Pliez's strategy in chapter 1 of focusing on the anchor points of global trading routes, in his analysis of Cairo, Salloum, Tripoli, and Yiwu. Another way this could be done is by following a single good on its journey across the globe, from manufacture through middlemen to consumption: following the "global commodity chain" as discussed by Aguiar in chapter 2, although he focuses on a single vast market in Guadalajara.

Globalization from below can also be studied through focusing on particular locales. This is what most of the chapters in this book do, but most characteristic of this approach are chapters 3 through 5. Rabossi in chapter 3 examines Ciudad del Este and its historical role as a supply center for imported goods headed for Brazil, and considers its emergence in terms of trade policies of far-off capitals in Beijing and Washington DC as well as regional governments. Mathews in chapter 4 considers Chungking Mansions in terms of the ideology of neoliberalism, an ideology of which Hong Kong is an exemplar—how does this ideology enable Chungking Mansions' existence? Telles in chapter 5 looks at São Paulo through the lens of legality/illegality and their intertwining existence throughout the world of globalization from below. All these chapters examine particular locales through a larger skein of influences worldwide; they are neither as broad and sweeping in focus as chapters 1 and 2, nor as specifically ethnographic as later chapters, but shed light onto crucial links in the chain, in focusing on the local level between the global and the individual.

Later chapters in the book, those of Part Two, explore globalization from below not in terms of routes or chains, but primarily through people who play specific roles in the system. The Smarts examine in chapter 6 a particular family of Hong Kong petty investors in China over thirty years; Milgram in chapter 7 focuses on a small group of Filipina entrepreneurs in their travels between the Philippines and Hong Kong, just as Gauthier in chapter 8 looks at a few particular "ant traders" between El Paso and Ciudad Juarez, and Yang looks at a number of African traders in Guangzhou in chapter 9. Bandyopadhyay in chapter 10, in his examination of Calcutta hawkers and malls and their interrelation, and Shepherd in chapter 11 in his analysis of a Washington DC street market in its tensions between the local and the global are somewhat more locale-based in their arguments than the preceding chapters, just as Alba Vega's final chapter focuses on the organization of Mexico City's street hawkers. These three chapters in some ways parallel chapters 3 through 5 in their mode of analysis, but all, in their fine-grained arguments, are focusing particularly on individuals, whose voices are prominently heard.

This book's first two chapters are thus about trade routes over a broad area, offering innovative attempts at multi-sited ethnography. All the other chapters in the book are located in one particular place, and most are about particular people. This fits anthropology's forte of ethnography—the detailed focus on particular people in particular places. In this book's ethnographic examinations of street hawkers in Calcutta, African traders in Guangzhou, Chinese market-vendors in Washington DC, hawker-political leaders in Mexico City, or petty entrepreneurs in Hong Kong or between the Philippines and Hong Kong, we learn a great deal about the practices of these particular people, and also something about the global connections of their livelihoods.

More theoretical discussions, such as that of Ribeiro in this book's conclusion, may help us to grasp globalization from below in its broadest panorama; but the kind of very specific discussion in these chapters is essential in understanding the nitty-gritty of what globalization from below consists of. Given all the uncertainties and lack of large-scale knowledge about globalization from below, the kind of analysis that you read in this book is as close as we can come to a comprehensive picture of what globalization from below looks like in the world today.

Globalization from below and globalization from above

Globalization from below has expanded throughout the world in recent years as a consequence of key transformations in the global economy (liberalization and deregulation, particularly China's), in politics (the growth of liberal democracy, and the collapse of the Soviet Union and the socialist block), in society (the spread of poverty and inequality, and mass international migration), and in technology (the revolution of information technologies and communication). The last transformation includes the internet, CD/DVD burners, and a new ease of transport for goods and people, enabling production, copying, transfer, and consumption of goods with speed, at low cost, and with acceptable quality.

As a number of chapters in this book point out, globalization from below is in many respects not opposed to globalization from above. This linkage of globalization from below with globalization from above is most clearly the case in terms of what is sought by those who engage in it. The international migrants, petty entrepreneurs, traders, and street hawkers who are the participants in globalization from below have the same desires as the secretaries, analysts, executives, bankers, and lawyers who are engaged in globalization from above, that of becoming affluent; but typically, given limitations of capital and the nature of the economic environment around them, they can only pursue affluence through informal and often not fully legal means. They seek to survive and become affluent by following the rules of the game around them. Many of those at work in the world of globalization from below have little or no idea that it constitutes something like "globalization from below" in contrast to "globalization from above"; this is simply the world in which they must survive and attempt to prosper.

Those who practice globalization from below don't seek to destroy capitalism, but to benefit from it; this is what every chapter in this book illustrates. Among all the participants in globalization from below portrayed in this book, there are no radicals or revolutionaries to be found, no opponents of globalization.[1] While there are indeed politicized makers of copies (Lin 2011: 57–63), mocking the dominant corporate capitalist world, there are not many, and in any case this book is not about such people. The people in this book, such as the street hawkers' union leaders described by Alba Vega in chapter 12 may indeed be intensely involved in local politics, but they are not seeking to overthrow the established economic order of their societies, but simply to make their livings within their societies, with whatever ways and means, and through whatever gaps and advantages they can find. The Calcutta hawkers described by Bandyopadhyay in chapter 10 do not hate the glittering malls that shadow their sidewalk wares; rather they use those malls, and benefit from the trade generated by those malls. The African traders depicted by Yang in chapter 9 may hate the way Chinese merchants try to cheat them, but they certainly do not hate capitalism. And this is true, more or less, for the entrepreneurs, traders, and hawkers portrayed in every chapter in this book.[2]

But of course the agents of globalization from above do shadow the lives of most of these people: Gauthier's "ant traders" and Milgram's small-scale entrepreneurs must worry about the border police and customs officials who may confiscate their goods, just as Aguiar's CD vendors and Shepherd's flea-market salespeople must always be on the lookout, like many of the other traders and vendors in this book. Telles in chapter 5 describes in detail the tangled relation between the legal and the illegal, the licit and the illicit, and how these two categories are finally inextricable. This is the case within all the socio-economic milieus described in this book. Every chapter of this book depicts activities that are, strictly speaking, illegal, such as taking goods over borders without official clearance, and making copies of copyrighted goods, but that are also, to a significant degree, tolerated as a nuisance or a necessity. It is fair to say that the legal is no more than that which is designated as such by the agents of globalization from above, and more or less enforced by those agents.

Globalization from below can prosper where the state has less capacity or will to regulate, whether from a sanitary point of view (food preparation and distribution in public places), a spatial point of view (merchandise being retailed in prohibited places, such as city streets or on public transport) or a fiscal point of view (the retail sale of products manufactured in businesses that do not pay taxes, which were introduced as contraband, or that have been pirated). However, this lack of formal regulation from above may be compensated for by a strong regulation from below, non-official and informal. Globalization may be embedded at the local level in a social, cultural, and political system that finds support in traditional familial structures and other social networks. It also may be embedded in political relationships fed by corporativism (state influence over a labor union or a group of street peddlers in which the state gives the organization a monopoly over certain areas in exchange for its political support and control over its selection of leaders) and clientelism (the exchange of favors for political support, as in the delivery of public goods and services by the state, generally to the poor, in exchange for political loyalty). This regulation makes it possible for globalization from below to work from an economic point of view; it is not a simple free-for-all.

There are moral issues involved in the practices of globalization from below, such as the making and selling of copies of goods, as we have discussed. The making of inferior copies of such goods as pharmaceuticals is undoubtedly morally wrong, since it may kill people, but making copies of other kinds of goods may be more ambiguous. Is copying a Louis Vuitton bag a moral offense? Perhaps, since it deprives Louis Vuitton of profits on the basis of its design creation, but perhaps not, since almost all of those who buy copies in the poorer areas of the world will never be able to afford the original. What of the producers of copy CDs and DVDs described by Aguiar and Bandyopadhyay, depriving artists of their royalties but providing the poor expensive goods on the cheap that, likewise, they might otherwise never be able to buy? What, perhaps more controversially, of those who make and sell copy Nokia or Samsung mobile phones, which involves appropriating the intellectual and technological labor involved in the development of these phones?

Even in this last case, for a poor consumer who can acquire a copy for an affordable price as against an original that is impossibly expensive, this may be a moot point. If both buyer and seller are aware that a copy is a copy, as is usually although not always the case in globalization from below, then morality is murky. Producers of the originals are deprived of profits for their creations, but consumers who otherwise would never be able to afford these goods are able to obtain them.[3] To what extent is this morality simply the agents of globalization from above imposing their own standards on the participants in globalization from below, seeking to deprive them of the fruits of globalization? We offer no clear-cut answer to this question, but do maintain that questions of morality need to be debated beyond the perspective of globalization from above alone. The chapters of this book provide glimpses into this expanded perspective on morality.

Globalization from above is enacted by states, whether the United States, Brazil, India, or China, and myriad corporations across the globe, attempting to regulate and restrict globalization from below in its copy goods, hawkers, and smuggling. These states and corporations are often under the sway of international financial institutions such as the World Trade Organization (WTO). Since economic liberalization and the signing of trade agreements (NAFTA, Mercosur), governments are pressured to comply with international agreements and to defend the interests of the capital they wish to attract, for example, in providing copyright protections for transnational companies.

Although globalization from below is more predominant in the so-called developing world than in the developed world, it is present today in every society on the globe: "globalization from below" is by no means synonymous with "developing-world globalization," for just as the multinational corporations of globalization from above are active in almost every country in the world, so too are the small entrepreneurs and traders of globalization from below. Because globalization from below is typically untaxed, it deprives governments of income that they seek. Thus, governments almost as a rule seek to turn globalization from below into globalization from above through three means: banking (those within globalization from below opening up bank accounts), formalization (businesses within globalization from below becoming formally registered), and fiscalization (those within globalization from below paying taxes).

Developed-world states pursue this more rigorously than developing-world states. Developing countries have greater poverty and social inequality and do not have unemployment insurance as many developed countries do. In many developing-world societies, globalization from below is the only form of globalization that exists: in the Congo, 90 percent of the economic activity was officially invisible twenty years ago (MacGaffey et al. 1991) and today as well; an only somewhat lower figure is the case for many developing-world economies across the globe.

For the most part, this is not because developing-world economies do not seek to regulate, but rather because they lack the means to do so, compared to their more regulated and policed developed-world counterparts. However, the lack of official or institutional regulation does not mean that there aren't regulations of any kind. Regulation exists, but as we discussed earlier (and as illustrated in Alba Vega's chapter 12), it is embedded in social, cultural, and political structures from below rather than from above, in community norms rather than in formal legal regulations.

Formal regulations also obviously exist: every country on earth has laws regarding what can be imported and exported, but in some places laws are more tightly enforced than others, due in part to the low pay received by government officials, making the lure of under-the-table payments all but irresistible.[4] However, even in the developed world, enforcement is necessarily lax. Nordstrom (2007: 117–122) estimates that less than 5 percent of the goods passing through the world's ports are ever inspected. The chapters by Gauthier, Mathews and Milgram in this book, among other chapters, show how even in the developed world, border controls are relatively lax, simply because with such a huge volume of goods passing over borders on a constant basis, anything more than cursory surveillance is impossible.

Indeed, everywhere in the world, globalization from below is impossible to stop; it is inevitable, although its scale differs from society to society today. We who edit this book believe that globalization from below is beneficial, in that it provides the poor of the world a taste of the goods of the rich, and enables hundreds of millions across the globe to make a living. However, even if we did not hold this view—even if we were to argue that globalization from below is an evil that must be suppressed—the fact is that in today's and tomorrow's world, this is impossible.

The kinds of economic networks discussed in this book pose a serious challenge to the ideas about economic policy and planning set forth by major institutional players of "globalization from above." The World Bank, the International Monetary Fund, and the World Trade Organization advocate through their policies neoliberal capitalism serving global corporations, creating greater global inequality and placing a "one-size-fits-all" straitjacket on developing-world economies (Peet 2009; Woods 2007). These policies result in a crushing load of debt on many developing-world economies. Globalization from below is in direct confrontation with the macroeconomics and development policy advocated by international financial institutions.

But globalization from below is also based on free-market principles. Globalization from below, in its evasion of state control at every possible turn, in this sense operates in accordance with neoliberalism, the ideology that the market should operate with only a minimum of control by the state, the ideology of these international financial institutions today. As earlier noted, globalization from below is anchored in the social, cultural, and political structures in the lives of those who practice it; in this sense, it does not represent the ravages of capital untrammeled, as described by scholars like Harvey in his well-known discussion of neoliberalism (2005). The ravages of globalization from above upon the developing world, as exemplified by the institutions mentioned earlier, is seen by many critics as an outgrowth of colonial policies of centuries past, with today's multinationals linked in spirit to the East India Company and the Hudson's Bay Company; we can see globalization from below in clear opposition to this, as the effort to sustain local practices and local communities as against the ravages of "rich countries' capitalism."

Nonetheless, it can be argued that in a global era of neoliberalism (Harvey 2005), those who practice globalization from below are in effect "out-neoliberalizing" those who embody globalization from above. This is, however, a warmer, more human form of neoliberalism, one that circumvents the laws of states, but that does not necessarily sever human social bonds, as does the globalization from above that envelops the world today as Ritzer (2007) among others has eloquently described.

The seminal role of China

The source of most of the goods discussed in this book is China. This is apparent in chapters ranging from the Smarts' depiction in chapter 6 of Hong Kong petty investors to Yang's discussion in chapter 9 of African traders in Guangzhou, seeking to buy at the source the goods their fellow citizens covet, to Pliez's discussion in chapter 1 of goods circulating from China to Egypt and Rabossi's discussion in chapter 3 of the goods in Ciudad del Este. This is also apparent in Gauthier's depiction of Mexican "ant traders" in Ciudad Juarez shopping at "los Chinos" and the CD traders discussed by Aguiar saying, "they come from China," and Shepherd's traders at the Eastern Market in Washington DC, railing against "the Chinese" even though few Chinese are to be seen there. China is an explicit or implicit presence in every one of this book's chapters.

This is the case, most obviously, because China has become the world's manufacturing powerhouse thanks to such factors as an abundant and cheap labor force, control and work discipline, economic reforms, and integration to the WTO in 2001. But it is not, at least not yet, a powerhouse of globalization from above. The products of globalization from above whose names everyone knows—iPhone, Nokia, Coca-Cola, and so on—have not been originally made by Chinese companies, whose brand names remain largely unknown beyond China.

A major feature of most Chinese manufacturing is goods of comparatively low price: goods that the developing world, as well as the developed world, seeks to buy not because of their flashiness and fashion, but because they are relatively inexpensive and of acceptable quality. The goods described in many of the chapters of this book are often at the lower end of quality among China-made goods, in that entrepreneurs bringing goods to less affluent areas of the world focus on price as the primary determinant of what they buy—this, rather than the overall quality of China-made goods as a whole, is the major reason why China-made goods are looked down upon by many in Africa and elsewhere. In any case, the fact remains that China is the overwhelming source of the goods that are the source of globalization from below.

Beyond this, and of critical importance in understanding China's role in globalization from below, is the fact that the rule of law remains quite flexible in China today, particularly in terms of copy goods. Pinheiro-Machado (2008) has shown how a product can go through several metamorphoses from its production in China until its final destination in a retail spot on a Brazilian street stall, switching from licit to illicit circuits and vice versa. Lin estimates that *shanzhai* phones—copy or knock-off phones—comprise 80 percent of the phones manufactured in China (2011: 21), and China is similarly lax in the production of many other kinds of goods. But even if the bulk of goods produced by China are not copies—and despite the statistics cited above, most of them, in realms beyond mobile phones and DVDs, are not—they are certainly cheap. If it weren't for China, globalization from below would not be happening, at least certainly not at its current scale.

One of China's most important roles in creating contemporary globalization lies in supplying African, South Asia, Latin America, and other developing-world areas with the goods of globalization, even if these goods are often shoddy or copied. An intellectual Congolese trader (quoted in Mathews 2011: 149) said that traders like him are "expanding the imaginations" of the poor, by showing them what high-quality goods are like—"we're bringing home goodness, even if it's copied [...]. They won't take for granted any more that everything around them must be broken and shabby," he claimed. As a reflective Kenyan trader said (quoted in Mathews 2011: 149), "Nobody in my country can buy an original brand of suit, or an original phone by a famous company. It's too expensive! But these copies can show them good things. They bring the world to Africa!"

Chinese goods, according to these traders, however much disdained by some buyers, may indeed have an extraordinary impact. This is the ultimate significance of China: it enables at least some of the fruits of global goodness, even if copied, to be spread throughout the world. Africa, as Allen and Hamnett have noted (1995: 2; see also Ferguson 2007: 25–49) is "off all kinds of maps." China in effect puts Africa on the map again, just as it puts developing countries across the globe on the map once again. It is because of China that consumers in these countries can enjoy the fruits of globalization. This, we argue, is one of China's most important contributions to globalization in the early twenty-first century.

China has been under increasing pressure to rein in its making of copy goods, which are a significant proportion of the goods of globalization it sends overseas— although what proportion is difficult to guess. At least some Chinese commentators say that copies should be celebrated, as the birth of a "*shanzhai* culture," a culture of copies (Lin 2011: 61), while many others, more or less echoing China's official line, say that the making of copy goods will die out as China develops in both its manufacturing prowess, and in the enforcement of its laws. China's emergence as the maker of goods for "globalization from below" really began only in the early 1990s, as the Smarts discuss in chapter 6; as they point out, China is seeking resolutely to climb up the value chain in what it manufactures. The chapters by Rabossi and Alba Vega discuss how China has displaced the United States as the primary source of contraband products in the two nodes of Ciudad del Este and Tepito. Barring large economic reversals, China will eventually price itself out of this market: in a few decades, some other center may well take its place as the world's cornucopia of globalization from below.

The future of globalization from below

We conclude this introduction with a long-term view. Many of the authors who discuss globalization from below imply that it will vanish as the world "progresses." Harrison and Huntington (2001) imply that "the informal economy" is a cultural impediment suffered by those societies that cannot lift themselves up to create structures for building large modern enterprises, an impediment that can be overcome but only slowly. Soto (2002) argues that if bureaucratic barriers to property ownership can be removed and laws changed to be more transparent, then many in the informal economy can move into the formal legitimate economy. Yunus maintains (2009) that establishing institutions for micro-credit can potentially solve the global problem of poverty, and by implication, the need for globalization from below, which is created through the maximization of profit by predatory states and corporations.

We who edit this book are sceptical about these arguments, however much we may be in sympathy with some of their ideals. As long as we have a world in which the most affluent 15 percent of the world's population controls most of the world's wealth and sets most of the world's rules, then globalization from below will continue, as the only way to counter this stranglehold. Furthermore, as that affluent 15 percent is increasingly learning, the walls to immigration in an era of easier global travel are becoming more and more porous. Globalization from below is not simply an echo of the past; rather, it is the wave of the future, as the developed world lurches from crisis to crisis, and the world's economic tectonic plates shift. We who write speculate that globalization from below may outlast globalization from above as this world continues in its history. At the very least, it seems clear that the chapters of this book describe a world that will be with us for a very long time to come.

Notes

1 Of course there are indeed many such opponents of globalization. See Pleyers (2011) for an analysis of those who in street demonstrations or social forums all over the world, from Seattle to Porto Alegre to Nairobi, contest globalization in its neoliberal form and propose more just and humane alternatives.
2 This is also true for the population of other regions of the world not included in this book, for example, the agents of globalization from below in Russia (Thorez 2008). It is also necessary to consider the important role international migrants have in globalization from below (Tarrius 2002). These are actors who aren't determined by a region, a country of origin, or a destination: emigrants, illegal, clandestine, or paperless, they are in a looking glass of "deterritorialization," "from here and there at the same time." These people too are essential for understanding the itineraries, the migratory logic, and the underground networks of globalization from below, although we haven't specifically examined them in this book.
3 Mathews has spoken to a Nokia employee off the record, who maintained that Nokia really didn't object to such copies, since those who bought them aspired to eventually own a "real" Nokia (2011: 148–149). However, Mathews has also spoken to a detective hired by Nokia to investigate copy sales in Hong Kong's Chungking Mansions who expressed great anger at what he saw as the craven immorality of those who make and sell copies. It is probably true that, all in all, copies hurt more than help the corporations of "globalization from above." It is also fair to say that the copies provided through globalization from below are what make the experience of globalization possible in much of the world.
4 In many less affluent ports-of-entry, caution is required in giving and receiving such payments (Mathews 2011: 138–139), due to the potential intervention of police and law enforcement. While in the Congo, bribes of customs officials can simply be handed over, in Nigeria, money must be left in a hidden spot to be picked up later, while in East African countries as well as India, the trick is to find a customs official who is alone and unobserved, or with whom one can communicate in advance. In places like Mexico, as well as Brazil, "ant traders" must also pay bribes—"informal taxes"—for right of passage, as Gauthier describes in chapter 8. In almost all of the world's states, enforcement of customs laws is at least intermittently attempted, but this, again, is more feasible in some places than in others.

References

Allen, J. and C. Hamnett (eds) (1995) *A Shrinking World? Global Unevenness and Inequality*, Oxford: Oxford University Press.
Arrighi, G. (2005) "Globalization in World Systems Perspective," in R. Appelbaum and W. Robinson, eds, *Critical Globalization Studies*, London: Routledge.
Ferguson, J. (2007) "Globalizing Africa? Observations from an Inconvenient Continent," in *Global Shadows: Africa in the Neoliberal World Order*, Durham: Duke University Press.
Harrison, L. and S. Huntington (2001) *Culture Matters: How Values Shape Human Progress*, New York: Basic Books.
Hart, K. (1973) "Informal Income Opportunities and Urban Employment in Ghana," *Journal of Modern African Studies* 11(1): 61–87.
Harvey, D. (2005) *A Brief History of Neoliberalism*, Oxford: Oxford University Press.
International Labor Office (ILO) (1972) "Employment, Incomes and Inequality: A Strategy for Increasing Productive Employment in Kenya," Geneva.
Karaganis, J. (ed.) (2011) *Media Piracy in Emerging Economies*, New York: Social Science Research Council Books.
Lautier, B. (2007) *L'Economie Informelle dans le Tiers Monde* [The Informal Economy in the Third World], Paris: La Découverte.
Lin, Y. C. J. (2011) *Fake Stuff: China and the Rise of Counterfeit Goods*, London: Routledge.

Lomnitz, L. A. (1977) *Networks and Marginality: Life in a Mexican Shantytown*, New York: Academic Press.

MacGaffey, J., with V. Mukohya, M. Beda, B. Schoepf, R. Nkera, and W. Enqundu (1991) *The Real Economy of Zaire: The Contribution of Smuggling and Other Unofficial Activities to National Wealth*, Philadelphia: University of Pennsylvania Press.

Mathews, G. (2011) *Ghetto at the Center of the World: Chungking Mansions, Hong Kong*, Chicago: University of Chicago Press.

Naím, M. (2006) *Illicit: How Smugglers, Traffickers, and Copycats are Hijacking the Global Economy*, New York: Anchor Books.

Neuwirth, R. (2011) *Stealth of Nations: The Global Rise of the Informal Economy*, New York: Pantheon.

Nordstrom, C. (2007) *Global Outlaws: Crime, Money, and Power in the Contemporary World*, Berkeley: University of California Press.

Peet, R. (2009) *Unholy Trinity: The IMF, World Bank and WTO*, 2nd ed., London: Zed Books.

Pinheiro-Machado, R. (2008) "China–Paraguai–Brasil: Uma Rota para Pensar a Economia Informal" [China–Paraguay–Brazil: A Route to Discuss the Informal Economy], *Revista Brasileira de Ciências Sociais* 23(67).

Pleyers, G. (2011) *Alter-Globalization: Becoming Actors in a Global Age*, Louvain, Belgium: Catholic University of Louvain.

Portes, A., M. Castells, and L. Benton (eds) (1989) *The Informal Economy: Studies in Advanced and Less Developed Countries*, Baltimore: Johns Hopkins University Press.

Ribeiro, G. L. (2006) "Economic Globalization from Below," *Etnográfica* X(2): 233–249.

—— (2009) "Non-hegemonic Globalizations. Alter-native Transnational Processes and Agents," *Anthropological Theory* 9(3): 1–33.

—— (2010) "A Globalização Popular e o Sistema Mundial Não-hegemônico" [Popular Globalization and the Non-hegemonic World System], *Revista Brasileira de Ciências Sociais* 25(74): 21–38.

Ritzer, G. (2007) *The Globalization of Nothing 2*, Thousand Oaks, CA: Pine Forge Press.

Soto, H. de (1987) *El Otro Sendero: La Revolución Informal* [The Other Path: The Informal Revolution], Mexico: Diana.

——(2002) *The Other Path: The Economic Answer to Terrorism*, New York: Basic Books.

Tarrius, A. (2002) *La Mondialisation par le Bas: Les Nouveaux Nomades de l'Economie Souterraine* [Globalization from Below: The New Nomads of the Underground Economy], Paris: Éditions Balland.

Thorez, J. (2008) "Bazars et Routes Commerciales en Asie Centrale: Transformations Post-soviétique et 'Mondialisation par le Bas'," [Commerical Bazaars and Routes in Central Asia: Post-Soviet Transformations in 'Globalization from Below'], *Revue Européenne des Migrations Internationales* 24(3): 167–189.

Tokman, V. E. (2007) "Integrating the Informal Sector in the Modernization Process," *Economic and Social Affairs*, DESA Working paper no 42, New York: United Nations.

Woods, N. (2007) *The Globalizers: The IMF, the World Bank, and Their Borrowers*, Cornell Studies in Money, Ithaca: Cornell University Press.

Yunus, M. (2009) *Creating a World Without Poverty: Social Business and the Future of Capitalism*, New York: Public Affairs.

Part One
Mapping globalization from below

Routes, nodes, laws

1

FOLLOWING THE NEW SILK ROAD BETWEEN YIWU AND CAIRO

Olivier Pliez

Introduction: multi-sited ethnography

What link can be established between Tripoli, capital of the former rogue state of Libya, the small Egyptian border town of Salloum, inhabited by Bedouins, the Egyptian metropolis of Cairo, and Yiwu, a market city three hours' drive from Shanghai? At first glance, the question may seem like a guessing game, but in fact it leads geographers, anthropologists, and other social scientists to face the increasing difficulty of working out the unexpected and often invisible connections between locations along the routes of "globalization from below." Appadurai (2000: 3) proposed the term "grassroots globalization" to characterize social forms relying "on strategies, visions, and horizons for globalization on behalf of the poor," but I will opt for the different proposition of Ribeiro (2009: 298), defining this form of globalization as a "'globalization from below' that is more linked to globalization's economic aspects than to its political ones." This is a way, according to Ribeiro, "to shed light on the hidden side of globalization's political economy, the one in which nation states' normative and repressive roles are [...] bypassed in the economic sphere." This is the "globalization from below" that this chapter will explore.

This chapter is based on a field investigation notebook kept between 2004 and 2009. Its intention is to highlight a key transnational trading route, one celebrated as the revival of the Silk Road (Molavi 2007; see also Stuttard 2000; Broadman 2007; Simpfendorfer 2009). The chapter seeks to show how places in the Middle East and North Africa (MENA) and China—industrial districts, ports, streets, or marketplaces—are linked together by actors working at different levels, dealing in more or less difficult geopolitical contexts to supply the market for consumption among the poor in Egypt and neighboring countries. This trading route forms a whole because of freight traffic and movements of people based on a logic which is barely perceptible on a local level, but which remains fundamental to the functioning of some very large networks of trade. Indeed, social scientists are facing the need to redefine continuities between spaces of production, negotiation, and consumption "from below" in a globalized context.

"Strategies of quite literally following connections, associations, and putative relationships are [...] at the very heart of designing multi-sited ethnographic research" (Marcus 1995: 97). Let's take this ethnographer's methodological proposals literally: he invites us to follow both goods and people, in order to grasp the scales and discontinuity of processes that can be observed in a precise place, while at the same time spread over different sites. Such a program is undeniably useful, even if we cannot neglect some serious critics. The sociologist Michael Burawoy is particularly persuasive when he declares that "by the end of its cultural turn, anthropology has lost its distinctive identity, having [...] sacrificed the idea of intensively studying a 'site' [...]. Bouncing from site to site, anthropologists easily substitute anecdotes and vignettes for serious field work, reproducing the cultural syncretism and hybridity of the peoples they observe" (Burawoy 2003: 674). Burawoy is not entirely wrong, but is to some extent depicting a caricature: to place under suspicion each researcher trying to follow goods, people, or a road is absurd. Is the strategy of "revisits" to sites advocated by Burawoy an antidote against the temptation of superficiality inherent in practicing multi-sited analysis? I don't think so. I consider that these methods are not antithetical but complementary strategies to be used in the difficult task of gaining a precise idea (generally without much statistical data, since it can be extremely difficult to gather) of transnational activities along the routes of globalization from below.

Therefore, I strive in this chapter to develop a multi-sited analysis by following the movement of garments and small commodities sold wholesale in Yiwu, China (Pliez 2007), labeled the world's largest wholesale market of small commodities, then transported through a mix of licit and illicit practices to Egypt, the largest consumption market of the Arab world, either directly or via the Libyan port of Tripoli.[1] I focus on blue jeans in this investigation because it is the product most visible in the warehouses and markets of Libya and Egypt and worn by urban Egyptian teenagers. However, instead of dealing with this issue through the flow of goods, I instead analyze in this chapter the anchoring points between these flows, the interactions between them, and the reshaped spatial scales which result from them. The routes of globalization from below are irregular and their anchoring points—borders, malls, marketplaces, and ports—vary depending on social, economic, and geopolitical contexts. These anchoring points are of interest to social scientists studying the spatial dynamics of global trade processes because the routes change more rapidly than the places they link. By identifying and mapping spaces related to transnational activities, at least the tip of the iceberg comprising the routes of economic globalization from below can be apprehended.

Egypt: a market of 40 million consumers for Chinese products

Egypt joined the World Trade Organization (WTO) from its inception in 1995, officially becoming a "star pupil" of the world agenda of trade liberalization. This had

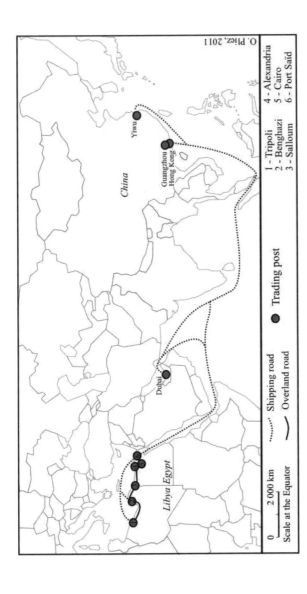

FIGURE 1.1 Places along a transnational trading road. Map by Olivier Pliez. Reproduced with permission

two essential consequences: first, the economic opening of the country rendered the existing tax-free areas null and void, and they were gradually dismantled; and second, Egypt's traditional business partners were to some extent supplanted. China soon took a dominant position and has been ranked third among Egypt's business partners in 2009 (with 7.1 percent of Egyptian foreign trade), behind the European Union (32.7 percent) and the United States (9.4 percent), with a commercial surplus of 3.84 billion euros (approx. 5.04 billion in US dollars) (Trade Egypt 2010).

These global statistics do not reveal the array of different kinds of products, as well as the practices of agents targeting one or another social level of consumption. It is difficult to distinguish between the importations of small or medium transnational agents and those of bigger firms. The issue of textile imports, for example, is not only particularly sensitive for the Egyptian clothing industry, whose workforce is char-acterized by oversupply and low productivity, but is also sensitive to the WTO schedule, which led to the abolition of quotas and tariffs on textiles between 2002 and 2004. Egypt feared the effects of such an opening and protected its textile industry from Chinese imports by putting technical obstacles in the way of these imports. But these protectionist measures, and the poor quality of local production, did not satisfy many Egyptian buyers, particularly those who were more modest in income; they tended to turn to China-made products.

Within the MENA region, in 2007 Egypt represented a vast consumer market of 76 million inhabitants. However, because of income disparities (GNP per capita is approximately EUR1,000), the Egyptian clothing market is divided up according to social levels and spatial locations, as follows (De Coster 2006):

- The wealthiest, comprising about 3.5 million consumers, have been buying quality products from Europe or North America for decades. In the last twenty years, Middle Eastern centers such as Dubai, Istanbul, and Beirut have been com-peting for this market, and are now themselves in competition with the luxurious commercial malls that are growing in number in central Cairo and its luxury suburbs, where gated communities have mushroomed (Zakaria 2006).
- The middle class, around 15 million people, shop for clothes and small commodities in the downtown Cairo area of Talaat Harb and in a few residential districts, as well as in other main Egyptian cities such as Alexandria.
- Aside from the above, an estimated 40 million people—leaving out the 20 percent of Egyptians living under living wage in 2005—comprise the enormous consumer market for cheap clothes, where Asian products, earlier manufactured in Thailand and Indonesia, and now in China, have replaced low-quality garments made in Egypt.

During the 1970s, both modest and wealthy Egyptians flocked to the port area of Port Saïd (Bruyas 2007) to buy imported duty-free goods often unavailable in the rest of the country. During this period, the Egyptian president, Anwar El Sadat, was attempting the first steps of economic opening, called the *Infitah* in Arabic. In the checkout lanes of the free zone, Port Saïd's shoppers mixed with dozens of traders and smugglers, who carried clothing and electronic products through customs in an unceasing shuttle. The demand was such that some Palestinian intermediaries offered clothes from Istanbul at lower prices than the ones imported through Port Saïd. The name has remained: one of the main wholesale clothing markets of Cairo, Jawhary, is also called the "Gaza Souk." Later, the importance of Port Saïd as a gateway for imports into Egypt gradually declined, and supply routes became diversified and progressively globalized during the 1990s.

Paradoxically, legislation encouraged the smuggling of imported garments during this period of strong state control of international trade. In Egypt customs duties were paid on imported material by the manufacturer, and provided that the final product was re-exported within one year, the manufacturer had the right to reclaim the already-paid duties in full. One estimate is that about US$300,000,000 worth of jeans coming from China were brought annually into Egypt and then, after being relabeled, were re-exported as final products made in Egypt to the USA, a practice made particularly profitable because of this law (see Bennet 1992).

In the 2000s, Egyptian legislation on international trade has become more flexible, but traders still seek ways to elude the law to maximize their profits. When Port Saïd lost its last attributes as a duty-free zone in 2002, the importers of Cairo and Alexandria got around quotas and taxes by delivering part of their goods to the closest low-tax container ports outside Egypt, such as those in Libya. These days, Chinese jeans or global gadgets sold on the Egyptian market often arrive from the Libyan ports of Tripoli and Benghazi by road, passing through the border village of Salloum, as I will now explore.[2]

Salloum: a Bedouin village and border warehouse

Twelve hours by road west of the Egyptian capital city is the Egyptian village of Salloum, on the Libyan border, where an intense movement of people and goods takes place. Egyptian emigration to Libya is a well-known phenomenon, which is both long-standing—it started at the beginning of the 1970s—and massive: officially 300,000 Egyptian migrants work in Libya (Zohry 2003). However, it is not the traffic of people which strikes the visitor to Salloum but the traffic of goods: not only Chinese blue jeans, but also all kinds of small products subject to quotas and/or customs duties in Egypt. Salloum, despite its apparent remoteness, is an essential link in the transnational route supplying Egypt from China via Dubai and Libya.

The profession of smuggler emerged from this informal but necessary tolerance at the border. On the Egyptian side, smuggling is openly practiced and considered an ordinary job by the actors in the border trade. They work at the request of the Egyptian forwarding agents who come to Salloum to take delivery of the goods that their Libyan counterparts send from Tripoli to the border. Smuggling usually means carrying loads of blue jeans or other goods (denim jeans from China were the main product smuggled into Egypt while I did field research in Salloum, but different types of small commodities and garments transit there according to opportunities and demand), walking from one side of the border to the other. The smugglers circumvent the Egyptian frontier post, pass through the Libyan customs check-point, and go into the Libyan village of Msaïd, and then make their way back with the goods they have picked up, always depending on the fluctuating tolerance of the customs officers. Once in Egypt, they load the goods into covered taxis commuting between the border and the warehouses on the main street of Salloum, ten kilometers away.

Smuggling is a commonplace activity here. For the porters and the conveyors, it does not represent something isolated and illegal but rather serves as an essential link in the importation of goods into Egypt. The blue jeans pass from the Libyan exporters' hands to those of their importing counterparts on the other side of the border; the rest of the business boils down to logistics depending on the conditions of the road. The smugglers may be men or women, Bedouins native to the Salloum region or Egyptians. Some of them came here after a first experience in smuggling in Port Saïd; others explain that they came because they "had heard of Salloum," preferring to work here than to emigrate to Libya or the Gulf countries to make a living. Most live in this border village so that they can work in different jobs relying on the border trade: as carriers of goods or drivers, but also money-changers or workers in the services that Salloum offers to residents, migrants, or travelers.

The commercial facilities of the locality reflect its two main functions: storage of goods and hospitality for those who make their living from these goods as well as those who stop in the village for just a few hours. The center of Salloum, along the main road, is very busy, especially early in the morning when the different players in the border trade take their breakfast before going up the hill to the frontier point, and after sunset, when everybody meets again downtown. Salloum's main street features about 230 businesses in a 900-meter stretch: coffeehouses, restaurants, phone shops, and shops of imported products as well as warehouses. There are also seven hotels to accommodate travelers, customs officers, and security forces.

Salloum's Bedouins are well entrenched in the border commercial chain, either as carriers of the parcels of blue jeans, or if they have enough money, as speculators on the sale or rent of warehouses on the other side of the border. The warehouses are simple rooms of ten meters square made up of racks and a front counter where the smugglers place their loads and the purchasers negotiate with them. Those goods generally do not remain on display for long, as Ahmed, one of the forwarding agents for Chinese jeans, who has been commuting between Cairo and Tripoli for twenty years, explained to me. Ahmed goes to the Libyan capital twice a month, and negotiates directly with the Libyan wholesalers who deliver cargo worth several thousand euros to the border. Then he picks up his order in Salloum and takes it to the wholesalers of Alexandria and Cairo, who sell the goods on the Egyptian market.

The trading post of Tripoli

Situated 20 hours west of Salloum by road, Tripoli has been returning to its historical role as a Mediterranean port and transnational commercial center due to its low import taxes and its location at the crossroads of migratory and trade flows between

FIGURE 1.2 Warehouses, small shops and taxis on the main street of Salloum. Photo by Olivier Pliez. Reproduced with permission

the Sahel (Sudan, Chad, and Niger) and North Africa (Tunisia, Algeria, and Egypt). The wealthy state of Libya, with its interventionist economic policy, controlled the national market by subsidizing the import of many consumer goods from the 1970s until the oil price counter-shock of the mid-1980s. During that period, the difference between the prices charged in Libya and those charged in neighboring states was so significant that smuggling networks were set up to export the subsidized goods illegally and sell them overseas (Boubakri 2000). The drop in oil prices in the mid-1980s and the embargoes on Libya (1982–1999) largely ended this economic activity and caused a drop in the national currency, the Libyan dinar. In just a few years, after public authorities reduced subsidies and low taxation was introduced, the players in the illegal re-exportation of goods from Libya turned Tripoli into a market for the re-exportation of imported goods from Asian markets (Pliez, 2004).

Today, hundreds of Libyan wholesalers and importers connected to Istanbul, Dubai and the East Asian industrial districts trade with North African, African and Egyptian re-exporters who oversee the supply of commercial chains several thousands of kilometers long. They have turned the central districts of Tripoli around the harbor into a vast storage area for markets, which are often ethnically oriented (such as the African market, the Chadian street, and the Rachid street area), stockrooms, and wholesale shops. Mid-range hotels accommodating foreign dealers and shopping malls attracting the shoppers of the capital have grown in number.

FIGURE 1.3 African souk in the old city of Tripoli, Libya. Photo by Olivier Pliez. Reproduced with permission

The old city of Tripoli and its surroundings have become an employment site for hundreds of sub-Saharan, North African, and Middle Eastern migrants at the lower levels of this transnational commercial chain, those who moved to Libya during the 1990s embargo (Bredeloup and Zongo 2005; Pliez 2006). They carry parcels, sew garments, or negotiate imported goods with wholesalers from Libya's neighboring countries—although of course all this has been changing with the Libyan revolution of 2011, whose ultimate outcomes remain to be seen.

Yiwu: a Chinese supermarket of the Arab world

> Of course, life has improved. We couldn't have imagined any of this ten years ago. This small town with mud houses now has an airport, a world trade center, skyscrapers, hundreds of factories, hotels, and two Middle Eastern restaurants with belly dancers. We hardly had any schooling, but our daughter studies marketing at college.
>
> *Jin Xiaoqin, owner of Yiwu Toys (Wang 2005)*

"Build the largest supermarket in the world. Build an international shopping paradise." The slogans on the walls of the main hall of the annual International Fair in Yiwu are not the incantation of some municipal officials in a small and isolated village of rural China, but the expression of the success of this "Made in China" showcase. Yiwu is indeed one of the central commercial centers in China, a world-scale low-price wholesale showroom specializing in the sale of "small commodities," i.e. small household goods, jewelry, razors, toys, and religious artifacts.

The easiest way to describe the market of Zhejiang, two hours away by train south of Shanghai, is to list its superlatives: the surface area of the markets exceeds 2.5 million square kilometers; 58,000 shops offer 400,000 different goods; and 80 trade fairs take place each year, the most important being the annual international fair which attracts 16,000 foreign visitors over three days. Yiwu is probably unique both for its scale and for the diversity of its products. However, despite the operators I met in this market who praise Yiwu as the "capital of small commodities," it remains primarily a textile area, with a third of its export sales clothing, 12 percent socks and 7 percent various other textiles (Yiwu Industry and Commerce Administrative Bureau 2006). The growing number of transnational buyers, who sometimes come with little money, is made possible by the fact that in Yiwu they can fill up a container with different types of product instead of only one product, as is often the case in other East Asian markets. Yiwu is known as a major center of copied goods in China, with about 80–90 percent of all goods offered for sale being counterfeit or goods infringing copyright (Chow 2003). Its prices are at the moment unbeatable. For all these reasons, in Yiwu one can find more products than anywhere else and a multitude of people from around the world can test their fortunes in small-scale transnational trade.

The International Trade Center (ITC), with a total of 17,000 shops, has provided an accessible center for Yiwu's specialized markets one year after China joined the

FIGURE 1.4 A trader and her Chinese translator in the halls of the ITC. Photo by Olivier Pliez. Reproduced with permission

WTO; three-fourths of the commercial transactions carried out in the city are concentrated here. In 2008, the Yiwu market was divided into five main markets (Binwang, ITC I, II, III, IV) and specialized streets bringing together a total of 620,000 booths of Chinese suppliers (Zhejiang China Small Commodities City Group 2009). It is at the heart of Yiwu's emergence as one of the world's major sources of the goods that fuel globalization from below.

In the 1970s, Yiwu was one of many small industrial cities in China, each of which specialized in the production of small commodities in accordance with the economic doctrine of that time: "one village, one product." But the economic liberalization led by Deng Xiaoping in the 1980s brought competition between these mono-specialized localities to attract Chinese customers in a competitive production market. In this context, driven by local trade operators with the support of public authorities (Chow 2003), Yiwu gradually became a local and then a regional trading city of the specialized mono-industries dispersed in the Zhejiang countryside (Ding 2007). A new stage was reached in the 1990s, when the operators who ran Yiwu's markets went into partnerships with private commercial operators located in other Chinese provinces. Together they created a network of markets to sell the goods produced around Yiwu: today, about fifty markets in twenty-five Chinese provinces are connected to the market of Yiwu (Sun and Martin 2008). They are usually located in the main cities of each province, and can be found in border provinces and in ports connected to South Korea or Japan. In 2001, the People's Republic of China (PRC) joined the World Trade Organization and attracted transnational trade operators that had dealt with Southeast Asian markets until the financial crisis of 1997. Today, two-thirds of the sales in Yiwu are within a huge world market:

TABLE 1.1 The main importing countries of Yiwu products

Rank	2002	2009 (first semester)
1	United Arab Emirates	United States
2	Russia	United Arab Emirates
3	United States	Spain
4	South Korea	Germany
5	Ukraine	Russia
6	Japan	Brazil
7	Saudi Arabia	Iran
8		Italy
9		Algeria
10		Canada

Source: Data sourced from China Commodity City: http://en.onccc.com

Exports from China to the Arab world have grown significantly with the increasing demand for consumer goods caused by the explosion of oil prices (Habibi 2006). Therefore, a trading outlet of major importance for the exports of Yiwu has opened towards the vast consumer market of the Middle Eastern and North African region looking for inexpensive products. In 2005, China ranked among the four principal exporting partners of 9 of the 19 countries of the MENA region, ranking first in Sudan and the United Arab Emirates (UAE) and second in Iran and Jordan. However, this increasing presence of Chinese imports in terms of volume is most striking in two states, namely Saudi Arabia, where China's market share doubled (from 3.6 to 7.2 percent) between 2000 and 2005 and the UAE, where it made a 320 percent jump during the same period (Habibi 2006).

There is a trade history linking Yiwu and Dubai, which was long the main trading interface between the Arab world and China. However, during the 2000s, many purchasers have come alone or in small collectives directly to Yiwu, circumventing Dubai, in order to find the lowest prices. They usually walk around in tandem with their interpreter, most often a young multilingual Chinese intermediary, and deal directly on site, having been provided with the names and addresses of their potential suppliers and of the districts where they will stay. Most of the Arab tradesmen report similar routes which led them to add China to their transnational trading destinations during the 2000s, after southern Europe in the 1980s and Turkey, the United Arab Emirates, and Southeast Asia in the 1990s. Often, they entered China step by step, first traveling to Hong Kong to buy Chinese goods (often staying at Chungking Mansions: see Mathews's chapter 4), and then going directly into mainland China to buy.

An Egyptian stationery importer I spoke with has been traveling to China for ten years to buy small low-cost articles (pens, erasers, etc). Five years ago, the French company which was his main supplier relocated its production to Shanghai. His French partner invited him to visit the Shanghai production site and the main markets of the area. So he went to Yiwu in 2003 but "only saw souks like the ones in Cairo: articles of bad quality sold on the pavement by small craftsmen." Skeptical and disappointed, he left after placing only one small order. But after fresh talks with his

French supplier and with other Egyptian importers he eventually changed his opinion: "Then I understood that Yiwu was an important trading city but that I had not understood its rules during my first visit. I needed to be guided." Today, Yiwu is his principal destination in China; he goes there every two months, each time for short stays of two to three days. He devotes this time to meeting his suppliers, and to looking at the huge showrooms of the International Trade City, and sleeps in Yiwu's new five-star hotel in the city center. "In the evening, the city is a little bit livelier than before" he says, especially in the vicinity of the "Arab district," which can be identified by the smell of kebab. This highlights one emergent feature of the city: the setting up of a hospitality structure for the foreigners who visit or live in Yiwu.

Muslim hospitality

The bonds of trade between Yiwu and Arab countries have resulted in the development of an Arab community of 3,500 residents (Al-sin al yowm: 2006) out of a total of 6,000 to 8,000 foreigners living in the city. The presence of so many Muslim tradesmen has led to the emergence of a so-called Arab district in downtown Yiwu,[3] a place where almost everything is written in Arabic. The tradesmen meet after 5:30 pm (when the International Trade Center closes its doors) in the Algerian, Egyptian, Iraqi, and Lebanese restaurants of the area. This district solves a crucial problem for these Muslim travelers: where to find halal food, food which conforms to the precepts of Islam, especially in a country where language problems are acute and where pork and alcohol are very popular.

FIGURE 1.5 Maedah Restaurant, the first Egyptian restaurant in Yiwu. Photo by Olivier Pliez. Reproduced with permission

Yiwu's resident Muslim traders and merchants, whether they are Arab, Asian or African, attract many Chinese Muslims as a consequence of their religion (there are some 20 million indigenous Muslims in China: Gladney 1994). While Yiwu has received a large number of migrants from inside China (at least 600,000) who come to work in industrial workshops, the migration of Muslims is mainly from the western autonomous regions of China (Ningxia and Xinjiang), and is mostly linked to the catering needs of the city's foreign Muslim visitors. For example, the Uighurs of Xinjiang, a Turkish-speaking group from Central Asia, have earned a good reputation as animal slaughterers and *mechoui* cooks. They can be found in every restaurant of the district, where they butcher sheep and grill the meat on barbecues every evening. The majority of these Muslims work for the managers or owners of the Arab district restaurants. However, as the manager of an Algerian restaurant confides, "Communicating with them is not so easy: their Arabic, their English, you don't understand their accent very well." Most of the Arab residents of Yiwu have learned some Chinese in order to try to get around the language problem.

A Muslim community in Yiwu is thus being built into the meshes of the geopolitical and commercial agreements which have defined the renewal of relations between the African and Asian continental blocks during the 2000s. Global networks can materialize in seemingly improbable places such as the previously mentioned "Arab district" in Yiwu, where Arab restaurant owners employ Chinese Muslims to cater for the busy traders, providing them with a place to negotiate and relax, a place where they can build ties with a degree of confidence. They share the same goal: to make money rapidly. They also share the same religious identity, that of Islam.

I consider the "Arab street" of Yiwu as an exemplary site of transnational commercial exchange networks from below. Ethnic enclaves have multiplied near supply sources located in the world's Asian factories. This is the case in Beijing (Gladney 1994), in Guangzhou (Bertoncello and Bredeloup 2007) and in Bangkok (Marchal 2007; Simone 2007). "The Muslim Street is Everywhere," suggested Abdoul Maliq Simone in describing the district of Soi Sukhumvit 3 in the Thai capital, which "anchors the intersection of Arabs and Africans from all over the world" (2007: 593). This is as relevant in Yiwu as in Bangkok. Today the secular links between Muslim worlds not only transcend states but also post-colonial north–south and center–periphery relationships, to provide coherence to the globalization of cultural, religious, and commercial exchanges (Dennerlein and Reetz 2007).

However, we cannot essentialize these interactions, because these enclaves are just one among many practical ways to make the global traffic flow more fluid. In the "Arab street" of Yiwu, the Arab restaurant owners and their Muslim Chinese employees cater to traders in a hurry; they also provide them with places of exchange and connectivity (Kesselring 2006). Is it any different in the harbor district of Tripoli or in the main street of Salloum, where traders, migrants, and occasional guests meet? Is it any different in Yiwu itself, where the Muslim enclave is next to the African, Russian, Hispanic, and Korean enclaves? Streets such as these bring people together for specific reasons, such as the language or the food (such as the importance of halal food for Muslims), but that might not be enough to explain the multiplication of

"Muslim streets." Moreover, the Arab street of Yiwu attracts as many Chinese people, who come to discover the culinary tastes of the Middle East, as it does foreign Muslims who spend a few days in the city.

Conclusion: the uncharted geography of transnational networks

Following the "new Silk Road" between China and Egypt and therefore emphasizing the links between these places is a methodological and heuristic means for anthropologists, geographers, and other social scientists to understand the focal sites of transnational networks. It enables us to put their characteristic commercial enclaves into perspective on a global scale, and also reminds us of the fact that these networks are not created spontaneously, but from layers of economic and social circumstances. This is the case not only at present, but also for the maritime trading posts of the ancient Mediterranean, the medieval Silk Roads, the trans-Saharan caravan roads which reached their height in the nineteenth century, and the foreign concessions of coastal China during the first decades of the twentieth century.

It is necessary to locate these on their own geographical scale. They are, as in the Xiaobei neighborhood of Guangzhou (see Yang's chapter 9), "a combined result of both so-called 'globalization from below' and a locality such as Guangzhou's commercial culture, religious traditions and trading networks" (Li, et al. 2007). They also should be located on a global market timescale: over the last twenty years, Arab migratory and trade routes have undergone radical changes. Until the 1980s, Arab merchants were in the port cities of Southern Europe (Peraldi 2005). During the 1990s, Arab merchants plied their trade in Turkey and the Gulf States. From there, they entered Southeast Asia step by step until the financial crisis of 1997 and the entry of China into the World Trade Organization in 2001. The 2000s represent the beginning of the Chinese phase of the globalization of these Arab routes.

And finally we must define these networks by their local contexts. The size of the Egyptian consumer market for low-price products, the fringe society of the Bedouin populations at the border between Egypt and Libya, the Libyan economy, founded both on oil and gas revenue and on an economic laissez-faire policy during the embargo of Libya (1982–1999), the involvement of both public and private local social actors in Yiwu, in the heart of one of the main Chinese "world factory" provinces, Zhejiang—all these factors are essential to the formation of focal sites of economic globalization from below along the global road from Cairo to Yiwu. Economic globalization from below in commercial exchanges creates new scales of observation for their discontinuous but strongly interconnected units of space. They are located at the intersection of migratory, production, and circulation areas, which are older and often distinctive, such as the Egyptian–Libyan migratory system. They involve a growing number of both local and transnational players.

The making of these places involves many uncertainties. Price competition, for example, can be limited by consumers' search for better quality products. The consequence is that tough competition triggers the development of trading posts located in production areas. All these sites are linked along global trade routes which are constantly renewed through the efforts of the commercial players who enliven these hubs. They must maintain low prices from the production sites to the retail sale of the goods. They must ensure good conditions of hospitality for the traders. And they must deal with many legal constraints, such as protectionist barriers, borders, national and international legislations, or the reversals of the world economic situation (AFP Asian Edition 2009).

The success and sustainability of the routes of globalization from below often vary according to the places they go through. The commercial enclaves are numerous and varied along the multiple roads that bind the continental blocks of Africa and Asia. They are commonly presented by the media and politicians as explanatory factors of the new geopolitical and commercial world. One does not talk about business from continent to continent or from country to country, but from place to place: places to buy (Yiwu), places to sell either to local wholesale dealers or to private individuals (Cairo), places to take delivery and to re-forward (Tripoli), and sometimes also places to divert goods (Salloum). Each of these places could be intensively studied, following spatial but also anthropological perspectives. The logic of the actors who follow the global routes, whether importers, smugglers, or migrants, and the logic of local actors, whether they accommodate (money changers, cooks), deal (peddlers, wholesalers, translators, traders), or manage (municipalities, boards of trade) are constantly embedded within the particularities of these places.

The connection between such places seems at first glance unlikely. It is the temporary result of social and spatial networks meshing in the 1990s and 2000s. What of today? After the bankruptcy of Dubaï in 2009, the Arab revolts of 2011 may be followed by profound changes along the transnational roads between China and the Arab world. In the course of those revolts, Cairo became the symbol of the aspirations of freedom of the Arab populations, Tripoli was a battlefield, and Sallum hosted refugees during the Libyan civil war. But this new geopolitical situation won't necessarily lead to the end of the new Silk Road. Transnational trade networks often lead to a dynamic constituting or reconstituting of places within changing territorial configurations, and new networks of trade may emerge. Whatever may come, it seems clear that understanding the connections explored in this chapter can serve to clarify the inconspicuous geography of the nodes and networks which link the world. They are a necessary complement to the metaphor of fluidity which is so often used to describe the flows of people and goods across the globe—a metaphor which is accurate, but which nonetheless tells only part of the story, the other part of which I have tried to tell here.

Notes

1 I investigated the cities of Tripoli (2003, 2005), Salloum (2005–2007), Cairo (2005–2007) and Yiwu (2006, 2009) for this chapter. I have also investigated marketplaces in Algeria (2000), the Libyan Sahara (1998, 2003) and Khartoum (2004, 2005), which are similarly well connected with the Gulf States—especially Dubai—and East Asia, although I do not discuss them in this chapter.

2 According to my investigations in Salloum in 2006, cotton denim blue jeans made in China were bought by peddlers at the Libyan border at about EGP20–25 (one US dollar was worth EGP3.5) and then sold in the seaside resort of Marsa Matrouh at EGP40–45, and in the metropolises of Alexandria and Cairo at EGP50–60.

3 I found different names for this area: *san mao chu* ("economic quarter no 3") is the former administrative name, recently renamed "Exotic Street" by the municipality; Chinese native speakers call it *maedah* (table in arabic) in reference to the first Arabic restaurant built in Yiwu; Arabic native speakers usually call it the Arab street, Arab restaurant (*alabo fan dian* in Chinese), or Maedah.

References

AFP Asian Edition (2009) "Global Crisis hits China's Huge Yiwu Market, but Optimism Remains," http://www.thefreelibrary.com/Global+crisis+hits+China's+huge+Yiwu+market, +but+optimism+remains-a01611783822 (accessed October 14, 2011).

Al-sin al yowm (2006) http://www.chinatoday.com.cn/Arabic/2006n/0612/index.htm (accessed October 14, 2011).

Appadurai, A. (2000) "Grassroots Globalization and the Research Imagination," *Public Culture* 12(1): 1–19.

Bennet, J. (1992) "Chinese Agency Indicted in Jeans Import Scheme," *New York Times*, October 6.

Bertoncello, B. and S. Bredeloup (2007) "The Emergence of New African 'Trading Posts' in Hong Kong and Guangzhou," *China Perspective* 218: 94–105.

Boubakri, H. (2000) "Echanges transfrontaliers et commerce parallèle aux frontières Tuniso-Libyennes" [Trans-Border Exchanges and Informal Trade through the Tunisia-Libya Border], *Monde Arabe, Maghreb Machrek* 170: 39–51.

Bredeloup, S. and M. Zongo (2005) "Quand les frères burkinabè de la petite Jamahiriyya s'arrêtent à Tripoli" [When the Burkinabè Brothers of the "Small Jamahiriyya" Stop in Tripoli], *Migrations entre les deux rives du Sahara* 36: 123–47.

Broadman, H. (2007) *Africa's Silk Road: China and India's New Economic Frontier*, Washington DC: World Bank Publications.

Bruyas, F. (2007) "'Méga-projets' nationaux et dynamiques identitaires locales: Le cas de Port-Saïd et des autres villes du Canal de Suez" [National 'Mega-Projects' and Dynamics of Local Identity: The Case of Port Saïd and other Cities of the Suez Canal], É. Denis, ed., *Villes et urbanisation des provinces égyptiennes. Vers l'écoumènopolis?* Paris/Le Caire: Karthala/Cedej.

Burawoy, M. (2003) "Revisits: An Outline of a Theory of Reflexive Ethnography," *American Sociological Review* 68(5): 645–79.

Chow, D. (2003) "Organized Crime, Local Protectionism, and the Trade in Counterfeit Goods in China," *China Economic Review* 14(4): 473–84.

De Coster, J. (2006) "New Egyptian Consumers Want China Retail Prices" *International Market News*, May 12.

Dennerlein, B. and D. Reetz (2007) "Continuity and Disparity: South–South Linkages in the Muslim World," *Comparative Studies of South Asia, Africa and the Middle East* 27(1): 3–6.

Ding, K. (2007), "Domestic Market-based Industrial Cluster Development in Modern China," Discussion Paper no. 88, IDE-JETRO, Tokyo, http://www.ide.go.jp/English/ Publish/Dp/pdf/088_ding.pdf (accessed October 14, 2011).

Gladney, D. (1994) "Sino-Middle Eastern Perspectives Since the Gulf War: Views from Below," *International Journal of Middle East Studies* 29(4): 677–691.

Habibi, N. (2006) "China Builds Growing Middle East Export Market Share, at the Expense of Competitors," *Al-Jazeera*, http://www.aljazeera.info/Opinion%20editorials/2006% 20Opinion%20Editorials/May/31%20o/China%20Builds%20Growing%20Middle%20East %20Export%20Market%20Share,%20At%20the%20Expense%20of%20Competitors%20By %20Nader%20Habibi.htm (accessed October 14, 2011).

Kesselring. S. (2006) "Pioneering Mobilities: New Patterns of Movement and Motility in a Mobile World," *Environment and Planning A* 38(2): 269–79.

Li, Z., D. Xue, M. Lyons, and A. Brown (2007) "Ethnic Enclave of Transnational Migrants in Guangzhou: A Case Study of Xiaobei," Conference on China's Urban Land and

Housing in the 21st Century, Hong Kong, December 13–15, 2007, http://www.hkbu.edu.hk/~curs/Abstracts%20and%20Fullpapers/05/07.doc (accessed October 14, 2011).

Marchal, R. (2007) "Hôtel Bangkok-Sahara," [The Bangkok-Sahara Hotel], in F. Adelkhah and J. F. Bayart, eds, *Voyages du Développement: Emigration, Commerce, Exil*, Paris: Karthala, Coll. Recherches internationales.

Marcus, G. (1995) "Ethnography in/of the World System: the Emergence of Multi-Sited Ethnography," *Annual Review of Anthropology* 24: 95–117.

Molavi, A. (2007) "The New Silk Road," *Washington Post*, April 9.

Peraldi, M. (2005) "Algerian Routes: Emancipation, Deterritorialisation and Transnationalism through Suitcase Trade," *History and Anthropology* 16: 47–61.

Pliez, O. (2004) "De l'immigration au transit? La Libye, dans l'espace migratoire euro-africain" [From Immigration to Transit? Libya in the Euro-African Migratory Space], in *La nouvelle Libye, géopolitique, espaces et sociétés au lendemain de l'embargo*, Paris: Karthala, 139–57.

——(2006) "Tripoli, vers l'effacement de l'africanité de la capitale libyenne?" [Tripoli: Towards the Blurring of the African Identity of the Libyan Capital?], *Migrations Société* 18(107).

——(2007) "Des jeans chinois dans les rues du Caire, ou les espaces discrets de la mondialisation" [Chinese Jeans on the Streets of Cairo: A Stroll Through the Discreet Places of Bottom-up Globalization], *Mappemonde* 88, http://mappemonde.mgm.fr/num16/articles/res07404.html (accessed October 14, 2011).

Ribeiro, G. (2009) "Non-hegemonic Globalizations: Alter-native Transnational Processes and Agents," *Anthropological Theory* 9: 1–33.

Simone, A. (2007) "The Muslim Street is Everywhere (and soon coming to a theater near you)," *Geoforum* 38(4): 593–96.

Simpfendorfer, B. (2009) *The New Silk Road: How a Rising Arab World is Turning Away from the West and Rediscovering China*, New York: Palgrave Macmillan.

Stuttard, J. (2000) *The New Silk Road: Secrets of Business Success in China Today*, New York: John Wiley & Sons.

Sun, Z. and P. Martin (2008) "The Role of Trading Cities in the Development of Chinese Business Clusters," *International Business Research* 1(2): 69–81, http://ccsenet.org/journal/index.php/ibr/article/viewFile/993/969 (accessed October 14, 2011).

Trade Egypt (2010) http://trade.ec.europa.eu/doclib/html/113375.htm (accessed October 14, 2011).

Wang, P. (2005) "Three Poems," *Manoa* 17(1): 106–11.

Yiwu Industry and Commerce Administrative Bureau (2006) *Complete Commercial Guide to China Commodity City – Yiwu, China*, vol. 1, Peking: China Youth Press.

Zakaria, E. (2006) "Role of Urban Greenway Systems in Planning Residential Communities: A Case Study from Egypt," *Landscape and Urban Planning* 76(1–4): 192–209.

Zhejiang China Small Commodities City Group (2009) http://www.onccc.com (accessed October 14, 2011).

Zohry, A. (2003) "The Place of Egypt in the Regional Migration System as a Receiving Country," *Revue Européenne des Migrations Internationales* 19(3), http://remi.revues.org/index2664.html (accessed September 7, 2009).

2

"THEY COME FROM CHINA"

Pirate CDs in Mexico in transnational perspective

José Carlos G. Aguiar

So far, the perspective of globalization "from above" has been dominant in the social sciences when studying the impact of global neoliberalism on urban economies. Globalization is described as a formal process defining international trade. Attention has been focused on top–down flows led by institutional actors or mechanisms (institutions for global governance, free-trade agreements, multinationals), that order the circulation of commodities across the globe. In this context, the urban space is the privileged enclave where investment and infrastructure are centralized (Harvey 1989; Smart and Smart 2003). The service industries, market liberalization, technological advancement in communications, and transport rely on the configuration of the city as a space of flows. The global city is the playground where the mobilization of commodities, people, and ideas becomes tangible (Sassen 2000, 2010).

However, global neoliberalism entails more than institutional reforms promoted by international organizations or firms in privileged urban enclaves. The intensification of connections and commercial relations on a global scale is also reflected in the economy and daily lives of "petty" actors. Street peddlers or retailers in marketplaces, for instance, participate from their "informal" or "marginal" position in this process. Perspectives "from below" (Portes 2000) have discussed the emergence of "popular globalization," the formation of a "non-hegemonic world-system" (Ribeiro 2007) where economic actors make use of the advantages of globalization in unpredicted ways. Non-institutional actors can also become agents of transnational economic relations, and create enclaves of globalization where investment and trade is not ordered by the formal structures of global governance (see Schendel and Abraham 2005). Many of these activities and agencies contest the legal system of global neoliberalism and the dominant position and interests of formal actors. This tension generates various kinds of conflicts related to governance of urban spaces, particularly visible in state programs to counter "new illegalities," as is the case for copied music or films on CDs.

The rise and intensification of trade routes across the globe and the introduction of digital technologies have promoted the emergence of a synchronized global market for cultural goods (see Featherstone 1990; Mathews 2000). These cultural patterns are characterized by exclusive consumerism and commercial profit. Alternatively to this model, non-hegemonic actors have set up transnational networks for trade in unauthorized copies of music and films, as well as other products. These developments have a far-reaching impact on the street economy and marketplaces in urban settings around the world. In particular, there is evidence of the emergence of a market for "piracy," visible in global commodity chains between China and Latin America that makes possible the circulation of pirate CDs, "fake" fashion accessories, and electronics. Piracy thus mirrors and benefits from the global market of cultural goods.

Hegemonic globalization ambiguously profits from the informal or illegal practices feeding global cities, as is the case in the use of undocumented working force and other semi-legal practices (Harvey 2000; Sassen 2000). The edges of the system of law have, however, never been as solid. The boundary between states and illegal actors is often obscure. These actors adapt according to changing interests, and engage in activities that rearticulate the limits between legality and illegality (Nugent and Asiwaju 1996; Schendel 2005), as is apparent in chapters throughout this book.

The relation between states and illegal actors has long intrigued anthropologists (Blok 1975; Gupta 1995; Chabal and Daloz 1999; Lomnitz 2000; Haller and Shore 2005). Hibou has argued that corruption and illegality constitute the state's "alter-ego" (1999): state actors participate in the exchange of favors, gifts, or bribes to expand their realm of power or profit from illegal activities. In practice, states and illegal actors are entrenched in a relation of mutual benefit, although the outcome from these exchanges is highly unpredictable, due to the net of ambiguous loyalties in which these actors are embedded (Aguiar 2009). Corruption cannot constitute foolproof mechanisms of cooperation between state and illegal actors; uncertainty and some degree of "error" are perceived as inherent in these negotiations.

Mexico is a suitable case for studying the rise of global commodity chains of pirate CDs. A conservative estimate is that 400 million blank CDs are smuggled into Mexico every year (PGR 2011). The smuggling of CDs is crucial for the domestic production of pirated music and films. In Mexico, CDs are copied, distributed and later sold for retail across the country in more than 52,000 retail points.[1] In the San Juan de Dios market, in Guadalajara, there are about 1,500 stalls retailing some kind of pirated goods. This marketplace has a pivotal function in the production and trade of bootleg goods, on both a local and international scale. From the San Juan de Dios market, CDs are sent to central and southern Mexico, and to South America. In Venezuela and Peru, Mexican pirate goods constitute a desired commodity.

This chapter presents ethnographic material gathered between 2003 and 2010 in the San Juan de Dios market. The data was collected from sellers, traders, municipal authorities, police officers, and the copyrights lobby. In this research, I observed the practices and agents related to trade in counterfeit goods, giving shape to a global commodity chain for pirate CDs. I first discuss commodity chains in a larger sense; from there, I discuss the Mexican trading conglomerates that import these CDs into

Mexico, and finally I examine traders on the ground in Guadalajara, and how they engage in their trade, before returning to a brief discussion of how this is linked to globalization from below.

Commodity chains: made in China

The mobilization of goods and resources between regions of the world can be found at least since the rise of modern European imperialism, particularly in the formation of commercial routes among metropolises and colonies (i.e. proto-commodity chains). At this stage, however, there was mobilization of mostly natural resources and little technology (Landes 1998).

In the second half of the twentieth century, globalization intensified the commercial and industrial relations between different regions of the world. The term "global commodity chains" was coined to capture the processes of production, transport, consumption, and disposal of goods in international and highly complex environments. This concept is helpful in studying lean production, internationalization of manufacture, and outsourcing:

> [It] describes the full range of activities which are required to bring a product or service from conception, through the intermediary phases of production [...] delivery to final consumers, and final disposal after use
>
> *(Kaplinsky 2000: 121)*

Due to the improvement and cost reduction of communication and transportation, industries progressively make more use of the differences between countries to be able to localize production in profitable locations. Labor-intensive activities are sourced to countries where manufacture is cheaper or less regulated. Countries with a lesser degree of labor regulation, offering fiscal advantages or a weak rule of law, are attractive to companies in order to internationalize production (Dicken 1992; Gereffi and Korzeniewicz 1994). This is a financially driven process which aims to reduce costs and maximize profit. As a consequence, productive processes have become more complex since they involve different locations for specific tasks. As Vind and Fold have noted (2010: 57):

> A commodity chain is the full range of activities carried out by firms and workers to bring a product from conception to final use. This includes activities such as research and development, design, sourcing of inputs, the various stages of production, and marketing. These activities can be contained within a single firm in a single place, but more often, and increasingly so, they are divided among different firms and different places.

The commodity chain perspective looks at the whole cycle of a product, including extraction, transformation, manufacture, consumption, and disposal. Thus, the analytical emphasis lies on the mobilization of values across locations; every link in the chain is localized in a different place to be able to generate profit and surplus:

> The greatest virtue of a commodity chain approach is its emphasis on process. Not only do commodities move extensively through chains, but the chains are scarcely static for a moment. The capitalist world-economy reveals itself via this kind of radiography as a fast-moving network of relations that nonetheless constantly reproduces a basic order that permits the endless accumulation of capital, or at least has thus far reproduced this basic order.
>
> *(Hopkins and Wallerstein 1994: 50)*

Although global commodity chains predominantly involve North-to-South relations (companies from industrialized nations going abroad), the internationalization of production has also engendered South-to-South exchanges. A suitable example of these new multidirectional relations is the trade between Latin America and China. Deng Xiaoping's economic reforms marked the beginning of China's transformation into the factory of the world. Next to its participation in industrialized countries, China is also interested in transition economies. The growing presence of China in the foreign policy and international trade in Latin America (Pérez Le-Fort 2006; Li 2007) has led to China becoming the most dynamic commercial partner of Latin America in the early 2000s. For instance, China's exports to Chile have grown around 20 percent per year (Claro and Delpiano 2006). However, Latin Americans have mixed feelings concerning these developments. On the one hand, China's participation is perceived as a source of economic growth and access to cheaper goods, which have also improved in quality. But China's participation is also seen as a threat, particularly to Mexico. Expanding imports from China in the US market have put Mexican exports under pressure. Mexico competes with China in the US market to position its products, such as clothing, electronics, auto parts, and furniture (Gallagher and Porzecanski 2008).

The fast-growing presence of Chinese imports in domestic markets cannot be understood without looking at the migration of Chinese entrepreneurs (Smart and Hsu 2004). Chinese modernity is the "ideological construction of transnational Chinese capitalism" (Ong 1997: 173), one that has resulted in the formation of a transnational entrepreneurial class, well organized in lobbies and associations of Chinese importers and traders. The construction of a hegemonic cultural solidarity among a greater community of Chinese beyond national borders provides the capital and expertise for China's takeoff. Production, transport, and wholesale and retail sales are organized by a community of Chinese linking the factories in China to a multitude of wholesale and retail outlets overseas.

In explaining Chinese entrepreneurs in Eastern Europe, Nyíri (2010: 1) observes that "entrepreneurial migration also began to other parts of the world that were undergoing similar economic transitions from closed, authoritarian systems to open economies." Transnational entrepreneurs function as a broker between the industries in China and the consumer markets abroad. With the formation of associations of traders, entrepreneurs safeguard their interests and, by extension, those of China in the southern hemisphere. The transfer of productive processes to China has had an ambiguous outcome. Some results were expected: the reduction of production costs, a cheaper provision of customer services, and the expansion of the consumer market. Other consequences have been unintended. The enlargement and internationalization of production has exposed the limitations and weaknesses of governance and control of global commodity chains.

The manufacturing and selling of varieties of counterfeit merchandises have increased in the past 20 years, and the product field has also been expanding consistently. The methods of making and selling fake or shoddy products are becoming more and more advanced. East and Southeast Asia play a leading role in the global market of counterfeit goods (Chang 2004). There are unregistered illegal factories as well as legal factories making and trading counterfeit commodities. Factories often manufacture original items in off-hours to supply the illegal market, and there is often no noticeable difference in the quality between an original and a fake:

> Private factories produce clothes and shoes with their own legal brand. Since their brands are not famous, they have limited sales volume and profits; they secretly manufacture and sell the same kind of products with famous brand names and sell them at a low price to obtain large profits.
>
> *(Xiu 2010: 12)*

As a consequence, the difference between original and counterfeit is often not a question of quality (since the same factory supplies both the legal and black market) but of property rights, of whether or not the factory pays the license to produce the copyrighted material. Similar situations have been documented in Latin American factories, such as the apparel industry in Guatemala. The neoliberal organization of production has unexpectedly created new conflicts concerning the control and legal definition of production:

> Manufacturers themselves report that as much as 80 percent of apparel production in and around Tecpán involves the use of pirated brands like Nike, Lacoste, Disney, and Abercrombie & Fitch. Manufacturers say that pirated logos, labels, and tags are easy to obtain. Local embroidery shops reproduce the most popular labels with varying degrees of verisimilitude. Many producers travel to markets or other factories in Totonicapán, Sacatepequez, or Guatemala City to purchase copied tags and labels in bulk. They can sometimes participate in grey market exchanges by purchasing tags, size stickers, and embroidered logos that have been smuggled out of *maquiladoras*.
>
> *(Thomas 2009: 4)*

In China, there are criminal organizations behind the production and export of bootleg and counterfeit goods (Xiu 2010). The networks are active in China but also at the international level, and are involved in various activities, including money laundering, weapons trafficking, the porn industry, and human smuggling. By adopting an assembly line method of operation, the networks coordinate the process of purchasing, manufacturing, transporting, and selling.

The "made in China" phenomenon has reached the urban spaces of Latin America, transforming the legal nature of the goods available on the streets and in the marketplaces, and the networks in which sellers are involved. The economy of counterfeit goods is illustrative of "popular globalization [...] organised in knots, marketplaces, and in fluxes" (Ribeiro 2007: 19). The transportation and importation is in the hands of transnational Chinese entrepreneurs, linking commercial circuits between China and Latin America (Rabossi 2004; Pinheiro-Machado 2008). The Chinese diaspora has formed an entrepreneurial elite, involved in both legal and illegal domains. Retail and smuggling of Chinese imports is visible in the networks of *paseros* and *sacoleiros* (Aguiar 2010) who mobilize goods across borders within South America. On the streets, sellers retail products that challenge the definition of legality and demonstrate the ambiguous impact of globalization on the economies of Latin American cities.

Transnational CD smuggling and the czar of piracy

Mexico has a limited production of blank CDs. According to the Mexican Association of Music Producers, AMPROFON (see note 1), there is only one CD factory in Mexico, and imports are necessary to meet the needs of the legal record industry. The music industry lobby estimates that two of every three CDs sold in Mexico are pirate. In 2006, 110 million counterfeit CDs were sold across the country; 56 million legal CDs were sold in the same period (IFPI 2006). Transnational smuggling provides the supply for the production of pirate CDs. The introduction of CDs into Mexico is the starting point of a commodity chain for the production, distribution, and wholesale and retail sale of illegal CDs. By examining two cases, I will analyze the rise of a global commodity chain for the smuggling and transport of CDs, constituting a transnational network between China, Mexico, and South America.

The first case is the Grupo Mekong (Mekong group), formed in 1999 by the Solís Heredia family. Thirteen family members joined the venture for the "trade, distribution, representation, supply, lease and consignation of all kinds of goods and merchandise of national or foreign origin" (*Reforma* 2003). The Solís are a family from Tepito, Mexico City, a well-known neighborhood controlled by criminal gangs. The Mekong group began with trade in blank CDs. The company quickly became the importer for the legal music industry, supplying CDs to national and foreign enterprises. CDs were produced in Taiwan and later in China, and transported to San Diego, California, where the CD manufacturers had a subsidiary company. Mekong picked up the CDs in San Diego and brought them to Mexico via the border city of Tijuana. Autotransportes Tonatiuh, a sub-company under the wing of Mekong group, was in charge of transport operations, from San Diego to Mexico City. One year after its foundation, the group expanded its activities to southern Mexico.

The booming activities of the Mekong group drew the attention of the Secretary of the General Attorney (PGR). The company was suspected of CD smuggling.

In December 2001, the federal police carried out a seizure in one of the warehouses of the group in Mexico City; 10 million discs were seized but no person was detained. But this did not mean the end of the enterprise; on the contrary, it gave a new impulse to it. The importation system was modified: Mekong supplied merchandise from different companies, while entrance points at the border diversified across the northern Mexican border.

By 2002, three years after its founding, the enterprise had already opened subsidiaries in a number of Mexican cities, among them Guadalajara. According to federal investigators, Mekong had become specialized in *contrabando técnico* (technical smuggling): the illegal introduction of foreign goods by means of forged paperwork or false declarations and tax payments. Established trading companies were used as legal screens to mask illegal activities. According to the PGR, Mekong was introducing millions of blank CDs to Mexico every year through tax evasion and bribes to customs officers. Mekong had also expanded its operations to southern Mexico and Central America, becoming a major player in the smuggling of blank CDs on a continental scale.

The first link of this chain is located in China. Guangzhou, the capital of Guangdong province in south China, is increasingly taking over Taipei's earlier role in the production of CDs and DVDs. Factories manufacturing CDs for companies such as Canon, LG, Sony, Verbatim, and Philips, work off-hours, and the overproduction supplies the illegal market. CDs are even branded with international labels. Yet, even if CDs seem to be original, they are illegal, since the production license is not paid to the company (*Reforma* 2006). Chinese smugglers and the Mekong group have various trade routes. The main route, as already mentioned, goes by sea from China to Taiwan and later the US. Once in the United States, the merchandise is sent by land to Mexico. Secondary routes are sea shipments arriving at Mexican harbors, primarily Lázaro Cárdenas and Manzanillo, on the Pacific Coast. CDs are also sent by air. However, even if Mekong developed networks in airports in China and Mexico City, the air route is more uncertain and expensive.

In 2002 the PGR started another investigation. The brothers were accused of using illegal resources, flouting copyright laws and engaging in activities comparable to smuggling. In December 2002, the federal police carried out a major raid in Mexico City, confiscating 7 million CDs from Mekong-related facilities. Two Solís brothers, Rafael and Daniel, were detained. The investigation concluded that they were supplying resources for the illegal reproduction of music; the PGR estimated that the group controlled around 50 percent of all smuggled CDs in Mexico: 200 to 250 million units. The brothers denied the accusations and argued that the seizure had been a setup by the police.

A few months after the detention of the Solís brothers in March 2003, information emerged concerning the protection that the local police were allegedly providing to the network. Mexico City's police force was accused of guarding convoys transporting merchandise; the press claimed to be in possession of photos of this as evidence. The Solís brothers were sent to prison to await sentencing. Once the case was turned over to the judiciary, the brothers claimed that the evidence had been fabricated, and successfully convinced the court that 26 million CDs and 30 million pesos in cash seized during police actions (December 2001–December 2002) was not solid enough evidence. The defense made use of a rarely successful resource called *desvanacimiento de datos* (dissolution of evidence) and the judge declared the Solís brothers innocent. Five months later they were freed. Shortly after their release, in December 2003, Judge Carenzo Rivas was removed. The Federal Judiciary had doubts regarding the trial and demanded that the case be re-examined. Warrants for the arrest of the brothers were served in June 2004. However, the judge was returned to office in June 2005, and received a retroactive salary for the months he had not been active. Six years after the warrants for the arrest against the Solís Heredia brothers were issued, they are still fugitive.

The Comercializadora Agaroniam is probably the second most important smuggling network after the Mekong group. This enterprise was established in 2002 by Ara Agaroniam, who was born in Yerevan, Armenia in 1945, and migrated to Mexico in the early 1990s. Agaroniam has been involved in various import companies since 1995. In February 2002, he registered the Comercializadora Agaroniam at the Federal Tax Office. The enterprise's listed activity is the importation of merchandise, like Russian vodka, to Mexico. Agaroniam was granted Mexican citizenship in 2003, and has developed a luxurious lifestyle. In contrast to the Solís brothers, who always stayed in their *barrio*, Tepito, Agaroniam acquired real estate in upper-class neighborhoods in Mexico City. From investigations carried out by the PGR, Agaroniam was suspected of introducing illegal merchandise, chiefly blank CDs, from Russia and China. The Mexican press quickly picked up the allegations and named him the *"zar de la piratería"* ("czar of piracy"), who sought to spread his network all across Latin America. Agaroniam, according to the PGR, was smuggling around 270 million CDs a year, with a profit of US$80 million. His warehouses were spread all over Mexico City, it was reported, the largest of which had a storage capacity of up to 25 million CDs.

The network under Agaroniam was formed by Syrians and Armenians resident in Mexico, but also included a number of Mexicans who often functioned as *prestanombres* (providing one's name as a cover). Mexican names are useful to ward off police attention when registering companies and filling out paperwork. Agaroniam also enjoyed police protection when transporting merchandise (*Reforma* 2005a), as was the case with Mekong. Agaroniam supplied *ambulantes* (peddlers) in Mexico City's downtown and Tepito, areas of the city characterized by informal commerce. In another parallel to the Solís brothers, Agaroniam successfully managed to expand his area of influence by opening subsidiaries in various Mexican states, including Jalisco. Agaroniam also dealt with the company Comercializadora Continental, based in Tacna, Peru (*Reforma* 2005b). In December 2004, the federal police confiscated 9.2 million CDs during a raid at one of Agaroniam's warehouses in Mexico City. The Treasury argued that Agaroniam had taken control over the structure that the Solís brothers had established for CD smuggling. An arrest warrant was issued in June 2005 against Agaroniam, but he too is still fugitive.

The Grupo Mekong and Comercializadora Agaroniam cases reveal how illegal networks reflect the international flows of goods and structures of trade typical of globalization. The enterprises include professional actors, accountants, and lawyers. They are organized in a funnel network that becomes transnational at two levels: supply (input of CDs), and sales (output of pirate CDs). They were introducing 400 to 600 million blank CDs per year from China to Mexico. Bearing in mind that the national market for piracy in Mexico is estimated at about 110 million CDs a year, the majority of the 400 to 600 million smuggled CDs is thus meant for export. Links in the chain run towards South America, as shown by Agaroniam's company in Peru. These networks do not work on a fully illegal or criminal basis, and this is what makes them so intriguing. Grupo Mekong and Comercializadora Agaroniam are established companies. These enterprises can be seen as the ultimate case of what in Mexico is often called *empresas fantasma* (ghost enterprises): companies legally con-stituted that serve as a smokescreen to facilitate illegal activities. (This is also the case for money laundering, where shops, hotels, restaurants, or other suitable businesses are used to legalize money.) In their structure and activities, they are successful in organizing globalization from below and constitute a side of global trade that challenges hegemonic actors and their interests.

Piracy in the San Juan de Dios market

Thus far I have described the international links at the input level in the global commodity chain for pirate CDs; I will now turn to the output level. The mobili-zation of blank CDs within Mexico, the production of pirate CDs, and their further distribution to other links are clearly territorialized processes. They take place among embedded actors, involving more autonomous, grounded agents at every stage, which allows for a fuller ethnographic description.

FIGURE 2.1 The San Juan de Dios market. Photo by José Carlos G. Aguiar. Reproduced with permission

Guadalajara is the second largest city of Mexico; the official census counted some 4 million inhabitants in the metropolitan area (2005), although it is commonly assumed that the population is well above 5 million. The city doubled its population in ten years (1995–2005), and has preserved its "traditional identity" with a characteristic historical center. Next to the Plaza Tapatia, the center's main square, stands the San Juan de Dios market, founded in the sixteenth century as a trading post linking the northern and central regions of the former Spanish colony.

This marketplace is still a pivotal trading point in the city. About 3,000 sellers work in the 1,600 stands in the three floors of the market building. The administration of the market estimates that up to 30,000 people a day come to the market on a busy week-end. The colorful and festive environment in the market that locals call "traditional" coexists with a number of illegal activities—prostitution, drug trafficking—with piracy the most remarkable one since the late 1980s. In ten years, the marketplace has under-gone a deep transformation: the local handicrafts and food have disappeared; more than a half of the stalls now sell some kind of counterfeit goods, including training shoes, clothing, software, perfumes and, above all, music and films. The San Juan de Dios market in Guadalajara is crucial for the production and sale of pirate CDs at a regional level.

Pirate CD retailers in stalls in the marketplace are the most visible link in the global commodity chain. Where do the CDs come from? "They come from China," I have often been told. Sellers in the San Juan de Dios know about the raw resources of piracy. However vague and imprecise their answers might be, it indicates the amount of knowledge available to the agent, defined by the position s/he occupies within the network. Knowledge is hierarchical, and suppliers administer information accordingly. Retailers in the San Juan de Dios market indeed know they are one link of a larger chain that includes transnational networks, but their position within the chain also limits their knowledge about the structure. Privileged informants, wholesalers themselves or sellers with good contacts, are aware that blank CDs arrive at the harbour of Manzanillo in the neighboring state of Colima, about 300 kilometers from Guadalajara.[2]

Here, shipments from China and Taiwan arrive in containers and are then trans-ported by land. From the marketplace in Guadalajara, as Roberto, a young tenant, pointed out, merchandise is distributed to other locations in Central Mexico:

> The strong ones bring it from China. As far as I understand, there are more people selling from here [to Tepito] than from there [Tepito] to here. That is because the merchandise enters through Manzanillo […]. The containers arrive in Manzanillo, then [the merchandise comes] here, and from here they distribute. They [the importers] are from here.

The big wholesalers can also be importers themselves; they mobilize the merchandise in Guadalajara and take care of the production process: *quemar* ("burning," copying) CDs. The typical retailer in the marketplace does not buy blank CDs and copy them; s/he obtains the finished product from a pirate entrepreneur.

In the past, some pirate entrepreneurs were smugglers, *fayuqueros*, who in the 1980s mobilized and sold wholesale electronics and clothing from the US in Mexico before

FIGURE 2.2 Stands in the San Juan de Dios marketplace. Photo by José Carlos G. Aguiar. Reproduced with permission

the opening of commercial borders. At present, there is a new generation of piracy entrepreneurs in the San Juan de Dios market, led by young men with university educations who have envisioned the whole structure and run it from one end of the chain to the other, bringing CDs directly from China or the US. Aside from these large pirate entrepreneurs, there are also small-scale burners, who copy material for their own retail activities. This is, however, quite a marginal phenomenon. Most retailers in the San Juan de Dios market source their merchandise from pirate entrepreneurs in the market, and are not involved in production themselves. But there is no such thing as a typical pirate retailer; they all work at different levels and with different degrees of autonomy.

Digital technology has made it possible to reproduce music and film material with the same quality as the original in almost no time and at very low cost. The transition from videocassettes to CDs and later DVDs—from magnetic to digital technology—is a key factor for understanding the velocity of the spread of piracy. Burning CDs is not a labor-intensive or capital-intensive undertaking. CDs are inexpensive: the wholesale price in the San Juan de Dios market is US$0.10. CDs can be copied fast and easily, and the invested capital can be rapidly retrieved. A *torre* (tower: a desktop computer) with seven copying drives costs about 7,000 pesos (US$636). With seven drives simultaneously burning CDs, one desktop computer can produce 350 or more discs a day. Pirate entrepreneurs set up *laboratorios* (factories) with many computers in service, which multiplies the daily production rate. A *laboratorio* consists of three to five computers, and one day of production can deliver some 2,000 discs, depending on the processing speed of the computer and the CD burner (*Mural* 2005a, 2005b).

FIGURE 2.3 Pirate goods for sale. Photo by José Carlos G. Aguiar. Reproduced with permission

Stalls in the San Juan de Dios market are quite small (4 × 2 meters, depending on the zone), and there is not sufficient space to set up a factory. Beyond this, the administration of the market might raise questions about the activity. *Laboratorios* are thus rarely situated in the marketplace; rather, they are located in warehouses in the surrounding streets, or in houses in quiet neighborhoods nearby. Nevertheless, there are a few market tenants who have a computer at their stall, from which they may continuously copy material for their own retail sales, engaging in production and vending at the same time.

Another important element in the supply is the original data to copy, the music or films that entrepreneurs reproduce. Only very few piracy entrepreneurs succeed in building up a network reaching the music and film industry. Sergio (a pseudonym) was a *fayuquero* and often traveled to Los Angeles, where he had a contact who was working for a video distribution company. Before films are released in the DVD market, the distribution companies or subsidiaries edit catalogues for the season for their clients to announce and promote coming releases. Sergio had access to these services and this provided him material before its market release. This kind of mechanism becomes visible when much-anticipated albums or films are already on sale in the pirate market before their official release.[3] Other entrepreneurs provide material from music or video stores; there are also recordings of screenings in movie theaters, but the bulk of the films and music is downloaded from the internet.

Once the music or film has been copied onto the CD, the disc must be boxed. This is a crucial part of the production process; the films or songs recorded on a CD may not vary that much in terms of audio quality from one retailer to another, but there are clear differences in packaging that provide evidence as to the legal or illegal origin of the product. "*Lo que cambia es su presentación*" ("just the packaging is different"), a retailer assures me when explaining the packaging of the product, which determines its price. Some CDs are sold in plain envelopes or plastic sleeves, which makes them cheaper. Other CDs are packaged in cases, with a hand-written or computer-printed cover indicating the singer, the album, or the film. At the top in the quality chart, there are CDs or DVDs boxed in fancier cases, with covers that give the impression of being original; these are the most expensive. Packaging the pirate CDs is a micro-process that, in contrast to burning, takes place entirely inside the San Juan de Dios market. All necessary materials relating to packaging can be found here. On the third floor of the market building there are a number of stalls that only sell CD and DVD covers. Some of these covers are printed offset, while others have been copied using a regular color copy machine. Stickers with photos of film stars or movie titles are also on sale; they can be placed on the front of a pirate CD. There are also stalls where CD and DVD cases can be bought in packages of ten units or more.

The seller, who is typically an autonomous agent, can decide for him- or herself which titles to sell. Retailers choose albums and films on the basis of what they already see on display in the market—perhaps not the best business strategy, since sellers are competing for the same buyers. Retailers may also make a decision on the advice of the *proveedor* (supplier), who informs the retailer as to *estrenos* (new releases) which may be highly profitable. Vendors in some cases make their own lists with titles they want, asking the supplier to find and reproduce the material. This allows vendors to offer a larger catalogue to customers, like *quema de discos bajo pedido* (CD burning on request), whereby clients ask retailers for specific titles.

Pirate sellers in the San Juan de Dios market generally serve as brokers between the entrepreneur (manufacturer or provider) and a retailer or the final consumer. The majority of the sellers are males in their late teens or early twenties working for a "boss." When a customer requests a title that is unavailable, the young retailer may reply, "I don't have it here, but wait, let me check"; then the retailer may go to the next stall and ask if they have the title. There is also an exchange of money between young retailers, lending and borrowing banknotes or coins to be able to give change. These two practices, checking for titles from other stalls and lending and borrowing money, imply an open flow of giving and taking between stalls that often belong to the same owner or entrepreneur.

"Here there are people [buyers] who sell in *tianguis* [street markets], people who come from Aguascalientes, Zacatecas, Vallarta, from many places," says a pirate CD retailer about his customers. Guadalajara is the second largest point of wholesale, behind Tepito in Mexico City. Supply in the San Juan de Dios market has created a region for pirate CDs; the neighboring states of Colima, Aguascalientes, Zacatecas, Durango, and Nayarit all depend on the San Juan de Dios market for their supply of pirate CDs and DVDs.

When looking at the distances between retailers and the distribution centers in sub-regions, it is clear that retailers do not travel far to source their merchandise. This is the case for economic reasons, but it also reduces risk. Uncertainty prevails in the event of a police roadblock when driving home with a trunkload of illegal CDs. As I was told:

> What is sold in Guadalajara is made in Guadalajara. To bring it from Mexico City is very risky because the federal police or the PGR can catch you on the road, and it obviously is illegal merchandise and you run the risk of getting the merchandise confiscated. So, merchandise is made here in Guadalajara to reduce that risk, and here it is also distributed and sold.

Even if arrangements between police agents and retailers are common, the police do not have what might be termed a "collective morality." In Mexico, the police are woven into a complex fabric made of different loyalties (Aguiar forthcoming). The police officer continually adapts to a changing environment, based on an equation between the institutional expectations of the policeman as a public servant and his own personal interests. This makes the outcome of the negotiation between pirate sellers or smugglers and enforcing officers unpredictable. Transport of large volumes of merchandise, therefore, always poses a risk. Trips ought to be short; this allows retailers to frequently restock and not risk losing large amounts of merchandise.

Final remarks: China–Latin America from below

The mobilization of blank CDs across continents provides evidence of trading regions in the context of globalization which are not dominated by hegemonic actors. In the global commodity chain of pirate CDs, Chinese, Armenian, and Mexican agents become involved. They are integrated in the links of the chain, and show the particularities and limits of their participation.

The participation of Chinese and Taiwanese networks in the liminal economy of Latin America becomes observable when looking at the commodity chain of pirate CDs in Mexico. Commercial relations between the two regions are by no means a new phenomenon. In the sixteenth century the commercial ties between the Americas and the Far East were already intense; the trade route between Acapulco and Manila was, for instance, one of the busiest and most profitable of its time (Headrick 2010: 40–41). However, the commercial ties described in this chapter are not controlled by colonial powers or institutional actors, but are organized by agents who switch between legal and illegal domains. Established, formal enterprises help as a smokescreen to run commodity chains where the goods shift in their legality. In some links the goods are legal but they turn into illegal commodities once reaching a new location or when undergoing a transformative process such as copying protected data on a CD.

By partially taxing merchandise, declaring one kind of merchandise and introducing a different kind, or by bribing authorities, the Grupo Mekong and the Comercializadora Agoraniam have been successful in neutralizing surveillance at the national borders of a number of countries to illegally transport goods. The San Juan de Dios market constitutes a territory where the chain becomes tangible, in the productive process of the commodity as much as in the relations between entrepreneurs and sellers. What, then, is the relation between piracy and global neoliberalism? Does the commodity chain of pirate CDs mimic globalization? In other words, is it a substitute or a leeching off the formal processes of global trade?

Blank CDs are essential to the commodity chain; they constitute the technological and physical support for the production of piracy. But many other commodities are also mobilized through the chain joining China and Mexico, such as counterfeit clothing, shoes, jewelry, and electronics, that demonstrate diversity in the trading relations from below. And much of this trade is not counterfeit.

The position of Chinese and Taiwanese actors in the commodity chain has its particularities. Unlike such activities in Latin American countries like Brazil, Colombia, or Venezuela, Asian traders in Mexico do not participate in retail. Chinese networks come in contact in the import of CDs, but they do not organize the chain as pirate entrepreneurs do in the San Juan de Dios market. Chinese traders do not own retail stalls in the marketplace. They have bought buildings around the market area, but are not integrated into this space of popular commerce. They are either not interested in partaking in retail or do not possess the political capital to be able to obtain retail points in highly politicized arenas, as marketplaces in Mexico are, territories mediated by political parties and leaders. "*Los Chinos*" (regardless if they are from Taiwan, Hong Kong, or Japan) do not represent a direct threat to sellers in the marketplace or to the entrepreneurs in the commodity chain for pirate CDs in the San Juan de Dios market.

The commodity chain surrounding the pirate economy explicitly shows that globalization is not only about legal or formal exchanges between regions;

globalization becomes visible as well in the rise of illegal economies in which local and transnational actors are linked, creating new commercial regions. The global commodity chain for pirate CDs reveals a liberal entrepreneurial environment, which is characterized by a specificity of functions at every link, specialized knowledge, and open competition.

Notes

1 Mario Arturo Díaz (AMPROFON legal representative), in discussion with the author, June 25, 2005.
2 Manzanillo is also an important harbor for the transport of drugs. While controls harden at the border between Mexico and the US, as Gauthier describes in chapter 8, harbors serve as hubs where drugs and smuggled merchandise can easily pass through.
3 This was the case with the Romance albums by the Mexican singer Luis Miguel, as a scandal broke out when it became known that workers from the production company were bribed to provide a copy of the album to smugglers.

References

Aguiar, J. C. G. (2009) "Nuevas ilegalidades en el orden global. Piratería y la escenificación del estado de derecho en México" [New Illegalities in the Global Order. Piracy and the Rule of Law in Mexico], *Foro Internacional* 196: 403–24.
——(2010) *Stretching the Border: Smuggling Practices and the Control of Illegality in South America*, New Voices Series 6, Santiago: Global Consortium on Security Transformation (GCST).
——(forthcoming) "Policing New Illegalities: Piracy, Raids and *Madrinas*," in W. Pansters, ed., *Violence, Coercion, and State-Making in Twentieth-Century Mexico: The Other Half of the Centaur*, Palo Alto: Stanford University Press.
Blok, A. (1975) *The Mafia of a Sicilian Village, 1850–1960: A Study of Violent Peasant Entrepreneurs*, London: William Cowes Sons.
Chabal, P. and J. P. Daloz (1999) *Africa Works: Disorder as Political Instrument*, Bloomington: Indiana University Press.
Chang, H. (2004) "Fake Logos, Fake Theory, Fake Globalization," *Inter-Asia Cultural Studies* 5(2): 222–36.
Claro, S. and R. Delpiano (2006) "Competencia China: buena, variada y barata" [Chinese Competitiveness: Good, Assorted and Cheap], *Estudios Públicos* 104: 307–29.
Dicken, P. (1992) *Global Shift: The Internationalization of Economic Activity*, New York: Guilford Press.
Featherstone, M. (1990) *Global Culture*, London: Sage.
Gallagher, K. and R. Porzecanski (2008) "China Matters: China's Economic Impact in Latin America," *Latin American Research Review* 43(1): 185–200.
Gereffi, G. and M. Korzeniewicz (eds) (1994) *Commodity Chains and Global Capitalism*, Westport: Praeger.
Gupta, A. (1995) "Blurred Boundaries: The Discourse of Corruption, the Culture of Politics, and the Imagined State," *American Ethnologist* 22: 375–402.
Haller, D. and C. Shore (2005) *Corruption: Anthropological Perspectives*, London: Pluto.
Harvey, D. (1989) *The Condition of Postmodernity: An Enquiry into the Origins of Cultural Change*, Oxford: Blackwell.
——(2000) *Spaces of Hope*, Edinburgh: Edinburgh University Press.
Headrick, D. R. (2010) *Power Over Peoples: Technology, Environments, and Western Imperialism, 1400 to the Present*, Princeton: Princeton University Press.
Hibou, B. (1999) "The 'Social Capital' of the State as an Agent of Deception," in J.-F. Bayart, S. Ellis, and B. Hibou, eds, *The Criminalization of the State in Africa*, Bloomington: Indiana University Press.

Hopkins, T. and I. Wallerstein (1994) "Commodity Chains in the Capitalist World-Economy Prior to 1800," in G. Gereffi and M. Korzeniewicz, eds, *Commodity Chains and Global Capitalism*, Westport: Praeger, 17–51.

IFPI (International Federation of the Phonographic Industry) (2006) "The Recording Industry 2006 Piracy Report," http://www.ifpi.org/content/library/piracy-report2006.pdf (accessed August 28, 2010).

Kaplinsky, R. (2000) "Spreading the Gains from Globalisation: What Can Be Learned from Value Chain Analysis?", *Journal of Development Studies* 37(2): 117–46.

Landes, D. (1998) *The Wealth and Poverty of Nations: Why Some are so Rich and Some so Poor*, London: Brown & Company.

Li, H. (2007) "Red Star Over Latin America," *Nacla Report on the Americas*. 40(5): 23–27.

Lomnitz, C. (ed.) (2000) *Vicios públicos, virtudes privadas: la corrupción en México* [Public Vices, Private Virtues: Corruption in Mexico], Mexico City: University of Chicago/CIESAS.

Mathews, G. (2000) *Global Culture/Individual Identity: Searching for Home in the Cultural Supermarket*, London: Routledge.

Mural [newspaper] (2005a) "Tiran negocio de megapiratas" [Pirate Mega Business Put Down] February 2.

——(2005b) "Entrega su mujer a esposo y 'pirata'" [Woman Hands in her Man and 'Pirate'] April 16.

Nugent, P. and A. I. Asiwaju (eds) (1996) *African Boundaries: Barriers, Conduits, Opportunities*, London: Pinter.

Nyiri, P. (2010) *Chinese Entrepreneurs in Poor Countries: A Transnational 'Middleman Minority' and its Futures*, Amsterdam: Vrije Universiteit.

Ong, A. (1997) "Chinese Modernities: Narratives of Nation and of Capitalism," in A. Ong and D. Nonini, eds, *Ungrounded Empires: The Cultural Politics of Modern Chinese Transnationalism*, New York: Routledge, 171–97.

Pérez Le-Fort, M. (2006) "China y América Latina: estrategias bajo una hegemonía transitoria" [China and Latin America: Strategies under a Transitory Hegemony], *Nueva Sociedad* 203: 89–101.

PGR (Procuraduría General de la República) [Secretary of the General Attorney] (2006) http://www.pgr.gob.mx (accessed January 9, 2006).

——(2011) "Delitos de propiedad intelectual, industrial y derechos de autor. Situación Inicial" [Intellectual and Industrial Property and Copyrights Offenses. Initial Situation], Mexico, http://www.pgr.gob.mx/Combate%20a%20la%20Delincuencia/Delitos%20Federales/Delitos%20en%20materia%20de%20derechos%20de%20autor/Delitos%20en%20materia%20de%20derechos%20de%20autor.asp#/ (accessed March 12, 2011).

Pinheiro-Machado, R. (2008) "China-Paraguai-Brasil: Uma rota para pensar a economia informal" [China-Paraguay-Brazil: a route to think the informal economy], *Revista Brasileira de Ciências Sociais* 23(67): 117–33.

Portes, A. (2000) "Globalization from Below: The Rise of Transnational Communities," in D. Kalb *et al.* eds, *The Ends of Globalization*, Oxford: Rowman & Littlefeld.

Rabossi, F. (2004) "Nas Ruas de Ciudad del Este: Vidas e Vendas num Mercado de Fronteira" [In the streets of Ciudad del Este: Lives and Sales in a Border Market], PhD Dissertation, Universidade Federal do Rio de Janeiro.

Reforma [newspaper] (2003) "Inician Carrera en la Peralvillo" [They Start their Career at the Peralvillo], January 26.

——(2005a) "Detectan Custodia de Policía Capitalina" [Metropolitan Police Custody is Found], June 13.

——(2005b) "Erige Armenio en 2 Años Imperio del CD Pirata" [Armenian Builds up an Emporium for Pirate CDs in Two Years], June 13.

——(2006) "Investigan Red Para Piratería" [Investigation of piracy network], January 26.

Ribeiro, G. (2007) "El sistema mundial no-hegemónico y la globalización popular" [The world Non-hegemonic System and Popular Globalization], *Série Anthropologia* 410, Brasília: Universidade de Brasília, Departamento de Antropologia.

Sassen, S. (2000) *Cities in a World Economy*, Thousand Oaks: Pine Forge Press.
——(2010) "Global Inter-City networks and Commodity Chains: Any Intersections?" *Global Networks* 10(1): 150–63.
Schendel, W. van (2005) *The Bengal Borderland: Beyond State and Nation in South Asia*, London: Anthem Press.
Schendel, W. van and I. Abraham (eds) (2005) *Illicit Flows and Criminal Things: States, Borders, and the Other Side of Globalization*, Bloomington: Indiana University Press.
Smart, A. and J. Y. Hsu (2004) "The Chinese Diaspora, Foreign Investment and Economic Development in China," *The Review of International Affairs* 3(4): 544–66.
Smart, A. and J. Smart (2003) "Urbanization and the Global Perspective," *Annual Review of Anthropology* 32: 263–85.
Thomas, K. (2009) "Structural Adjustment, Spatial Imaginaries, and 'Piracy' in Guatemala's Apparel Industry," *Anthropology of Work Review* XXX(1): 1–10.
Vind, I. and N. Fold (2010) "City Networks and Commodity Chains: Identifying Global Flows and Local Connections in Ho Chi Minh City," *Global Networks* 10(1): 54–74.
Xiu, L. (2010) "Organized Crime and the Black Economy in China," *Working Paper Series* 7, Santiago: Global Consortium on Security Transformation.

3

CIUDAD DEL ESTE AND BRAZILIAN CIRCUITS OF COMMERCIAL DISTRIBUTION

Fernando Rabossi

Located on the eastern border of Paraguay, Ciudad del Este is a huge marketplace for imported goods from all around the world, especially from China and East Asia. What started as a shopping tourist destination at the end of the 1960s became the supply center of imported goods for traders from all around Brazil, flooding street markets, shops and shopping-malls with commodities. To understand this transformation and the changes that ended up restricting those circuits of commerce mainly to informal actors, we need to grasp the complex interrelationships between governmental practices, entrepreneurial strategies, geopolitical interests, and the workings of thousands of people that make the flows of goods from different parts of the world possible.

The concepts of "economic globalization from below" (Ribeiro 2006: 234) and "low-end globalization" (Mathews 2007: 170) help us to understand Ciudad del Este in a larger context, as part of a social and economic geography where goods flow through the interstices of regulations and where "'alternative' transnational agents disregard or bypass the normative and regulating power of nation-states" (Ribeiro, 2006: 247). The processes that led Ciudad del Este to become a node of international trade and the phases that it experienced in its short history offer interesting material to reflect on these and the related concept of "non-hegemonic globalization" (Ribeiro 2007, 2010).

In this chapter I first present a historical account of the development of the region that will allow us to understand the multiple dimensions and actors involved in the structuring of that world: the Brazilian and Paraguayan governments, the Lebanese and Chinese traders, and the circuits of smuggling and the emergence and consolidation of the *sacoleiros* circuits. Then I examine these circuits: their extent and functioning, and the differences that articulate them. Finally, I discuss the complementary nature between perspectives "from below" and "from above" to understand the workings of global circuits that usually remain outside the main narratives of globalization.[1]

Encountering Ciudad del Este

When I started fieldwork in the Paraguayan Ciudad del Este in 1999, the circulation over the bridge that connected the city with the neighboring city of Foz do Iguaçu in Brazil was incredible. Every day, thousands of cars, buses, motorcycles and bicycles moved people and parcels either side of the border through the Friendship Bridge, as it is called. To Paraguay, the parcels mainly included Brazilian merchandise that flooded the Paraguayan internal market through different mechanisms of introduction and commercialization. To Brazil, the parcels were mainly imported goods from other parts of the world, mostly from China and Taiwan.

At that time, thousands of Brazilians arrived every day in Ciudad del Este to buy the products that they would sell, back in their home cities. These small traders, known as *sacoleiros,* came from places as far away as São Paulo (1,062 km), Rio de Janeiro (1,507 km), Brasília (1,598 km), Feira de Santana (2,677 km) or, Caruaru (3,568 km). The word *sacoleiro* comes from the word *sacola* (bag), and it is taken from the big bags that are used to carry merchandise. *Sacoleiros* are also known as *muambeiros,* persons who carry smuggled products. They arrive by bus—regular ones or ones rented for the occasion and presented as tourist excursions—and return with bags full of merchandise that will be commercialized among acquaintances, in shops and shopping centers, or in the popular markets and the commercial districts that started to specialize in imported goods since the 1990s.

FIGURE 3.1 Traffic jam in Ciudad del Este, 2001. Photo by Fernando Rabossi. Reproduced with permission

Despite my surprise at the huge numbers of people and things that were moved through the border, all those involved in the business said that the movement at the turn of the century was only a shadow of what it had been previously. It is difficult to come up with accurate numbers, but some estimates of the traders I spoke with were that during the peak years of 1994–1995, more than 60,000 Brazilians buyers arrived weekly in Ciudad del Este. By 1999–2001, estimates were of less than 20,000 buyers. The significance of this flux can be seen in the proliferation of popular markets fed by products that came from Paraguay in almost all Brazilian cities. But these products are not only restricted to popular consumption. Certain goods—electronic and computer devices, for example—were, and still are, consumed by middle- and upper-class sectors. Let me now explain the recent history of this region, in order to understand Ciudad del Este's rise and recent decline as a world entrepôt of trade.

The radical transformation of a region

The borders of Brazil, Paraguay and Argentina meet in a corner that came to be known during the 1980s as the Triple Frontera, or the Tri-Border Area as it is known in English. The use of this generic name for that particular place was the result of its regular usage in the media (especially in Argentina and Brazil) and its incorporation in official discourses during the 1990s. (It was officially recognized in 1998 in the *Plan de Seguridad para la Triple Frontera*; the name of the security plan to be applied in that region signed by the members the regional common market, Mercosur.) This usage appeared together with accusations of trafficking in all kinds of things, and the presence of organized gangs as well as, reputedly, Islamic terrorists. After the bombing of the Israeli Embassy (1992) and an Israeli association (1994) in Buenos Aires, the border region was denounced as having been the logistical base from where the attacks were planned and prepared.

Compared with other confluences of three international borders, the first distinction that draws attention is the presence of important cities on all sides of the different borders. Puerto Iguazú in Argentina and Foz do Iguaçu in Brazil are cities separated by the Iguassu River, a few kilometers down from the famous Iguassu Falls. On the Paraná River lies the international border that separates Paraguay from Brazil; across from the Brazilian Foz do Iguaçu is the Paraguayan city of Ciudad del Este. Some kilometers north of both cities, on the Paraná River, is located the world's largest hydroelectric plant in power output, Itaipu.

Until the end of the nineteenth century, the region surrounding the confluence of the Paraná and Iguassu rivers was not incorporated under the institutional frames of their respective states. The processes of occupation of the territory that displaced its indigenous population had been related to the appropriation of *yerba mate* and wood, but property titles were given only after 1870. The date is not accidental and reflects the interest of these different governments in seizing their territories after the end of the War of the Triple Alliance fought between Paraguay and the allied forces of Brazil, Argentina and Uruguay from 1864 to 1870, a war that ended in the bloody defeat of Paraguay.

The Paraguayan side was incorporated in 1879 into one of the largest plantations (*latifundio*) of the region, remaining outside of any significant population movement until the foundation of Ciudad del Este under the name Puerto Presidente Stroessner in 1957. (Stroessner ruled Paraguay from 1954 to 1989. After the coup d'état that deposed him in 1989, the name of the city was changed to Ciudad del Este. For simplicity's sake, I will use this name even when I discuss the city before 1989.) In the case of Brazil, at the end of the nineteenth century, the War Ministry sent a military commission to open a road that connected the west of Paraná Estate with the rest of the territory. The city of Foz do Iguaçu was set up at the mouth of the Iguassu River in 1889. During the 1880s, the Argentinian side was sold to private owners. The town that later would be known as Puerto Iguazú emerged as a small village, linked to the appropriation of *yerba mate* and wood, and also to the emerging commerce with the city on the other side of the river.

The first half of the twentieth century witnessed the slow but growing presence of state institutions, both on the Brazilian and the Argentinian side, farming colonists, and the incorporation of the region in regional flows of merchandise. That included not only the traditional production of *yerba mate* and wood, but also products that followed more specific regional demands, as for example, the flow of tires from Brazil to Argentina, escaping the strict control over rubber and derived products that the US established over Brazil during World War II. During the 1940s and 1950s, several agreements opened the possibility for Paraguay to escape from its landlocked position via Brazil. These agreements included the construction of a corridor of roads from Asunción, Paraguay's capital, to the Brazilian Atlantic coast, where Paraguay gained harbor facilities that guaranteed a channel for its exports and imports. Ciudad del Este was one of the steps in the construction of that corridor. It was founded a year after the agreement for the construction of the bridge that would connect both countries. The Friendship Bridge was inaugurated, in its finished version, in 1965.

Although the costly conditions imposed on Paraguay by Argentina to reach the sea through its rivers stand as the main reason in the historical narratives for the Paraguayan shift to Brazil, other elements also are key to understanding this transformation. These include the Paraguayan political situation and the Argentinian place in it (Argentina was the main economic regional presence in Paraguay until the 1960s, having also an important place in Paraguayan politics); the hesitant position of both countries during World War II; the US support for Brazil in its relations with Paraguay as a way of countering the influence of the countries of the Axis; and the Brazilian change of focus in its international policy, which renewed its interest in Hispanic America.

The development of the region continued in the 1970s, with the Paraguayan economic boom. The Paraguayan east, which had been opened to settlement since the 1950s and occupied mostly by Brazilians colonists (in 1963, Stroessner's government revoked the prohibition to sell land located in the frontier strip to foreigners), experienced an incredible expansion. During the 1970s, the rise of international prices of soybeans—which were mainly cultivated by Brazilian producers—and cotton created a boom for Paraguayan exports. Parallel to that agricultural expansion, the construction of the Itaipu dam (1975–1984) between Brazil and Paraguay had a profound impact on the Paraguayan economy. Together and intermingled with these processes, the consolidation of commercial exchange between both countries transformed the face of the border region. The Alto Paraná, whose capital city is Ciudad del Este, is one of the states comprising the Paraguayan east, and experienced a dramatic demographic explosion over 50 years. In 1950, the total population of the state was 9,531; in 2002 it was 558,672.

The construction of the Itaipu dam led to a radical transformation of Foz do Iguaçu and Ciudad del Este;[2] increasingly after the completion of the dam, commerce came to occupy an extraordinary position. The commercial ties between Paraguay and Brazil cannot be understood outside this matrix of relationships. Puerto Iguazú, in the Argentinian side, also played an important role in the commercial activity of the region until the first half of the 1990s, especially after the completion of the bridge that connected it with Foz do Iguaçu in 1985, the Tancredo Neves Bridge.

Commercial platforms: connections and complexities

The harbor facilities given to Paraguay on the Atlantic coast made Ciudad del Este the main entrance of imports to the country. The Paraguayan government implemented a policy of tax exemptions on imported goods restricted to the city, as a way of attracting foreign buyers. Imported products were taxed as "products intended for tourist consumption," which, depending on the product, fluctuated at around 6 percent of the value of the product. The city consolidated as an important commercial center. Goods came from all around the world but, progressively, more and more from East Asia. The Paraguayan side of the bridge grew with this commerce and so did the Brazilian side, which saw the emergence of commercial houses around the exit of the bridge in the late 1970s. Foz do Iguaçu functioned, basically, as an entrepôt of Brazilian goods for their importation to Paraguay until the consolidation of the Mercosur in the mid-1990s, when the export of Brazilian goods came directly from production centers instead.

Most of the traders and exporters are of Arab origin, mainly Lebanese. Some came long ago to Brazil, generally arriving in São Paulo and moving later to the countryside as peddlers and merchants. The older ones are proud of having been the traders that opened the Paraguayan market to Brazilian goods since the end of the 1950s. The possibility of operating on the other side of the border dealing with imported products diversified the opportunities for trade in the border region. The dynamism implicit in these possibilities turned the region into an attractive destination for the relatives and acquaintances of these traders, who left Lebanon during the civil war and particularly after Israel's invasions.

As has been noted in research on Arab and Muslim communities in Brazil, Foz de Iguaçu became their city of arrival in the country (Nasser Filho 2006; Carloto 2007). The youth of these migrants—most were between 20 and 40 years old—and their religious affiliation altered the face of the community (Arruda 2007). The extent of this transformation became apparent during the 1980s, with the emergence of new

FIGURE 3.2 Ciudad del Este, downtown. Photo by Fernando Rabossi. Reproduced with permission

institutions—welfare societies, mosques, cultural associations—and public demonstrations by these new immigrants linked to events in their countries of origin (Rabossi 2007, 2010). In the heyday of the border trade, during the first half of the 1990s, community representatives and journalists estimated that more than 12,000 Arab immigrants and their descendants lived in the region; 80 percent were assumed to have come from Lebanon. After the commercial crises that affected the region around 2000, and the controls and harassments that migrants from the Middle East received after September 11, 2001, many left the region. But even today, the Arab presence in Foz do Iguaçu city center is apparent. Men smoking their hookahs in public bars, women wearing their chadors in the street, and shops with Arabian delicacies such as *sfihas* and *kebabs* can be seen.

Chinese immigrants initially came from Taiwan and Hong Kong, but since the 1990s, they have been coming primarily from mainland China. Numbers are difficult to establish, but according to community leaders and news reports, there are no less than 30,000 Chinese in the region. The category "Chinese" is used to designate both mainland Chinese and Taiwanese, and also Koreans. Like the category "Arab," "Chinese" is a generic category used by Paraguayans and Brazilians to designate those who are perceived to be in control of commerce. If at first glance, in Foz de Iguaçu the Arab presence is marked, in Ciudad del Este the Chinese presence is more significant, particularly in the city center, where just a few blocks from the bridge one can find Chinese restaurants and groceries, and residential buildings almost completely occupied by Chinese.

FIGURE 3.3 Chiang Kai Shek statue at the China Park. Photo by Fernando Rabossi. Reproduced with permission

The presence of Chinese immigrants dates from the 1960s, when some started to arrive in Paraguay. The anti-communist regime of Alfredo Stroessner aligned Paraguay with the government of Taiwan. Paraguay is the only South American country that maintains diplomatic relationships with the Republic of China (ROC) and does not recognize the People's Republic of China. The statue in front of the city hall exemplifies that connection. Under the figure of a bald man with a cane in his right hand, wearing a Mao suit, as it is known in the West, one can read: "Tribute to Generalissimo Chiang Kai Shek, President of the Republic of China 1947–1975."[3]

The presence of Wang Sheng as an ambassador of the ROC in Paraguay from 1983 to 1991 was fundamental in the consolidation of the ties between Paraguay and Taiwan and in the articulation of the Chinese community in that country.[4] These ties explain the institutional character that the Taiwanese presence has had in Ciudad del Este. Examples are the public inscription of donations by the government of Taiwan (for example, new police vans in Ciudad del Este have "Donation from the Republic of China" stamped on their doors, accompanied by the Taiwanese and Paraguayan flags), the presence of the Chinatrust Commercial Bank, and the Orient Industrial Estate located in outlying areas of Ciudad del Este, where some Chinese entrepreneurs assemble electric ventilators, table lamps, Christmas trees and umbrellas. Paraguay is an important target for the international aid of the Taiwanese government. Usually, Chinese immigrants have remained outside the public scene as individuals, and when they appear, they do it through Chinese institutional frames of representation:

government institutions, Buddha's Light International Association, or their own organizations, such as the Chinese–Paraguayan Chamber of Commerce.

Since the 1990s, mainland Chinese migrants have outnumbered the Taiwanese in the border region, articulating the region through commercial circuits with the People's Republic of China. Because the ROC remains the official face of China in Ciudad del Este, mainland Chinese migrants became dependent on services organized by the Taiwanese, especially regarding schools and cultural activities. Rosana Pinheiro-Machado, who analyzed the commercial circuits between mainland China and Paraguay and the migration of mainland Chinese to Ciudad del Este, speaks of a process of "Taiwanization" of the mainland Chinese migrants in Ciudad del Este (Pinheiro-Machado 2009: 240ff). The growing commercial ties of the People's Republic of China is a crucial element to understand the political importance that the ROC pays to Paraguay. (For a good description of Taiwan's economic diplomacy, see Tubilewicz 2007.)

In terms of residence, many traders of "Arab" and "Chinese" origin have their stores in Ciudad del Este but live in Foz do Iguaçu (and not vice versa). However, they are not the only ones who cross the bridge every morning. In 1999, it was calculated that 15,000 Brazilians living in Foz do Iguaçu worked in Ciudad del Este. Today, the number may be smaller due to the transformation of controls in Paraguay and at the border; however, thousands of Brazilians residents still work there. All of them work in the city center in shops, commercial galleries, malls or in the street. Almost 5,000 Brazilians work as shopkeepers, shop assistants or employees at stores, repairing houses, and in the bars and restaurants inside the galleries. There are also the food kiosks attended by Brazilian owners and employees, and thousands of *laranjas* waiting in particular streets or inside commercial galleries. What is a *laranja*? The quota of products that a Brazilian can bring as accompanied luggage without paying taxes is, nowadays, the equivalent of US$300 per month. The buyers that come to Ciudad del Este are resellers, and they buy goods for amounts several times greater than that figure. The options that she/he has are to take the risk of passing the customs in one trip, to go and to return several times, or to divide the volume of the purchase in parcels that are given to someone else to transport across the border. That is the work of a *laranja*. Besides carrying merchandise, they are renting their right to enter their quota in Brazil. Sometimes, they are also in charge of doing the shopping.

At the stores or on the streets, thousands of Paraguayans earn their living by selling, changing money, transporting and handling goods, and in all the logistic operations necessary for a market of that scale to function. Almost all of them are internal migrants, many of them coming from a peasant background.

Ciudad del Este has occupied an important place, both as a node for distribution and commercialization of imported goods and as a site of localization of commercial diasporas. It has served both as a market of provision for thousands of resellers and as a corridor for the traffic of all products and services that can be imagined—or at least, that is what is often proclaimed, shamefully or proudly. The scale that it assumes is related to the role that it has played as a provision center for the Brazilian and other Latin American markets. In this sense, as a node of international commerce, we must envision the circuits of provision and of distribution in order to understand its functioning.

The elements presented so far give us some clues to grasp these circuits. Until the late 1980s, American or European products came from their places of production. Merchandise from Asia—first from Japan, then from Taiwan and Korea, and later from mainland China—arrived via re-export markets. Miami was the main source of imported goods in Puerto Presidente Stroessner. The description of the city that appeared at that time in the British weekly *The Economist* is symptomatic of that portrait:

> The city, founded 20 years ago, lies where Paraguay meets both Argentina and Brazil. The commodities it deals in are desk-top computers, Scotch whisky, authentic Levis, children's toys, even cars. The customers are Brazilian and Argentines who cannot buy such things at home because their governments have for decades "protected" them from good cheap imports in favor of bad, expensive home products.
>
> (The Economist *1990: 42*)

The portrait should be interpreted according to the political agenda of the time—and the position assumed by the magazine—characterized by a plea for the "free" market. In this agenda, the border between Paraguay and Brazil was the forefront of the free and competitive market at the early 1990s, a portrait that would change radically some years later after the consolidation of a new security agenda.[5] Nevertheless, the description sheds some light on the importance of Ciudad del Este in the provision of trendy and luxury goods.

Slowly during the 1980s and clearly during the 1990s, the commercial channels that supplied the city changed. Miami remained an important market for Ciudad del Este, but its place was completely eclipsed by direct links with East Asia and alternative re-export markets such as Panama. As trade routes changed, so did business partners and contacts. These changes were reflected in the growing importance of Chinese merchants and migration in the city, and also in the kinds of merchandise commercialized and the ways of commercializing products: not only in shops with attendants, but also in self-service places. This transformation was reflected in the changing profile of buyers—increasing in number—and the kinds of merchandise that were sold: cheap and replaceable. Instead of replacing the old circuits, they superimposed over them, changing the relative weight of trends, types of merchandise and connections. As we will see, the same trend applies to buyers and the circuits of distribution.

Sacoleiro circuits

Until the 1970s, tourists were the regular customers in Ciudad del Este. They arrived not only to buy imported products but also to gamble at the casino—something that has been prohibited in Brazil since 1946. From being a complement for those visiting Iguassu Falls—located some kilometers below the city—buying and gambling in Ciudad del Este became the main attractions for a growing number of visitors.

Together with the tourists, there were other actors that took advantage of the offer of imported goods. They could be perceived occasionally when an accident or a seizure of some smuggled cargo presented a huge amount of merchandise, such as whiskey, electronics or computers. Flights linking airstrips located near the border with estates in the interior of southern and southeastern Brazil seem to have been one of the privileged mechanisms for the introduction of goods. One of the first articles published in an international journal on Ciudad Presidente Stroessner reported precisely this kind of mechanism (Cohen 1988). One of the Brazilian traders interviewed for that article said that he sent between three to six planes every week full of computers from Paraguay to São Paulo. With the fall of Stroessner in 1989, these circuits of large-scale smuggling appeared in the Paraguayan media, showing governors and former governors, mayors and former mayors, national officials and relatives as being important actors in the business. The Brazilian partners were also important people.

However, during the 1980s, the control that they had earlier had over the flows of imported goods in Brazil came under dispute. A growing number of retailers were competing with them: the *sacoleiros*. For a combination of reasons, the *sacoleiros* managed to open and to expand a space of non-compliance to import regulations. First, in 1976, in a context of international crisis with money shortages, the Brazilian government instituted a compulsory deposit for any person who wanted to travel abroad as a way of keeping money inside the country. The measure did not apply to neighboring countries, and Ciudad del Este became the main destination for those who sought imported goods. This measure also had a crucial impact on the development of internal tourism, establishing regular transportation circuits to the border region. Abolished years later, the compulsory deposit popularized the city as a commercial destination.

In the same period, some commercial houses of Ciudad del Este started to send articles to Brazilian consumers at home. The system rested on informal delivery channels that involved several persons carrying the orders to their destination. In a sense, the system regularized the existence of people earning their living by crossing the border carrying merchandise.

Beyond this, taking advantage of the reduction of taxes for exportation, some firms and individuals started to reintroduce Brazilian goods exported to Paraguay to be sold informally at a better price in Brazil. The striking case was that of cigarettes. The biggest Brazilian tobacco company, a branch of British-American Tobacco, exported to Paraguay huge amounts of cigarettes that were reintroduced to Brazil to be sold without taxes.[6] The numbers of people involved and the practice of introducing goods that were not supposed to be reintroduced, consolidated channels and networks of people who learned to live on that practice.

The *sacoleiro* circuits were consolidated in the context of several agreements between the Paraguayan and Brazilian governments—Itaipu and the colonization of the Paraguayan east—together with the proliferation of irregular practices by regular enterprises, commercial representatives and official actors. In the context of those agreements and the proliferation of irregular practices, the systematic control of *sacoleiros* was not an urgent matter. Instead of being hidden, the conditions of possibility of the trade—at least at the frontier—rested on their numbers: the massive scale of the practices made systematic control impossible.

At the border, being registered was a matter of luck, so the strategies developed by the *sacoleiros* tried to reduce the possibility of being stopped and/or of losing all their merchandise. They multiplied the crossings—by themselves or with others paying for the crossing—or they made a single passage when the conditions were appropriate, i.e. when the police or the customs officials allowed free passage. Once they made their way to their own cities, the multitude disaggregated and sought to go unnoticed, for example, by leaving the bus before arriving at the bus station—a public scenario making them easy target for inspections. On the roads, the *sacoleiros* were targeted by the different police that knew the routes and the frequencies of the buses. Sometimes, the controls were part of the institution's planned activities. More often, however, they were individual decisions by the police aimed at getting some money from the *sacoleiros*.

The scale reached by this commerce shows the huge expansion of the Brazilian internal market and the importance of informal distributional channels for its provision. These channels are also important for the distribution of internal production (Rabossi 2008). During the 1990s, thousands of Brazilians traveled to Ciudad del Este to buy goods to resell in their cities. Street markets or particular areas of old marketplaces in Brazil got the name of Paraguay: the Paraguayan fairs of Brasilia (Federal District) or Caruaru (Pernambuco State), the *Feiraguai* de Feira de Santana (Bahia State)—a mixture of *feira* (fair or market) and *Paraguai* (as Paraguay is written in Portuguese). In all of them, the imported goods brought by *sacoleiros* from Ciudad del Este were offered.

The circuits of *sacoleiros* did not restrict themselves to popular markets for the lower classes. They were also crucial in provisioning shops and individual providers to the middle and upper classes. At least until the end of the 1990s, the social composition of the *sacoleiros* was also heterogeneous; resembling the social complexity described in the case of long-distance trade after the fall of the Soviet bloc (Hann and Hann 1992; Konstantinov 1996; Konstantinov, Kressel and Thuen 1998).

Among the *sacoleiros* engaged in the long-distance trade to Paraguay at the end of the 1980s and the beginning of the 1990s, there are accounts that describe the immersion in the trade as a way of escaping from unemployment and poor wages. But there are other accounts that signaled a conscious choice for the possibilities opening in a growing commerce. It is not uncommon to find people who left their stable jobs, even at public companies or offices—something very appreciated in Brazil— to try to follow their aspirations: a house, a car or a shop. Until the mid-1990s, to make those aspirations real through this path was something quite plausible.

Some *sacoleiros* managed to capitalize themselves and to start their own businesses in Brazil. Others remained in the circuits of Ciudad del Este but lost their money in an assault or their merchandise in a police raid, and needed to sell their car or house in order to get the money to follow the circuits of commerce again. At the end of the 1990s, the possibilities of losing merchandise increased due to the multiplication of controls.

The 1990s were years of expansion and contraction of the *sacoleiro* circuits in Ciudad del Este, with 1994–1995 being their peak years. The emergence of the

Southern Common Market (Mercosur)—the regional trade agreement between Brazil, Argentina, Uruguay and Paraguay—and the confluence in the reduction of taxes for imported goods in 1995, modified the privileged place that Ciudad del Este had enjoyed for many years. São Paulo, gradually, became the importation center of Brazil, being nowadays the provision market for the Paraguayan fairs in Brazilian cities. Since the end of the 1990s and throughout the last decade, *sacoleiros* have been systematically controlled and repressed. However, although reduced, *sacoleiro* circuits are still important in certain type of goods, such as computers and digital technology.

"From below" and "from above": complementary perspectives on globalization

As the preposition indicates, the expression "from below" points out a particular perspective on globalization. The phrase indicates where that perspective is constructed: from everyday practices in the streets, by looking at the people that make their livings beyond the registers and tax offices of the state, and far from the scenarios described in the common portraits of global flows. However, the open dimension that these practices assume and the presence that they have in the lives of millions of people indicate that its under-representation is a matter of perspective and not just a problem of it being part of a different domain.

If "from below" is a perspective that emerges out of the uncomfortable feeling produced by the fact that portraits of globalization are being drawn exclusively from a perspective "from above"—the perspective of Capital, the State, the Law, the Media, and all the hegemonic systemic devices with capital letters—the challenge is to disrupt these portraits superimposing those perspectives, but not by replacing one for the other, nor by postulating different universes or systems.

The circuits that cross over at Ciudad del Este show the complexity that structures certain flows of international trade. The articulations that produced that world—the harbor facilities given by the Brazilian government to Paraguay, the connections with Taiwan or the commercial strategies of international brands, to mention just a few—are something more than conditions of possibility. They are the variables that structure that world and they are indispensable to understand both the legal and the illegal circuits, the smuggling routes of the officials and of the thousands of *sacoleiros*, the channels of luxury goods and of trinkets.

From the point of view of the actors, as Josiah Heyman and Alan Smart have put it, illegal practices should be considered as an option and a resource used by some groups at certain moments (Heyman and Smart 1999: 13). They are not abnormal behaviors or particular subcultures.

That option was used by thousands of resellers, who pretended to be tourists returning home with their accompanying luggage: the *sacoleiros* that prospered in and out of Ciudad del Este in the 1990s. But this option was used not only by them. Both in terms of the products that are sold and of the distribution channels that operate from Ciudad del Este, there is no clear-cut distinction between legality and illegality. Instead, we can consider legality and illegality as phases in the trajectory of the goods or in the cycles of the circuit. Something legally produced could be under-evaluated or miscounted to get a reduction in the taxes that have to be paid at the port of arrival. It could be sold in an authorized shop but acquired by a reseller who will enter his country claiming the merchandise for his own consumption, offering it later in his formalized shop. We can trace a similar swinging trajectory starting with something produced without recognizing the proprietorship of others over processes or symbols associated with certain merchandise.

But if legality and illegality are phases that switch on and off at different moments, the distinction between legal and illegal is the operator that differentiates actors and processes, allowing certain practices to be prosecuted or else tolerated, and either criminalizing or promoting certain actors or phenomena. Showing the interconnec-tions that structure these worlds by analyzing them from below and from above will help us understand the way these distinctions are produced and the consequences that they have in the world today.

Notes

1 This paper is based on fieldwork research undertaken in the region of the confluence of the borders of Paraguay, Brazil and Argentina for 11 months between 1999 and 2001 and successive visits in 2006, 2008 and 2009. The historical material presented in the paper was gathered in interviews, local media and historical records. The main arguments were presented as my PhD (Rabossi 2004).

2 Foz do Iguaçu's population jumped from 33,966 before the construction of the dam in 1970, to 136,321 inhabitants in 1980. The population of Ciudad del Este was 18,315 in 1973 and in 1981 reached 98,300 inhabitants. Nowadays, Foz do Iguaçu has 256,081 inhabitants (DOU 2010: 114). The urban area of Ciudad del Este also includes the districts of Presidente Franco, Hernandarias and Minga Guazú, totaling 389,891 people (DGEEC 2003).

3 The words on two sides of the monument—in Chinese and in Spanish—are not very helpful in identifying him: "[W]e want a just peace, not a peace based on submission to an aggressor. With the aggressor there cannot be coexistence, much less appeasement." By 2001, the plaque in the front had been stolen. The difficulty in identifying the figure in the statue is even greater considering the huge red flags that stand behind him, marking the head-office of the Partido Colorado (Red Party), officially known as the Asociación Nacional Republicana. This emphasis on red is not associated with communism but with Stroessner. His Colorado Party governed Paraguay for almost all the twentieth cen-tury, with anti-communism one of its main political principles.

4 Wan Sheng was a key figure in the Kuomingtang and in the Republic of China in Taiwan, being a confidant of Chiang Ching-kuo, Chiang Kai Shek's son and later Premier and President of Taiwan. He was general of the ROC Army and was the head of the military academy of Taiwan, where some Paraguayan officials were trained. His ambassadorship in Paraguay was a kind of political exile "in service," where he was sent because of the political power that he was accumulating, especially in front of the Americans. For an analysis of Wan Sheng's period in Paraguay, see Marks 1998.

5 Eight years later, for example, analyzing the possibilities of the Mercosur to become a customs union, an article that appeared in the same magazine presented a very different picture. "One worry is the lawless area around Ciudad del Este, where Paraguay borders both Argentina and Brazil. Its neighbors—and the United States—suspect this to be a haunt not only of drugs and arms-traffickers but Islamist terrorists" (*The Economist*, 1998: 32). Because of the emerging agenda against Islamic terrorism, the consumer glamor of

previous years disappeared, replaced by an image focusing exclusively on the illegalities of the region.
6 This policy was not restricted to Brazil but was a global strategy of British-American Tobacco, as was shown in the problems that the company faced in Great Britain as reported in CPI 2000a, 2000b; Campbell 2000a, 2000b; House of Commons 2000. For Brazil, see Evelin 1998 and *Valor Econômico* 2002a; 2000b.

References

Arruda, A. (2007) "A presença libanesa em Foz do Iguaçu (Brasil) e Ciudad del Este (Paraguai)" [The Lebanese presence in Foz do Iguaçu (Brazil) and Ciudad del Este (Paraguay)], Master's Dissertation, Social Sciences, University of Brasília.

Campbell, D. (2000a) "Planning, Organization and Management of Cigarette Smuggling by British American Tobacco PLC, and Related Issues," *Memorandum by Mr. Duncan Campbell* (TB 51), Health Committee, House of Commons, United Kingdom Parliament: London.

——(2000b) "Smuggling in Africa by British American Tobacco PLC: Obstruction of Access to Evidence," *Supplementary Memorandum by Duncan Campbell* (TB51A), Health Committee, House of Commons, United Kingdom Parliament: London.

Carloto, D. (2007) "O espaço de representação da comunidade árabe-muçulmana de Foz do Iguaçu-PR e Londrina-PR: da diáspora à multiterritorialidade" [The Arab-Muslim Community Representational Space in Foz do Iguaçu and Londrina: From Diaspora to Multi-Territoriality], Master's Dissertation, Geography, Curitiba: Universidade Federal do Paraná.

Cohen, R. (1988) "Paraguay Provides a Haven for Smugglers: Brazil and Argentina Grumble But Can't Slow the Traffic," *The Wall Street Journal,* December 23.

CPI (Center for Public Integrity) (2000a) "Major Tobacco Multinational Implicated in Cigarette Smuggling, Tax Evasion, Documents Shows," M. Beelman, D. Campbell, M. T. Ronderos, and E. Schelzig, International Consortium of Investigative Journalists, Center for Public Integrity Investigative Report, January 31.

——(2000b) "Global Reach of Tobacco Company's Involvement in Cigarette Smuggling Exposed in Company Papers," M. Beelman, D. Campbell, M. T. Ronderos and E. Schelzig, International Consortium of Investigative Journalists, Center for Public Integrity Investigative Report, February 2.

DGEEC (2003) "Paraguay total: resultados preliminares" [Total Paraguay: Preliminary Results], Fernando de la Mora: DGEEC.

DOU (2010). Fundação Instituto Brasileiro de Geografia e Estatística (Resolução N° 6). [Brazilian Institute of Geography and Statistics Foundation (Resolution 6)], *Diario Oficial da União* CXLVII (211), Brasilia: Imprensa Nacional.

Economist, The (1990) "The Gentlemen Go By," 316: 42, September 1.

——(1998) "Back and Forth," 345: 32–3, December 20– January 2.

Evelin, G. (1998) "Cigarro é Perjudical ao Fisco" [Cigarettes are Harmful to the Treasury], *Revista Istoé,* September 2.

Hann, C. and I. Hann (1992) "Samovars and Sex on Turkey's Russian Markets," *Anthropology Today* 8(4): 3–6.

Heyman, J. and A. Smart (1999) "State and Illegal Practices: An Overview," in J. Heyman, ed., *State and Illegal Practices,* New York: Berg, 1–24.

House of Commons (2000) "The Tobacco Industry and the Health Risks of Smoking. Second Report, Session 1999-2000," Health Committee, House of Commons, United Kingdom Parliament: London.

Konstantinov, Y. (1996) "Patterns of Reinterpretation: Trader-Tourism in the Balkans (Bulgaria) as a Picaresque Metaphorical Enactment of Post-Totalitarianism," *American Ethnologist* 23(4): 762–82.

Konstantinov, Y., G. Kressel and T. Thuen (1998) "Outclassed by Former Outcasts: Petty Trading in Varna," *American Ethnologist* 25 (4): 729–45.

Marks, T. (1998) *Counterrevolution in China: Wang Sheng and the Kuomintang*, London: Frank Cass Publishers.

Mathews, G. (2007) "Chungking Mansions: A Center of 'Low-End Globalization,'"*Ethnology* XLVI(2): 169–83.

Nasser Filho, O. (2006) *O Crescente e a Estrela na terra dos pinheirais: os árabes muçulmanos em Curitiba (1945–1984)* [The Crescent and the Star in the Pine Forest Land: The Muslim Arabs in Curitiba 1945–1984], Master's Thesis, History, Curitiba: Universidade Federal do Paraná.

Pinheiro-Machado, R. (2009) *Made in China: Produção e circulação de mercadorias no circuito China-Paraguai-Brasil* [Made in China: Production and Circulation of Goods in the China-Paraguay-Brazil Circuit], PhD Thesis, Social Anthropology, Porto Alegre: Universidade Federal de Rio Grande do Sul.

Rabossi, F. (2004) *Nas ruas de Ciudad del Este: vidas e vendas num mercado de fronteira* [On Ciudad del Este's Streets: Lives and Sales in a Border Market], PhD Thesis, Social Anthropology, Rio de Janeiro: Universidade Federal de Rio de Janeiro.

——(2007) "Árabes e muçulmanos em Foz do Iguaçu e Ciudad del Este: Notas para uma re-interpretação" [Arabs and Muslims in Foz do Iguaçu and Ciudad del Este: Notes for a Reinterpretation], in G. Seyferth, H. Póvoa, M. C. Zanini and M. Santos, eds, *Mundos em Movimento: Ensaios sobre Migrações* [Worlds in Movement: Essays on Migration], Santa Maria: Editora da Universidade Federal de Santa Maria, 287–312.

——(2008) "En la ruta de las confecciones" [On the Clothing Route], *Crítica en Desarrollo* 2: 151–71.

——(2010) "Interações e estereótipos: os 'árabes' de Foz do Iguaçu e Ciudad del Este a partir do comércio de fronteira" [Interactions and Stereotypes: The 'Arabs' of Foz do Iguaçu and Ciudad del Este Considered from the Standpoint of Border Commerce] in A. Pacelli, C. Vainer, H. Póvoa Neto and M. Santos, eds, *A Experiência Migrante: Entre Deslocamentos e Reconstruções* [The Migrant Experience: Between Dislocations and Reconstructions], Rio de Janeiro: Garamond, 249–65.

Ribeiro, G. L. (2006) "Economic Globalization from Below," *Etnográfica* X(2): 233–49.

——(2007) "El sistema mundial no-hegemónico y la globalización popular" [The Non-Hegemonic World System and Economic Globalization from Below], *Série Antropología* 410, Brasília: DAN/UnB.

——(2010) "A globalização popular e o sistema mundial não-hegemônico" [Economic Globalization from Below and the Non-Hegemonic World System], *Revista Brasileira de Ciências Sociais* 25 (74): 21–38.

Tubilewicz, C. (2007) *Taiwan and Post-Communist Europe: Shopping for Allies*, London: Routledge.

Valor Econômico [newspaper] (2002a) "Para cada paraguaio, 8 maços por dia" [For Each Paraguayan, Eight Packets of Cigarettes per Day], May 8.

——(2002b) "Vendas foram sempre legais, diz companhia" [Sales Have Always Been Legal, Company Says], May 9.

4

NEOLIBERALISM AND GLOBALIZATION FROM BELOW IN CHUNGKING MANSIONS, HONG KONG

Gordon Mathews

"Globalization from below," or "low-end globalization" (Mathews 2007, 2011)—the transnational flow of people and goods involving relatively small amounts of capital and informal, sometimes semi-legal or illegal transactions—can be seen across the globe. Central nodes of globalization from below include Guangzhou, Yiwu, Mexico City, Guadalajara, Kolkata, Cairo, and São Paolo, as chapters of this book explore. These nodes serve as places where producers can meet large-scale buyers of goods, or where large wholesalers can meet smaller-scale traders who sell goods to retail buyers. This book, while not providing an encyclopedic coverage of these nodes, gives a broad global depiction, and shows how these nodes function in the global distribution of goods.

The cities mentioned above are (despite China's growing wealth) all within what can be described as "the developing world." While there are indeed nodes of globalization from below in "the developed world," such as the market described by Shepherd in Washington DC in chapter 11, as well as various sites in New York City (Stoller 2002), London, and Paris (see MacGaffey and Bazenguissa-Ganga 2000), among other cities, these are comparatively small-scale. Why is this form of globalization apparently most often found in the developing world and less so in the developed world?

One reason is simply that the developed world tends to shut out people from the developing world. Despite the fact that increases in migration would ultimately make the world economically much better off according to many economists (see Stalker 2008: 134; Hayter 2004: 158), the developed world as a whole displays a terror of being overrun by the developing world, as is attested by the panics over immigration that have taken place in Australia, Western Europe, and the United States in recent years. Africans, Latin Americans, and South Asians are typically not allowed entry into the United States, Australia, Western Europe, or Japan without stringent screening and very stingily issued visas.

A second reason is the fact that globalization from below may typically involve activities that are beyond the full scrutiny of the law, laws which tend to be more rigorously and rigidly followed in developed-world societies than in developing-world societies. Money exchanged through globalization from below is generally exchanged outside the realm of the formal economy. If "dirty money" is defined as money "generated outside of the formal economy" (Nordstrom 2007: 93), then most of the money generated through globalization from below is "dirty," although buyers and sellers in the developing world will almost certainly not see it as dirty. Primarily for these two reasons—the shutting out of people and the stringency of law enforcement—nodes of globalization from below tend not to be prominent within the developed world.

However, there are a few places in the developed world that are indeed central nodes of low-end globalization, both because of liberal immigration policies and also because of minimal application of the law. This chapter describes one of them, Chungking Mansions, Hong Kong, a building that is a transit point for a significant percentage of the mobile phones, computers, watches, and clothing that passes from manufacturers in south China to, eventually, consumers in Africa, South Asia, and throughout the developing world. In this chapter, I first describe Chungking Mansions, and what goes on in the building. I then explore the reasons why Chungking Mansions exists. Then I examine neoliberalism as the villain of contemporary anthropology, and explore how the ideology of neoliberalism—in all the inequalities it breeds—is what makes low-end globalization in a place like Chungking Mansions possible. Finally, I speculate as to the possibility of a different and perhaps more just version of neoliberalism in a world without borders—a world in which not just capital but also labor is rendered free.

Chungking Mansions: place and people

Chungking Mansions is a dilapidated 17-story structure full of cheap guesthouses, restaurants, and retail and wholesale businesses, located in the heart of Hong Kong's tourist district of Tsim Sha Tsui (see Mathews 2011). It is where small entrepreneurs from Asia and sub-Saharan Africa and other regions come to seek goods for resale back in their home countries. It is also where workers on tourist permits from South Asia struggle to survive on substandard wages; it is where asylum seekers in flight from persecution or deprivation in their home societies come to temporarily escape and perhaps make a living; and it is where tourists from across the world come, seeking cheap accommodations and perhaps adventure. Chungking Mansions is perhaps the most cosmopolitan building in the world, with people from across the globe jostling within its crowded confines. I have counted people from 130 different nationalities within the guestbooks of its 90 legal hostels and guesthouses.

Chungking Mansions was opened in 1962, intended for the well-off by some accounts. But with no unified ownership, each of the hundreds of owners could do wholly as he or she pleased, and the building rapidly deteriorated, making a mockery of its name; by the early 1970s Chungking Mansions was already blighted. In the

FIGURE 4.1 Chungking Mansions. Photo by Gordon Mathews. Reproduced with permission

1970s and 1980s, many Western backpackers passed through Chungking Mansions' guesthouses; the building was prominently featured in the *Lonely Planet* guides as a backpacker magnet because it was so cheap. In this era Chungking Mansions also became a center for South Asian merchants living in Hong Kong, who began a number of restaurants and other businesses catering to Western as well as South Asian clientele. In 1988, a fire killed a Danish tourist, who dove out of an eleventh-floor window on a mattress attempting to escape the flames; this attracted worldwide media coverage, and calls for Chungking Mansions to be torn down. In 1993, Chungking Mansions lost power for 10 days. By the late 1990s, Africans began coming to Chungking Mansions; by the early 2000s, they made up over half of those staying in the building. In 2005, closed circuit TV cameras were installed throughout the building, making it considerably safer, and the building underwent a modest facelift as well—although it remains, indubitably, "the infamous Chungking Mansions" (simply google the above sobriquet to find hundreds of such descriptions of the building).

There are four major groups of people in Chungking Mansions: traders, owners/ managers and their employees, asylum seekers, and tourists. Traders make up, at most times of the year, the majority of the people one sees in the building. Well over half are from Africa. They buy a vast range of products: mobile phones, clothing, watches, and computers are most prominent within Chungking Mansions, but also various other goods around Hong Kong and south China, such as building materials, furniture, electronic equipment, and used car parts. Some traders carry goods in their luggage, up to 32 kilos allowed by such airlines as Biman and Ethiopian; others pay the extra costs of airfreight, while still others rent or share containers.

Many of these traders buy used or copy goods. For mobile phones, for example, there are "14-day phones," European models that have been returned to the manufacturer by their original owners within a 14 day period, and are now resold at a steep discount; "refab phones" that have had their motherboards repaired or replaced in China; new made-in-China branded phones; used phones; and copy phones at several different levels of quality and price, made-in-China knockoffs of European and Japanese phones for a fraction of the cost and with a fraction of the life expectancy of the original model. I estimate, based on my knowledge of different phone stalls in the building, that 20 percent of the phones in use in sub-Saharan Africa in 2008 passed through Chungking Mansions, although of course, as with other trade in economic globalization from below, the exact figure can never be known. Phone stalls in the building sold an average of 15,000–20,000 phones a month in 2007–2008, various store employees have indicated. There were one hundred phone stalls in Chungking Mansions, and thus some 20 million phone sales per year in Chungking Mansions. There were 126 million mobile phone subscriptions in sub-Saharan Africa in 2007, according to scholar of mobile communications Richard Ling (personal communication), with many users having multiple subscriptions. Thus the assumption of 20 percent seems broadly plausible (see Mathews 2011: 105–150; Shadbolt 2009). Traders have occasionally told me that my estimates are far too low.

Some traders stay in Chungking Mansions for a week or a month or more, and do their business within the building and its environs. Others stay in Chungking Mansions only long enough to procure their visas to get into mainland China, buying directly from factories there. It's often said by traders that for clothing or building tiles or other such large goods, China is better than Hong Kong for doing business, but for electronics and mobile phones, Hong Kong is better, since Hong Kong dealers of these goods are somewhat more trustworthy, offering limited guarantees that their

FIGURE 4.2 African traders at the entrance to Chungking Mansions. Photo by Gordon Mathews. Reproduced with permission

counterparts in China do not. It is also often said that to really make money, a trader needs to go into south China, but that this is also very risky; commerce in Chungking Mansions offers less likelihood of making a fortune, but also much less likelihood of losing one's shirt: "it's really easy to get cheated in China," traders often say, a circumstance that Yang describes in chapter 9. Because many African countries' banks do not offer letters of credit or other financial instruments accepted in Hong Kong or Chinese banks, many traders carry tens of thousands of dollars in cash, typically US dollars—they carry their family's fortunes. Traders have told me they estimate that only half of first-time traders from Africa can make enough of a profit to come back a second time, with the rest never seen again in Chungking Mansions.

Traders represent the heart of globalization from below in Chungking Mansions, but Chungking Mansions' other groups are also involved, directly or indirectly. The majority of the hundreds of owners of the building's properties are Chinese, many of whom emigrated from the mainland decades ago and bought property in the one place in Hong Kong that they could afford. These owners today more or less embody "the Hong Kong dream" in working hard over the decades to create successful businesses such as guesthouses, and raising children who have become teachers or accountants and want nothing to do with Chungking Mansions. Some of these owners still live and work in Chungking Mansions, but most have withdrawn from day-to-day management and simply receive rental checks from the South Asians they have hired

FIGURE 4.3 Business scene, Chungking Mansions. Photo by Gordon Mathews. Reproduced with permission

as managers. These South Asians—most often Pakistanis and Indians—have Hong Kong residence rights and sometimes have lived in Hong Kong for generations (see White 1994), but nonetheless may feel alienated from Hong Kong's Chineseness—many feel that Chungking Mansions is the only place in Hong Kong that seems like home. Most of the food stalls in Chungking Mansions are South Asian, and there are many Indian video outlets; television in the building features Indian, Pakistani, and Nepalese channels, like nowhere else in Hong Kong.

South Asian managers in turn often hire their fellow countrymen to work for them (they are virtually always male, as are 80–90 percent of the people in Chungking Mansions)—most often those on 14-day tourist entry, twice extendable. A surprising number of these temporary workers come from a single Muslim Kolkata neighborhood, Kidderpore. They are paid remarkably little (around US$400 per month), but can pay for 60–100 percent of their plane tickets to and from India by carrying goods for traders: typically clothing into India and foodstuffs such as *dal* or Indian rice into Hong Kong. Some of these Indian temporary employees are married to teachers and civil servants who remain in India, but it still pays for them to come to Hong Kong. If they are caught, the penalties are severe, but they are almost impossible to catch: as soon as immigration police enter Chungking Mansions, mobile phones are used *en masse* by friends and lookouts, and the illegal workers scatter, morphing into customers and passers-by. I went back to Kidderpore with one of these workers, and saw how the paltry wages he made in Hong Kong supported his family, paying for the weddings of his two sisters, the rebuilding of his family home, and the purchase of his pride and joy, his motorcycle: he is his family's biggest wage-earner.

There are also asylum seekers. There are some 7,000 asylum seekers in Hong Kong, mostly from South Asian and African countries; a large number congregate at Chungking Mansions. There are NGOs in Chungking Mansions set up to serve them, but the majority never show themselves in any NGO but simply go to work. Many asylum seekers are "bogus," in the sense that they have left their countries in order to seek better economic opportunities for themselves; others are quite "genuine," fleeing political, religious or ethnic persecution. And many asylum seekers are in the middle: they have genuine reason to fear for their lives, having faced threats from neighbors, employers, or creditors. But these reasons do not fit the narrow UNHCR (UN Refugee Agency) guidelines, involving ethnic, religious, or political persecution, defining who constitutes a "genuine" asylum seeker.

Asylum seekers are not legally allowed to work, and some live on charity in Hong Kong, often from church groups; but many do indeed work, in order to support their families back home. I witnessed a fireworks display on China's National Day of October 1 with a young Somali asylum seeker, who, to my surprise, began to cry: the fireworks brought back the bombs bursting in the air over Mogadishu, and memories of dead family members. These asylum seekers all barely scrape by in Hong Kong, on minimal subsidies from charities or the Hong Kong government, or from their own illegal work, and await the long drawn-out process by which their fates are decided.

There are other groups too in Chungking Mansions: heroin addicts, mostly Nepalese, sex workers from a dozen countries, and also Indonesian and Filipina maids who frequent the building on their day off from their Hong Kong employers. But the last really large group in the building is tourists, coming to Chungking Mansions because it is by far the cheapest place to stay in Hong Kong: increasing numbers of mainland Chinese tourists have been coming into the building, only to be shocked by what they find: "I thought Hong Kong was part of China! Why are all these Africans and Indians here?" Some tourists also come for the adventurousness of the place, especially older Western hippies and new young backpackers. Tourists tend not to hang out in the building, but go off during the day to see the Hong Kong sites; but they too are part of Chungking Mansions' panoply.

Why does this center of globalization from below, smack in the middle of some of Hong Kong's most expensive real estate, exist? There are three reasons. Most immediately, there is the building itself, in the cheapness of its goods, as well as of its beds and meals. These exist because of the particular history of the building. The incorporated owners of the building—at least up until the past few years—have been remarkably weak; thus the building has steadily deteriorated until recently. Partly because there is no unified ownership, property developers cannot buy the building and tear it down, to build a more expensive structure, as has happened to numerous nearby buildings. The building has been a gold mine for many of its owners and managers over the decades. Those who subdivided apartments to make guesthouses with many tiny rooms for minimal prices, and those who have set up mobile phone stalls and restaurants have often made very good livings indeed. The building's relatively low rents enable cheap prices that, with enough volume, generate considerable profits. Chungking Mansions, reflecting its more or less decrepit state, remains a draw throughout much of the developing world, as a cheap place to live, eat, and do business within the extraordinarily expensive city of Hong Kong.

Second is the emergence of China as a world manufacturing center. Low-end entrepreneurs from throughout the developing world, particularly from Africa and South Asia, flock to Chungking Mansions so that they can buy Chinese goods, whether in Hong Kong or over the border in China; Chungking Mansions is the entrepôt of globalization from below between China and the rest of the world. Hong Kong, as it has long been throughout its history, continues to serve as the gateway to China for these entrepreneurs. This is a new development in recent decades; only in the 1990s did south China truly begin to emerge as the world's economic powerhouse, after decades of quiescence (Lin 1997), and only in this era did large numbers of African and other global traders begin converging on Chungking Mansions, making the building the center of globalization from below that it is today. As China itself continues to open up, Chungking Mansions' salience may begin to ebb; already there are many more Africans in Guangzhou than in Chungking Mansions, and with more and more flights going directly into China, Hong Kong and Chungking Mansions may be bypassed. But as of this writing, this has not yet happened.

The final reason for Chungking Mansions' existence, between Chungking Mansions' particulars and China's vastness, is Hong Kong itself, particularly its visa regulations. In many developed countries, visitors from the developing world must obtain a visa prior to arrival; if they do not have a visa, they are immediately put on the next plane home. In Hong Kong, visitors from most developing countries can obtain visa-free entry at the airport: 14 days for those from some nationalities (India, Gabon, Niger, the Philippines), 30 days (Bahrain, Thailand, Uganda) or 90 days (Brazil, Egypt, Kenya, Tanzania) for others (Immigration Department 2011). This enables entrepreneurs from most countries in Africa and Asia to easily come to Hong Kong and engage in business. This comparatively relaxed visa regime in Hong Kong is a policy reflecting the government's ideology of neoliberalism, making Chungking Mansions possible. In the pages that follow, I will first discuss neoliberalism as an ideology, and then discuss neoliberalism's particular role in the shaping of Chungking Mansions.

Neoliberalism

Neoliberalism may be defined, most simply and straightforwardly, as an ideology emphasizing the market as the ultimate arbiter of value, and advocating minimal restriction of the market by states. "Neoliberalism," as Leitner *et al.* write (2007: 11), "seeks to articulate an imaginary that equates freedom with the autonomous individual, with market rationality as the mechanism through which responsible individuals can maximize their rights and wealth, and with a borderless 24/7 world."

The anthropological mainstream, and the mainstream of social science as a whole, views neoliberalism as a profound evil. Pierre Bourdieu writes that through neoliberalism, "a Darwinian world emerges—it is the struggle of all against all at all levels of the hierarchy [...] The neoliberal utopia tends to embody itself in the reality of a kind of infernal machine" (1998). Simon Clarke writes that "Neoliberalism has conquered the commanding heights of global intellectual, political, and economic power, all of which are mobilised to realise the neoliberal project of subjecting the whole world's population to the judgement and morality of capital" (2005: 58). Neoliberalism has been tarnished by the financial crisis afflicting the developed capitalist world since 2008, but as of this writing, the ideology remains dominant. Neoliberalism is depicted in a darkly negative way in virtually every ethnographic article I have read: it is generally depicted as representing the forces of rampant global capitalism destroying all possibility of indigenous resistance.

There is an extensive theoretical literature on neoliberalism, its causes, permutations, and effects (see Saad-Filho and Johnston 2005; Harvey 2006). "One of the signal triumphs of neoliberalism as a contemporary ideology," Alejandro Colas comments, "has been the appropriation of 'globalisation' as a process denoting the universal, boundless and irreversible spread of market imperatives in the reproduction of states and societies around the world" (2005: 71). Hong Kong has long been at the forefront of this process; "in Hong Kong […] the transnational *is* the local," Watson has written (1997: 80). Hong Kong is consistently named the freest economy in the world (InvestHK 2011; Index of Economic Freedom 2011), the economy most unbound by the strictures of state bureaucracy. The freedom of the Hong Kong economy is to some extent mythical: property developers and other magnates in fact have inordinate influence on government policy (Bowring 2006). Nonetheless, neoliberalism has long been the dominant ideology of Hong Kong (Mathews, Ma and Lui 2008: 15–17).

Chungking Mansions exists in large part because of Hong Kong's reigning neoliberal ideology; but what takes place in Chungking Mansions goes against some of the common observations of theorizing on neoliberalism. Tehranian (2004: 22) has written that "the nation-state system runs against the fact of an increasing global economy in which capital, trade, and investment are mobile but people are held back within the confines of the territorial states." This is indeed very true of the world as a whole. However, Chungking Mansions attracts its merchants from around the world exactly because in the low-level capitalism of Chungking Mansions, face-to-face relations are all that can be trusted. "If you make orders via the internet and never come to see your orders, you will be robbed," I have been told by African traders.

This is particularly the case for businesspeople going to south China, where cheating by manufacturers is rampant, in, for example, supplying clothes of inferior quality or wrong sizes, unless the entrepreneur is there to inspect every detail of the order and its shipment. Reliable capital, trade, and investment demand the physical presence of the investor. Those who come to Chungking Mansions are those who have the money and resources to come, given Hong Kong's relatively relaxed visa policies. These entrepreneurs have the capital to come to Chungking Mansions and buy the goods they buy that enables them to more or less exploit their fellow countrypeople who stay at home.

Santos (2004: 297) has written that "it is commonly agreed that one of the main features of the period of disorganized capitalism is a new international division of labor in the terms of which industrial capital from the core is moving to the periphery, where cheaper labor is located, establishing factories to produce manufactured goods for export to the worldwide market." This, again, is true in the world as a whole, and certainly in Hong Kong: this is why in the 1980s, so many Hong Kong factories relocated in south China—the pursuit of cheaper labor (see Smart and Smart, chapter 6). However, this is exactly not the case in Chungking Mansions—many African traders come from countries that are not even on the periphery of international industrial capital, but rather altogether "off all kinds of maps" (Allen and Hamnett 1995: 2).

They come to Chungking Mansions to buy from what might be seen as the "low-end manufacturing" of China—manufacturing that is gaining prestige in the world, but that is widely seen by the entrepreneurs I speak with as being not fully trustworthy but alluring because of its low price. The African countries whose entrepreneurs come to Chungking Mansions manufacture virtually nothing: these entrepreneurs buy goods ranging from canned food (Mauritius) to paper (Zimbabwe) to used car parts (Tanzania, Kenya) to building tiles (Mali), to clothing, watches, and mobile phones (Africa-wide). Chungking Mansions involves not rich countries sending their manufacturing to poor countries, but rather, extremely poor countries seeking manufactured goods from less poor countries becoming rich: not the manufacturing core exiled to the periphery, but rather the extreme periphery seeking goods of the semi-periphery because they are cheap.

In these ways, Chunking Mansions illustrates a broad congruence with neoliberalism, and also a particular uniqueness that goes against some of the dominant trends of neoliberalism because it represents globalization from below rather than globalization from above. Let me now explore some of the specific ways in which neoliberalism, as enacted through Hong Kong government policies, shapes Chungking Mansions.

Neoliberalism and the shaping of Chungking Mansions

One prominent fact attesting to Hong Kong's neoliberal regime is that Hong Kong can at present be so easily entered, as earlier discussed; the Hong Kong government does not play a restrictive role in the issuance of visas, as compared to most other developed countries. Neoliberalism is played out in the way that the state—the Hong Kong government—allows the market to work largely unimpeded, simply by letting most travelers in (Hong Kong is largely autonomous from China in its immigration policies). The traders and illegal workers in Chungking Mansions come in without visas for the most part, as "tourists"; immigration personnel know full well what they are doing, given their passports' multiple stamps, but largely ignore it.

This is not always the case, and some possibly illegal workers are given more limited entry periods. Furthermore, since 2005, Sri Lanka, Nepal, the Congo, and Bangladesh have had their visa-free access to Hong Kong revoked; Nigeria and Pakistan had their visa-free access revoked in earlier years. These restrictions have taken place largely because of worries about drug smuggling (Nigeria and Nepal, whose nationals have been involved in incidents of heroin shipments coming to Hong Kong), something that even market-oriented immigration policies such as those of Hong Kong cannot allow. They have also taken place because of fears of Hong Kong being swamped by asylum seekers, threatening Hong Kong's relatively open immigration policy.

However, by and large, Hong Kong remains remarkably easy to enter. Hong Kong visas that must be obtained in advance must be applied for through the Chinese Embassy in one's home country, and may take many weeks to acquire. On the other hand, if one can obtain entrance into Hong Kong at the airport upon arrival in Hong Kong, a visa to mainland China can often be obtained in Chungking Mansions within just a few hours, through the numerous cut-rate visa services that exist. The state, whether Hong Kong or China, thus maintains a degree of control over borders, but the market circumvents or moves nimbly around these borders. This is very different from Japan, or the United States, or the United Kingdom, where, as earlier noted, tourists from the developing world must have a tourist visa acquired in advance of their arrival, or else they will be sent straight back home.

A second fact attesting to Hong Kong's neoliberal regime is that financial transactions are so easily accomplished in Hong Kong. In China, money exchange is tightly regulated—in Guangzhou's equivalent of Chungking Mansions, the Tianxiu Building, where many Middle Eastern and African traders are to be found, changing money is illegal, although it is done all the time; one illegal money changer was murdered several years ago, I've been told, pushed out of the top floor of the building after having been divested of cash. However, there are 15 or more legal money changers in Chungking Mansions, and also many alternative informal means of sending one's money back home, whether that home is Nigeria, Pakistan, or even Somalia.

These informal means of transferring money, unless there is a robbery, are as a rule ignored by Hong Kong authorities. In most countries, including the United States, the government seeks to take a slice of one's profits from financial transactions, as in, for example, the capital gains tax; this does not happen in Hong Kong, where the government keeps out. I met a Japanese investor who works for a large brokerage firm in Tokyo. He comes to stay in Chungking Mansions several weekends each year; on Fridays, before his weekends, he invests tens of thousands of US dollars in hedge funds with a local bank. In Japan, the government charges 20 percent from all such purchases, while in Hong Kong the government takes nothing.

A third fact attesting to Hong Kong's neoliberal regime is that the police generally don't crack down on illegal workers, or copies, or prostitution, or on any of the violations to be found throughout Chungking Mansions, as long as no one complains. This differs from what Milgram discusses in chapter 7: she reveals considerable police harassment of her Filipina entrepreneurs in Hong Kong. This may be largely because police can't easily crack down on many violations in Chungking Mansions simply because they are so conspicuous: as soon as the police walk in its one main entrance (even if they are undercover they are still very easily recognizable, coming to a place where Hong Kong Chinese don't usually come), every illegal worker in the building vanishes, melting into the crowd.

It may be that the police practice neoliberal tolerance in Chungking Mansions simply because violators of the law are more easily apprehended elsewhere; but in Chungking Mansions, they do indeed practice such tolerance. I interviewed a senior police officer who revealed much about how the police operate. He said, concerning sex work, "You can't go arrest a sex worker for simply standing around. You can't even ask her questions. You can only do that on the basis of complaints. All the police can do is check IDs and see if these people are legally here in Hong Kong." Concerning copy phone sales, he said, "the Customs and Excise Department won't do anything unless there is a complaint. As long as deception takes place only in Africa, then the police will not act." In other words, if the buyer and seller both know that phones are copies and are satisfied with their transaction, then the police keep out. As for illegal immigrants, he said, "The younger policemen bring asylum seekers, while older policeman say, 'why are you causing problems for us?' We need interpreters for these people, and there's lots of paperwork. Leave it alone."

The police step in only in the case of clear-cut crime such as robbery or murder; otherwise, unless there is a complaint upon which they must act, the police keep out. Foucault, in *Discipline and Punish* (1977), portrays the process whereby the French state manufactured delinquency and created the need for police in order to more completely control its citizenry. In the context of Chungking Mansions, what we see is the opposite of this: the state enables the police to largely withdraw, to let its residents go about their business as usual, whether legal or illegal. This is not because of any sense of beneficence towards South Asians and Africans—Hong Kong is at least as racist as anywhere else in the world—but simply because enforcing the law to the letter requires too much trouble and paperwork, and might take away from Hong Kong's own profits: thus it is better for the police not to intervene in any way unless they must. The police do act to combat drug-dealing, robbery and violent altercations—if there are physical altercations, they generally show up in little more than a minute, as I've seen several times. Immigration police do pursue those with expired visas. But in other areas, the police usually stay out.

A fourth fact attesting to Hong Kong's neoliberalism is that borders are so porous in letting in goods from China. Many of the phone sellers I know in Chungking Mansions sell copy phones brought in from China, across the border into Hong Kong. These phone sellers often have their illegal employees bring the phones across the border, but no one bothers them; in one Pakistani man's words, "I just look confident, and Hong Kong customs never bothers me." Copy phones are insignificant compared to illegal drugs or other goods harmful to public health sometimes brought into Hong Kong; the latter are indeed often confiscated. Still, it is revealing just how much the Hong Kong government seems to allow: partly because the Hong Kong–China border is the busiest in the world, but partly too because the Hong Kong government prefers not to act too vigorously. All these facts portray neoliberalism in action, and the philosophy of "limited state, strong market" at work in Chungking Mansions: let the market proceed unfettered, with the state, through police and immigration authorities, intervening only as it absolutely must. This is neoliberal ideology at its fullest.

We have seen how the social scientific literature portrays neoliberalism in a very negative light. Yet, in Chungking Mansions, a positive side of neoliberalism cannot be denied. People from more or less warring societies the world over come to Chungking Mansions (India versus Pakistan particularly come to mind, but also civil-war-wracked societies like Somalia and Sri Lanka, and more broadly, Muslims and Christians, both of whom are richly represented in Chungking Mansions), and do not tend to fight with each other, as they might in their home countries. As a Pakistani said to me vis-à-vis Indians, "I do not like them; they are not my friends. But I am here to make money, as they are here to make money. We cannot afford to fight."

Fights do break out from time to time—between Sikhs and Muslims, between Muslims and Christians, between Indians and Pakistanis, and between Nigerians and other Africans, among other groups, and of course within these different groups as well—but these fights are comparatively infrequent. All in all, compared to many of the societies from which its traders and workers come, Chungking Mansions is remarkably peaceful. The general attitude of Chungking Mansions is, as shown above, that the pursuit of profit makes ethnic and religious discord no more than an unwelcome distraction. In this sense, we can say that neoliberalism is successful: what may be the most globalized building in the world is generally non-violent due to the common pursuit of more or less legal profit by all who sojourn there. Neoliberalism works, in this instance, as a creator of global peace.

Ethnic tension is generally more significant in Chungking Mansions' people's minds than class tension, the tension between rich and poor, which, surprisingly, hardly ever seems to arise. This is despite the fact that the gap between rich and poor, between the shop owner and the illegal employee, between the African entrepreneur and his countryman who is an asylum seeker, is vast. One young illegal worker I know often complained to me about how his boss, the restaurant owner, exploits him, making 20 times more money than he does while doing almost no work, while he himself scrubs tables and washes dishes from 7 a.m. until well after midnight every day. But his dream, he told me, was to go into business and own a restaurant, just like his boss, exploiting future versions of his young self. An asylum seeker I knew illegally worked for his relative in a phone stall, earning HK$2,300 a month in a stall that nets HK$100,000 a month, almost all going to his relative. His dream was to break free of this relative and cut his own deals, becoming a business magnate himself, he told me, something he was sure that he could do if only he put in enough effort. (Indeed, eventually he did become a minor magnate, as a successful phone wholesaler and marrying, largely for the sake of a residence permit, a Hongkonger. But for every one success like him, there are 100 or more failures.)

Thus, the system itself, in all its inequalities, is almost never questioned, but only one's own place in the system. Why? One reason is that the people in Chungking Mansions are not intellectuals but workers struggling to make a living: it is not for them to question the world they find themselves in, but rather to do the best they can within its structures. A second reason is that everyone in Chungking Mansions, by the very fact that they (or their parents or grandparents) were able to board a plane or a boat and come to a place that may be thousands of miles from their home societies, is among the successful in their home societies. Chungking Mansions is basically a "club of the third-world successful," including those at its lowest stations. The basic assumptions held by people in Chungking Mansions thus tend to conform to the neoliberal paradigm that has benefited them; even if they are exploited, they are nonetheless winners in the global game of accumulation of money and power. The poor in Chungking Mansions are highly unlikely to become rich—the illegal workers probably won't gain Hong Kong residency; the asylum seekers will probably be rejected in their claims. But the poor and the rich alike buy into the basic neoliberal assumptions of Chungking Mansions.

The real victims of Chungking Mansions may be not those who labor at its lower edges, however heartrending their individual stories may be, but rather those in traders' home countries who buy the Chungking Mansions' entrepreneurs' shoddy products at inflated prices; their voices are not heard at Chungking Mansions, although I have heard many different arguments as to whether these consumers are or are not exploited. One mobile-phone entrepreneur said, "In my country, poor people can't afford real phones, and they like the status that the copy brand name gives them. They know what they're buying, that it will work for only a month or two." Another said, "I sell copy phones in villages in the country, never in the city. I'll never go back there. So who cares?" But another gave a more positive view: "Of course we're helping our country in our trading. Before, only a very tiny number of people in my country had mobile phones, but now almost everyone does. That's because we bring them the phones." These traders, like traders everywhere, charge whatever the market will bear; they spend little time thinking about global justice.

In the exploitation apparent within the building, Chungking Mansions is really no different from anywhere else in Hong Kong or in China—it features the same vast gaps of rich and poor. It differs only in that it is more visible: instead of the exploitation of faceless corporations, Chungking Mansions enables exploitation by individual entrepreneurs whose faces those who are exploited may know well. If those at the lower rungs of the ladder in Chungking Mansions truly knew that they could never get out of poverty, perhaps they would rise up in anger. But they do not know, or in any case do not choose to know, and so the neoliberal haven of Chungking Mansions continues on as peacefully as ever, a laboratory for the humming motors of globalization from below.

Conclusion: Chungking Mansions, neoliberalism, and globalization from below

In this chapter, I have argued that nodes of globalization from below are underrepresented in the developed world because that world largely shuts out people from the developing world, and stringently enforces legal codes, making informal trade difficult. But Chungking Mansions is an exception: in the wealthy city of Hong Kong, Chungking Mansions is a thriving center of globalization from below.

It is able to flourish, I've argued, because of the particular history of the building, and because of China's emergence as the economic powerhouse of globalization from below, but especially because of Hong Kong's neoliberalism. This has enabled Chungking Mansions' existence. Hong Kong, unlike other developed-world societies, can be easily entered by people from the developing world; financial transactions can be easily accomplished; the police stay at arm's length from minor illegalities; and the border with China is porous. Neoliberalism enables the pursuit of wealth without the encumbrances of ethnic, national, or class conflict. Neoliberalism, in short, works within this place. Whether it also works for the far-flung customers of the goods that pass through Chungking Mansions is another question. But the building itself is rendered more peaceable than it otherwise would be because of the ideology of neoliberalism.

In the introduction to this book, we argued that globalization from below, often rooted in the social, cultural, and political structures in the lives of those who practice it, may differ from the unfettered capitalism of globalization from above. But we also argued that those who practice globalization from below are in effect "out-neoliberalizing" those who embody globalization from above in their ability to follow the paths of the world market unimpeded by the strictures of state control. This is apparent in Chungking Mansions. Family and social connections are often profound, in, for example, the Kolkata temporary workers who labor for their extended families back home, the African traders bearing all their family fortunes in their pockets to be augmented or lost, and the Pakistanis from the same home neighborhood who now are employer and employee in a Chungking Mansions phone stall. At the same time, these very small entrepreneurs of globalization from below can almost always outwit the agents from globalization from above: the undercover police, the customs agents, the private detectives hired by Nokia, almost always come up empty-handed in their search for illegalities.

But these denizens of globalization from below are nonetheless ultimately losers: the entrepreneurs depicted in this chapter and in all the chapters of this book are like mice nibbling at crumbs fallen from the tables of kings. In Chungking Mansions, the wealth accrued by its merchants and entrepreneurs is a tiny drop in the bucket compared to the vast sums at play in the skyscrapers of Central District across Hong Kong harbor. That world of wealth across the harbor is both the ultimate source and ultimate beneficiary of Hong Kong's neoliberalism: a world that no one in Chungking Mansions can hope to enter.

It is often proclaimed that we live in a global age of neoliberalism, but it is striking that this neoliberalism allows for the globalization of capital but not of labor. "Today working people of all countries are asked to accept continuing globalization, in which capital is free to go wherever it wants. By that token, migrants must have the same freedom" (Bacon 2008: 261; see also Hayter 2004: 3). It seems that in this situation, ideologies of neoliberalism are utilized so long as they enable the rich to get richer and the poor to stay poor; they serve as a way in which the developed world can justify its ongoing exploitation of the developing world. Chungking Mansions is one place in the developed world where the globalization of labor is to some extent allowed, as we have seen. But this is partly because Chungking Mansions is an ethnic island in the middle of Chinese Hong Kong; because the developing-world workers in Hong Kong's heart are kept apart from the Chinese who make up 94 percent of Hong Kong's population (many of whom would never think to enter Chungking Mansions), they are rendered tolerable and invisible to that vast majority.

Neoliberalism by definition can never be just, since it inevitably represents the rich profiting at the expense of the poor. Nonetheless, one can imagine a *more* just and inclusive global neoliberalism, one that would favor not just the movement of capital but also labor. Many social critics of late (Pecoud and Guchteneire 2007, Hayter 2004, Marfleet 2006, Bacon 2008) have advocated that the global regime of national passport controls be abolished, to let the market alone decide where workers from across the globe might go in search of opportunities for employment and wealth. If this radical step were taken, then the immigration regimes that have been fundamental to states over the past century would give way, and there would be a massive influx of the poor traveling to the cities of the rich in search of freedom or work, no doubt leading to initial chaos, but perhaps eventually to greater global prosperity and equality.

The ultimate costs and benefits of open borders is a huge issue, one that I cannot explore in this brief chapter: but what would be the effect of open borders on globalization from below? This would be no salvation, and much exploitation would doubtless remain. But it would serve to breach the wall separating the developed world from the developing world, globalization from above and globalization from below. In this sense, it seems at least possible that Chungking Mansions, an island of decrepitude in Hong Kong's touristic heart, is in its relative freedom from state control a window into the world's future: a glimpse into how globalization from below may increasingly shape not just the developing world but the developed world, as the future of us all. That world, while still no doubt exploitative, might be a better world than the one we live in today.

References

Allen, J. and C. Hamnett (eds) (1995) *A Shrinking World? Global Unevenness and Inequality*, Oxford: Oxford University Press.

Bacon, D. (2008) *Illegal People: How Globalization Creates Migration and Criminalizes Immigration*, Boston: Beacon Press.

Bourdieu, P. (1998) "The Essence of Neoliberalism: Utopia of Endless Exploitation," *Le Monde Diplomatique*, December, English edition: http://mondediplo.com/ (accessed July 7, 2007).

Bowring, P. (2006) "Economic Freedom? It Depends Where You Stand," *International Herald Tribune*, January 9.

Clarke, S. (2005) "The Neoliberal Theory of Society," in A. Saad-Filho and D. Johnston, eds, *Neoliberalism: A Critical Reader*, London: Pluto Press.

Colas, A. (2005) "Neoliberalism, Globalisation and International Relations," in A. Saad-Filho and D. Johnston, eds, *Neoliberalism: A Critical Reader*, London: Pluto Press.

Foucault, M. (1977) *Discipline and Punish: The Birth of the Prison*, trans. A. Sheridan, New York: Pantheon Books.

Harvey, D. (2006) *A Brief History of Neoliberalism*, New York: Oxford University Press.

Hayter, T. (2004) *Open Borders: The Case Against Immigration Controls*, 2nd ed., London: Pluto Press.

Immigration Department (2011), Government of the Hong Kong Special Administrative Region, http://www.immd.gov.hk/ehtml/hkvisas_4.htm (accessed August 30, 2011).

Index of Economic Freedom (2011) http://www.heritage.org/index/ (accessed August 30, 2011).

InvestHK (2011) The Government of Hong Kong, Special Administrative Region, http://www.investhk.gov.hk/static/whyhk/world-s-freest-economy-free-trade-hong-kong-free-market-economy-en.html (accessed August 30, 2011).

Leitner, H., J. Peck, and E. Shephard (eds) (2007) *Contesting Neoliberalism: Urban Frontiers*, New York: Guilford.

Lin, G. C. S. (1997) *Red Capitalism in South China: Growth and Development of the Pearl River Delta*, Vancouver: University of British Columbia Press.

MacGaffey, J. and R. Bazenguissa-Ganga (2000) *Congo–Paris: Transnational Traders on the Margins of the Law*, Bloomington: Indiana University Press.

Marfleet, P. (2006) *Refugees in a Global Era*, Houndsmill: Palgrave MacMillan.

Mathews, G. (2007) "Chungking Mansions: A Center of 'Low-End Globalization'," *Ethnology* XLVI(2): 169–83.

——(2011) *Ghetto at the Center of the World: Chungking Mansions, Hong Kong*, Chicago: University of Chicago Press.

Mathews, G., E. K. W. Ma and T. L. Lui (2008) *Hong Kong, China: Learning to Belong to a Nation*, London: Routledge.

Nordstrom, C. (2007) *Global Outlaws: Crime, Money, and Power in the Contemporary World*, Berkeley: University of California Press.

Pecoud, A. and P. Guchteneire (eds) (2007) *Migration Without Borders: Essays on the Free Movement of People*, Paris: UNESCO/New York: Berghahn.

Saad-Filho, A. and D. Johnston (2005) *Neoliberalism: A Critical Reader*, London: Pluto Press.

Santos, B. S. (2004) "Transnational Third Worlds," in J. Friedman and S. Randeria, eds, *Worlds on the Move: Globalization, Migration, and Cultural Security*, London: I. B. Tauris.

Shadbolt, P. (2009) "Where Africa Goes to Buy its Mobile Phones," *Financial Times*, 31 January.

Stalker, P. (2008) *The No-Nonsense Guide to International Migration*, Oxford: New Internationalist Publications.

Stoller, P. (2002) *Money Has No Smell: The Africanization of New York City*, Chicago: University of Chicago Press.

Tehranian, M. (2004) "Cultural Security and Global Governance: International Migration and Negotiations of Identity," in J. Friedman and S. Randeria, eds, *Worlds on the Move: Globalization, Migration, and Cultural Security*, London: I. B. Tauris.

Watson, J. (ed.) (1997) *Golden Arches East: McDonald's in East Asia*, Stanford: Stanford University Press.

White, B. S. (1994) *Turbans and Traders: Hong Kong's Indian Communities*, New York: Oxford University Press.

5

ILLEGALISMS AND THE CITY OF SÃO PAULO

Vera da Silva Telles

Doralice

Doralice, age 40, lives on the outskirts of São Paulo with her husband and son, as well as her mother, a brother and a nephew. Doralice works as a housekeeper by day at three different houses, but her earnings are irregular. As she has cooking skills widely celebrated by the family, there was a time when she decided to sell bread and scones that she prepared during the day. She sold them every night near the grounds of a hospital from a makeshift stand in her husband's van. The venture was not very successful and after a few months it was abandoned.

But Doralice is a hardworking woman who does not miss any opportunity to earn more for her family. Therefore, for example, she does not hesitate when the opportunity arises to assemble a kiosk of pirated CDs in a neighborhood near her home. It is a rather modest retail outlet, but one that activates networks of all kinds, starting with the boys from a slum next door who are called on to sell during the day while she goes to her job. There is also a varied mix of intermediaries passing through the neighborhood, but this largely overflows the local boundaries: a close relative made contact with a CD dealer, an obscure type with shady relations with a dark "studio" where CDs are copied and where dealers buy their products, in a business that is now widely expansive and present everywhere in the city. Doralice cannot reconstruct the path the CDs have traveled before reaching their modest point of sale—from a certain point the path is, one might say, "blurry."

She knows very well how life is and is aware that she would not be able to fund her business somewhere more high-profile and more profitable. I asked her why she did not choose a more profitable location, which would provide access to the "suppliers," an access further guaranteed by relationships of trust and close links with the family. The answer was clear: she would not have the capital to pay taxes or else pay off the police, and much less so to offset losses in the event of a police bust. In any event,

Doralice lacks the clout needed to deal with the representatives that infest informal-illegal businesses, who wield the power of blackmail and extortion, defining to a large extent, the ways in which these markets are organized and distributed in urban spaces (Misse 2006). So therefore, she must be content with paltry earnings from a poor kiosk located in a very poor area. The wages are indeed paltry and unreliable, because very often suppliers or intermediaries disappear, having been arrested or victimized in the perverse and violent world of market protection, or because relations of trust were broken (due to betrayals, disputes, disloyalties) at some point in this network where connections between the points of the poorest parts of the city and the circuitry of an increasingly globalized wealth are made. Indeed, it was for this reason that she gave up the business.

Doralice is decidedly far from being an entrepreneur. What she was doing was no more than the odd job, one among many other means to deal with the urgencies of life. Thus, for example, in tight times she does not hesitate to call on a widespread network that operates in the fraudulent prescriptions market to obtain the medicine on which her husband's life depends. These pass from large pharmacies in the region, profitable to those (pharmacists and clerks on duty, with officials looking the other way) who invent methods to make the purchase and sale of these prescriptions a resource to complement the extremely low wages paid in the formal job market. Doralice became so familiar with this black market of prescriptions that she herself, at times, becomes an intermediary or broker, earning a few more dollars each time an afflicted neighbor (almost always women, rarely men) comes to solicit her "know-how" and "relationships" to resolve an urgent domestic problem. At other times and in other circumstances, Doralice finds no moral reason to reject the chance offered by an acquaintance and neighbor of confidence to put an order for "flour" in her bag, get on a bus, cross the city and quietly bring the goods to their destination, bringing back a modest profit, but one that will make all the difference in the household budget. As she says, "I am not doing anything wrong, I do not steal, I do not kill"— she is doing what she can in this instance, as in many other circumstances of her life.

There could be much more to say about the routes of this not very meek housewife, but let us leave her here, to examine the larger issues apparent from her story. Following the path of the CDs and drugs and fraudulent prescriptions she momentarily deals in is a pursuit that could inform an entire research agenda. This could lead us through the strands of overlapping networks of which the informal market today is made, and enable us to reconstruct the chain of connections which define the channels through which these goods travel, as well as to do an ethnography of the practical negotiations created at these points of concentrated relations and mediations.

The fact is that today social life appears to be permeated by a growing universe of illegality that passes through the circuits of the informal expanding economy and expanding city, and of trade of illegal goods and trafficking of drugs and their globalized flows, with its capillaries in social networks and urban practices. This is how the story of Doralice is of interest. It represents a game situated in the scales that overlap and intertwine in "lateral mobility," to advance an argument to be made on the following pages, of this urban character, increasingly common in our cities, which moves in the blurry boundaries between informal and illegal along routes between uncertain work and means of survival, conforming to the moment and circumstances.

To be sure, it is always possible to say that this situation is nothing new; simply a repeat of what has always been present in our cities. However, we little understand what happens if we consider situations like those described here as just an example of the "hustling" that has always been known in situations of poverty. From situations like these (and many others), we can discern the profiles of an urban world changed and redefined by contemporary forms of production and circulation of wealth, which activate the various circuits of the informal economy and are processed in uncertain and informal borders, illegal, and also illicit.

The fact is that ambiguous relations between the legal, illegal and illicit create a transversal phenomenon in contemporary experience. Many scholars of late have been calling attention to this transitivity between the informal, illegal and illicit, with concerns, more or less explicit, to distinguish the nature of the transgressions that operate within the informal economy.

We know well that this transitivity traces the history of our cities, not to mention the historical circumstances that have prevailed in the ever-expanding informal market. However, let me place the Brazilian situation under another set of references. In the first part of this chapter, based on research in Europe, I discuss the metaphor of "the city as bazaar," and consider the bazaar economy as a means of comprehending the borders of the legal, formal and licit, and the illegal, informal and illicit. In the second part, I locate and describe this within São Paulo.

The uncertain borders of the informal, illegal and illicit

Ruggiero and South (1997) have made use of the metaphor of the bazaar—*the city as a bazaar*—to describe the intersections between formal markets and informal markets, illegal or illicit, as they formed starting from 1980 in the urban centers of the core countries of contemporary capitalism. The metaphor evokes otherness in the "orientalism" associated with the bazaar, to call attention to the fact that this "bazaar" now lies embedded in the core of modern and Western urban economies. In the view of these authors, the city is where a broad gray area expands, making uncertain and undefined the borders between precarious and temporary employment, means of survival, and illegal or criminal activities. At the porous borders between legal and illegal, formal and informal, the figures of the contemporary urban worker travel, making use of, in discontinuous and intermittent form, legal and illegal opportunities that coexist and overlap in labor markets. This is "lateral mobility," as defined by the authors, for workers that oscillate between poorly paid jobs and illicit activities, between unemployment and minor street trafficking, negotiating each situation within a context of moral acceptability of their choices. This characterizes the urban bazaar: the intersection between irregular and illegal markets, the shuffling of legal and illegal, and the permanent displacement of their boundaries.

The "urban bazaar," according to the authors, began to take shape in the mid-1980s. In the case of England and the United States, this was a turning point for cutting rights and social benefits by conservative governments, and was the starting point for a new precariousness of work and redefinition of urban labor markets. In general terms, years of productive restructuring and flexible employment relations ended and eventually snuffed out for many the differences between work, unemployment and means of survival. In the same way, the so-called "informal" has installed itself in the dynamic core of production processes and has expanded the process of networks of subcontracting and various forms of precarious and uncertain work, always at the unclear boundaries between legal and illegal, and also between the illicit and criminal when it involves human trafficking for the myriad sweatshops that permeate these productive circuits (Ruggiero 2000).

These were also years in which the scales of illegal activities changed, being internationalized and reorganized under polarized forms, between, on the one hand, illicit businesses, in particular drug trafficking as connected with common urban crime, and on the other, the small street vendors who operate on the margins of the drug economy and pass between the street and prison. These are the "working poor" of drugs, who multiply to the extent that this retailing expands and includes urban dynamics: criminal modulation of post-Fordist capitalism, and "just-in-time" crime as defined by Ruggiero (2000), which responds to variability, fluctuations and differing locations of markets. In this sense, illicit activities, not just drug trafficking, give rise to urban economies at the points of intersection with expanding irregular markets, multiplying the opportunities for the movement of goods and products of dubious origin, which are traded in a multiform game of social interactions independent of their legal, illegal or illicit origin.

Certainly the questions raised by these authors are far from resolving a problem discussed by a vast body of literature on the drug economy in its various dimensions, scales and forms of location. But that is not really the point that matters in this discussion. What matters, instead, is to retain the frame in which the authors present their questions, placing the city—the urban bazaar—as the frame of reference to locate illegal markets in their interactions with urban dynamics.

Contemporary forms of production and circulation of wealth

The revisited notion of "the bazaar economy" (see Geertz 1979, a reference almost required by authors who currently utilize the notion of the "bazaar economy") circulates today among researchers who take the situations described by Ruggiero and South to a different level. It prompts interest in the metaphor of the bazaar to describe contemporary cities, offering a perspective that places the city as a framework to describe its ongoing processes. It is this that permits placing in perspective and in dialogue research dealing with the various circuits and networks of varying size that constitute the so-called underground economies of the French suburbs, the overlapping of activities and informal street markets, in which the flows of money, merchandise, goods of illicit origin and also drugs interact in a complex system of trade, inscribing themselves in a game of social relationships and consisting of the urban dynamics that overflow the narrow boundaries of the so-called *quartiers sensibles* (Kokoreff 2004).

There is the "second great transformation," to use Palidda's term (2002) as applied to the Italian industrial cores, transforming the modern and developed city of Milan, now crossed by all sorts of illegality on which illegal immigration hinges, and the wide circulation of contraband and pirated goods, coming then mainly from China and Southeast Asia, and the nebulous relations between the illegal, informal and illicit which follows the process of outsourcing or relocation of industrial production plants.

Moreover, studies that deal with the call for new migratory forms shed light on another vector in the formation of the "bazaar economy" in the path of other dimensions of reconfiguration of contemporary capitalism. In the French context, Michel Peraldi (1999, 2002) makes use of this notion to deal with urban dynamics redefined under the impact of circulation of goods and wealth that follow the broad circuits of migration where transnational networks of proliferating petty trade are structured. These are networks that cross borders, linking commercial centers spread throughout various points in the world located under various models of the so-called informal market expanding in first-world urban centers. This is especially the case in border cities, located at the points of connection between these various circuits, many located at arrival points for previous waves of migration, and which now are redefined in this mutant cartography of the contemporary world.

The pathways for movement of goods destined for popular markets in urban centers trace transnational networks of informal exchanges in the porous borders between legal and illegal, always touching the illegal markets (for drugs, weapons and human beings). Alongside what might be called a migration of poverty (the tragedy of illegal immigrants), we see forms of migration with no goal of settling in destination countries, mobilizing men and women who move between countries and regions, depending on circumstances and opportunities for trade and commerce: the "ants of globalization" or "the new nomads of the underground economy," as Tarrius puts it (2002). These are petty traders that practice what Peraldi calls "*commerce à la valise*" (that which is practiced by "*sacoleiros*" in Brazil, as well as African mobile-phone buyers in Hong Kong and Guangzhou—traders with bags and suitcases filled with products purchased elsewhere), involved in transnational commercial mechanisms that link products from the North and consumers in the South (see Peraldi 2007). Many of them are independent, while others operate under traders well-established at commercial warehouses, some as wholesalers who mobilize the "ants" for the supply of products that are negotiated in other locations afterwards. These itinerant populations operate in more or less extensive networks, following "the circulatory territories" (Tarrius 2002) woven by family and neighborhood links (sedentary nuclei of earlier migration waves), anchored in the various towns and villages through which people and products pass.

These are transnational migration pathways that allow the movement of goods and merchandise that would not arrive at street markets of the North or the South without these migrants. This is the argument put forward by Alain Tarrius (2007): the large economic actors of globalization mobilize the poor as consumers, as clients, and as smugglers, outside official rules and commercial agreements, allowing products to reach poor countries and poor people in rich countries. Thus, for example, we see consumer electronics (camcorders, laptops, MP3 players, DVD equipment, etc.)

coming from China, dumped by the thousands in Dubai, spreading through Eastern Europe and reaching the German and French borders thanks to cohorts of Afghans, Iranians, Georgians and more, all those "beaten in wars" that decimated the Caucasoid countries in recent times. These "new nomads," populations "in excess," follow the social networks built on trails of previous or recent diasporas and are carriers of circulatory expertise (e.g. whether to pass through borders, to circumvent the restrictions, controls and taxes), becoming large players in international transfers of goods.

Such expertise in this circulation, Tarrius suggests, fits with "a project of savage globalization," because it is outside the bounds of states: "to arrive at the far reaches of the planet, merchandise from these places is deprived of random fluctuations of national policies" (Tarrius 2007: 180). There are various forms of smuggling involving "the ants of globalization," and there is an increase in practices of counterfeiting and piracy that is widespread on all sides, often with the complicity or encouragement of the companies making the original goods, who are interested in putting their brand names into broader circulation, further expanding their markets in this sort of frontier expansion of capital into realms of "the poor," in growing consumer markets today throughout the world. In the last few years, the importance of China as a supplier of myriad goods at very low prices changed the scale of these processes, recomposing the transnational routes of circulation of merchandise and redesigning the cartography of urban markets and the centers of popular trade in the circuits that link these places (Pliez 2010; see the chapters by Pliez, Mathews and Yang in this volume).

These transnational networks through which goods and people circulate create conditions for circulation of goods that would not arrive at these markets in other situations, given embargoes, bans, border controls, and differences in income and wealth that make it difficult, if not impossible, to access these goods and commodities. In other words, such markets actually feed off such obstacles, bans and prohibitions related to the movement of goods between countries, beyond the rules and laws that codify the regulations in each country. It is here that the meaning of the "contemporary bazaar" is specified. It is not so much oral agreements (informal agreements, rules of trust, strength of giving one's word) nor the relational web that characterize them, but the ability to transcend and circumvent boundaries and differences that marks (and prevents) the movement between countries. The entire relational web is triggered and the entire range of expertise related to the movement is activated in the folds of the legal and the illegal, in the folds of political borders and the circulating territories in which they pass: bribes to customs officials, false documents, shady deals with tax authorities and police, influence peddling, buying of protection, deals with truck drivers, and so on. In this sense, Peraldi makes use of the term the "bazaar economy": a term that brings together traders established in their posts, street vendors, "*sacoleiros*" and consumers, as well as the web of relationships within this network of intermediaries and mediations, for which negotiations are made in the folds of legal and illegal, formal and informal. Each point of this web enables the movement of goods. These actors are in relational situations, called upon to constantly negotiate the "moral acceptability of their behavior" in a situation that "makes possible the coexistence of legality and illegality, and the permanent change of its limits" in terms of "negotiations, always located in public or private venues conditional on public or private mercantile exchanges" (Peraldi 1999: 56).[1]

This issue helps us to better understand the idea of the contemporary bazaar that was our starting point. There are two points to consider. First, if there is porosity in the borders of the legal and illegal, the formal and the informal, then it is also true that passage between these borders is not simple; if there is transitivity between these dimensions, this does not mean the border is undifferentiated. It is in these folds where political arrangements are found—corruption, extortion, repression, violence, markets of protection—that allow for widespread circulation of goods, and of itinerant merchandise and populations. In other words, in contrast to what is suggested by the metaphor of flows, the spaces are not smooth, and it is the rough edges, we might say, that are interesting to observe: for therein orbits the political face of the "contemporary bazaar."

This highlights, on a broader scale, the issue that Michel Misse has considered when discussing the political dynamics inscribed in the informal and illegal markets in Brazilian cities (2006): its link with another market, also illegal, found inside legal-official apparatuses, where "political merchandise" is handled (false documents, agreements, bribes, buying of protection, corruption) that relies on the functioning of these markets and is constituted within these forms of regulation. This is today a central issue in the functioning of contemporary capitalism. This wide circulation of people, goods and merchandise depends on these very political devices to circumvent or to skirt legal obstacles at borders and national spaces through which they pass. They are at the center of globalization from below. They also affect how this wide circulation of people and merchandise is located in the urban landscape and the centers of popular trade, guiding the political dynamics in these markets. This is what I attempt to show in the pages that follow.

Second, these games of power and political devices are at the very center of the functioning of these markets. This is important because here are inscribed areas of tension, conflict and dispute that dislocate, form and re-form the border between the legal and the illegal, between justice and force, agreements and violence. At the center of the economies and urban dynamics of cities are the proper borders of the economy and relations with the state that are redefined in the threads of the informal markets. This is a possible way to understand the area of contention at these frictional points with the law and the state. But it is also a path to be followed if we want to understand the ways in which, through its antecedents and means of location, this wide circulation of products and people redefines urban networks, social order, relations of power and a set of actors in situated contexts. And here the notion of the urban bazaar is of interest, inasmuch as it proposes an urban scale to describe displacements in the relations between informal, legal and illegal, in interactions with the urban pathways where wealth circulates, and in relations of power found at its points of intersection.

Urban dynamics redefined

The "urban bazaar" is not new. This movement between the informal and the illegal, perhaps the illicit, has always occurred in cities that have long had an expansive informal market, always close and tangential to the illicit markets that also have an important story to be told. However, if this long history were updated today, the order of things would be considerably different. Today, we have an urban scenario, crossed by economic circuits of a variety of scales that are superimposed on the informal markets, now connected to transnational economies that mobilize workers and activate informal means, also illegal, to circulate goods and merchandise.

We can see this by following the products that travel about the centers of popular commerce in the city of São Paulo, with legions of vendors that circulate products of varied origins, almost always dubious, putting into action local and territorialized negotiations, linking the informal and illegal circuits of transnational economies (contraband, piracy, counterfeits). The fact is that, from any one of these points of sales that proliferate in urban spaces, it is possible to observe a game situated in the intertwining scales and webs of mediations that affect the local urban dynamic. Thus, for example, the points of sales of pirated CDs, ubiquitous in the city, are super-imposed onto networks of many scales: the contraband blank CDs that arrive by the thousands from Paraguay, coming originally from China (see Aguiar, chapter 2); the clandestine sound labs controlled by entrepreneurs in illegal businesses (and, it appears, that are under control of Chinese groups); small producers of pirated items that supply stores in these areas of popular trade with a recording kit (equipment, printing, passwords, sources, etc.) for those with the resources and necessary ability; and the intermediaries that circulate the product among myriad points of sales throughout the city, mentioned in the beginning of this chapter. Here, other social webs are mobilized to guarantee and negotiate place, passing through kinship and neighborhood networks; the mafioso control of the sales points also activates in turn many other networks, some more obscure, alluding to the illicit (for example, local bosses of drug trafficking), but there also circulates "political merchandise" (purchases of protection, bribes), which depends on the routine of these activities.

In the center of the city, in the places where this broad trading market is currently located, this scale gains another dimension. In São Paulo city streets such as 25 de Março and Santa Ifigênia, traditional centers of popular trade, there is an astonishing concentration of vendors, small-time traders and storefront shops, along with a heterogeneous gamut of small businesses and services that comprise the urban economy of the region. The streets are filled with multitudes, a crowded mass of men and women of all kinds: everyday consumers from many areas of the city, including the most distant outlying areas; small traders in search of products to supply businesses spread throughout the city, and in the urban peripheries; *sacoleiros* coming from the heart of the city, as well as other states and countries of the Southern Cone (Uruguay and Argentina in particular) and Angolans, who mobilize, in turn, a mixed range of services and workers to travel across the Atlantic and make possible the purchase and transport of merchandise. During certain times of the year, such as the end of the year with its holiday parties, this crowd will top one million people per day. On 25 de Março, between 3 and 6 a.m. every day the so-called "sunrise market-fair" opens. Nearby, in the neighborhood of Brás, there are two more of these early-morning markets. At these markets some 5,000–7,000 tents form labyrinths of narrow corridors, packed with merchandise of all types, where men and women circulate, toting enormous plastic bags stuffed with purchases. This is a wholesale market, with an estimated count of 15,000–20,000 customers daily. Nearby, hundreds of buses are parked, around 200 each day, many of them chartered, coming to the interior of São Paulo from the states of Paraná, Santa Catarina and Minas Gerais, and some from the faraway northeastern states of Brazil, even some from neighboring countries, mainly Argentina (Freire, 2008). As can be seen, the flows of these diverse consumers pass through the pathways of an urban dynamic that goes far beyond the local perimeter. The same can be said, too, for the merchandise in circulation.

The paths the products travel until arriving at these places trace routes of varied lengths at the porous borders, sometimes indiscernible, formal and informal, legal and illegal (see the research by Carlos Freire, 2008, 2009, whom I closely follow here). On the one hand, there are the products from factories that utilize itinerant vendors as a distribution strategy outside official controls and regulations. These products may be leftovers, off-line products or defective, and this is a strategy to compete in the market when it is impossible to enter the formal circuit dominated by famous brands and high costs of doing business. There are myriad small textile workshops proliferating in the area and the urban peripheries that even expand into homes where workers do piecework, with the street vendor a conduit for moving products: an informal but in some cases not entirely illegal means of distribution. In other cases the products follow a more obscure path, together with the actual black market of famous brand labels—here, this itinerant trade seeps through the cracks of subcontracted networks activated by economic circuits, in this case the textile circuit, in a swift process of integration into globalized markets.

However, in the great majority of cases, the origin of products is practically indiscernible between piracy, fakes, cheap copies, smuggling and other forms of "embezzlement." This is nothing new. For some time *sacoleiros* have been carrying contraband along the Paraguay–São Paulo route (Rabossi 2005), supplying myriad points of sale distributed among itinerant and small local traders who operate in the blurred borders of the formal and informal. Through the 1990s, and more intensely beginning in 2000, Chinese traders began to predominate (Pinheiro-Machado 2008). They widely dominate storefront shops, controlling broad distribution of electronic products in addition to an infinite variety of products, primarily garments, plus knickknacks of all imaginable types. From container ships unloading in the port of Santos to the storefronts, the products pass through longer and more intricate networks of paths. It is a business that depends heavily on smuggling, demanding more complicated means to move merchandise (tax fraud, bribes, corruption), transport and storage schemes, and commercial devices to make distribution possible for untold quantities of products of dubious origin: genuine and original products that arrive by means of interception and embezzlement and regulatory fraud, sophisticated or sloppy fakes, cheap copies or "true fakes", as Alain Tarrius (2007) says, when describing this type of commerce in Eastern Europe. It is a considerable change of scale. As is well noted by Freire (2009) this change is what activates, amplifies and redefines these traditional centers of popular commerce between stores and street trade, with its legion of traveling vendors.

The networks, the routes and the pathways traveled by the products have all changed. The landscape of 25 de Março, Santa Ifigênia and their surroundings have also changed. The Chinese presence now predominates. It is possible to find Chinese entrepreneurs in the blurred businesses of "import–export," or in obscure real estate businesses. There is evidence that enterprising Chinese are investing heavily in this area. Old factories that once housed industries that closed during the 1980s have been remodeled as huge warehouses. It is hard to know how this business is done, but there is evidence that it is through one-time cash payments. The fact is that the size and quantities of these acquisitions seem to be directly affecting the real estate market of the region.[2]

However, most important is the Chinese presence in warren-like shopping arcades. These arcades have multiplied in recent years, as additions to older structures, and consequently their internal spaces have been reformulated to receive a volume of business, people and merchandise on a scale unimaginable a few years ago.

Law Kin Chong, named as the largest smuggler of pirated goods by the "Comissão Parlamentar de Inquérito" (CPI: the Parliamentary Investigation Commission, established in São Paulo in 2004 to investigate piracy and tax evasion), is the owner of an arcade on 25 de Março, and has businesses in two other streets, the three most important commercial locations in the region, as well as merchandise warehouses close by and stores in other regions of the city. He was cited by the CPI, but in his defense said he is just a real estate entrepreneur, who rents the kiosks inside the arcades, not having any responsibility for what is sold in these areas. He was imprisoned not for contraband ("unproven") but for "evidence of bribery" in trying to bribe federal agents of the CPI.

As Freire notes (2009), the stores became a strategic device for the wide circulation and distribution of merchandise, in a complementary relationship with street commerce. Inside, the Chinese presence reigns in the kiosks, staffed by a legion of salesmen who are for the most part undocumented immigrants from mainland China, according to CPI. The circulation of people has also changed in scale, becoming a teeming mass of customers in search of products of all kinds. Street vendors also load up on products that will later be resold on the street. The small or large entrepreneurs of illegal businesses also find in these malls the products that they need—perhaps equipment for a small laboratory of pirated CDs, or more obscure schemes for the exchange and negotiation of products of origin, possibly stolen or "deviated" from official routes. As Freire says (2009: 25), the arcades are also places of capitalization for other economic enterprises, and function, to use the terms of Ruggiero and South (1997), as a "balcony of opportunities" whenever they are ready to assume the intrinsic risks for distribution of these products.

In the street trade, the same products are displayed as in the arcade, and, for the most part, the clientele is the same. At times, street vendors and suppliers, who control sales points, negotiate the way the street spaces are occupied. The fact is that street sales offer more profits and faster circulation of products than established trade. And, as Freire emphasizes (2009), vendors are strategic operators for this ample circulation of products of uncertain origin.

In the folds of the legal and the illegal: games of power and areas of dispute

Formal and informal, legal and illegal activities: everything is entangled and jumbled in these centers of popular trade. This is, above all, a varied composition of formal and informal procedures, legal and illegal, that puts into circulation a broad spectrum of merchandise. Between tax evasion, frauds, piracy, counterfeits, contraband, and varied forms of "embezzlements," the products travel through different means of transgression of laws and formal rules until arriving at the end consumer (Pinheiro-Machado 2008).

Here, everything is shuffled and entangled, with a provenance that is perhaps indistinguishable for the consumer who cares little about the legal or illegal origin of the transacted product. We return here to the legal–illegal folds. It is precisely at this point that business is done, opportunities appear and wealth circulates. After all, it is a market that, strictly speaking, feeds off the legal controls and barriers, and generates wealth through invented artifices and negotiations to bypass restrictions, controls, regulations (see Tarrius, 2007; Peraldi, 2002, 2007). As Fernando Rabossi says in his study on the *sacoleiros* that transit the border with Paraguay (Ciudad del Este), it has a "particular link between rules and practices" that needs to be understood, a "dynamic around the rules" that is basic to understanding the distribution of possibilities and opportunities that make street sales a form of making a living (Rabossi, 2005: 169). More concretely, and this is the focus of the research of Carlos Freire (2009), in these folds of the legal–illegal, negotiation practices are put in place, operating as points of anchor of varied and overlapping economic circuits, passing through legal and illegal, formal and informal, unfolding in real commercial devices on which depends this broad circulation of good, merchandise, products and people.

However, none of this would function without its connection to another market, also illegal, where transactions of political merchandise can be found, in terms, as we have said, proposed by Michel Misse (2006). This is where many other networks and actors come into play that interface with public power (taxes, city management, local councilmen, police forces) oscillating between agreements for sharing in profits, "buying people off" (bribes, corruption), exchanging favors and clientelism, and protection and extortion practices that are more or less violent depending on the context, and on micro-situational politics and alliances. As emphasized by Freire (2009), the ways that political merchandise circulates is predicated on the practical regulations of these channeled flows. And this is central to understanding the dynamics inscribed in these forms of the urban economy today. This is the political dynamic inscribed in the very functioning of these markets. But the market is not an abstract entity. It is composed of a system of exchanges, of social interactions, social exchanges, and relations of power. There are three points to be observed.

First, the means through which merchandise is transacted and political merchandise circumscribed into the networks where wealth circulates, is something like a surplus derived from corruption and extortion practices, appropriated (and expropriated) in the difficult lives of workers, and puts into play actors and operators of these markets.

Second, it is in this terrain that political games become armed, oscillating between mafia agreements and transactions, tolerance and repression, shady deals and open conflicts, and very frequently pitched in warlike campaigns involving vendors, city regulators, urban managers and police. Here, there is an area of conflicts and disputes that is dislocated and differentiated depending on the location of these markets and the origin of the products, interests involved, political conveniences and the political clout of the actors in the scene.

Third, in this game, oscillating between tolerance, consensual transgression and repression, another schism is created, transverse to the territories of this market, but marking the difference between illegal entrepreneurs and small storekeepers and street vendors that put this vast circulation of products of dubious origins into circulation. This is a unique risk management, says Carlos Freire (2009): the entrepreneurs of the illegal businesses, primarily involved in smuggling and piracy, covered by legal façades afforded by their storefront shops, put in place varied devices to neutralize possibilities of criminal responsibility for this illegal commerce. For them, consequences in a worst-case scenario are more of the white-collar sort (tax fraud, tax evasion, cheating). The risks related to smuggling and other illegalities in the journey of this merchandise are transferred to the small vendors and traders, on which more overt controls and repression are focused (Freire 2009).

Let me take up once again the issues discussed in the previous pages: the folds of the legal and the illegal, and the procedures put in place to circumvent legal restrictions circumscribed in areas of force and conflict. It is exactly here that the relations of power are configured and inscribed in the transaction of political merchandise. More than a corruption problem, the ways in which this political market function can be viewed, in the fine analysis of Misse (2006) as commercially exchanged mechanisms of expropriation of the sovereignty of the state in its prerogatives of law and order. This is why the ethnography of these markets unfolds as a political ethnography, with the state seen from this point of view as the nerve center of these economies.

There are many agents, procedures and practices that move between formal-legal situations and extralegal proceedings heading into arbitration, expropriation and open violence. Strictly speaking, this also constitutes the displacement of the borders between legal and illegal that accompanies these forms of production and circulation of wealth. But this is also a disputed area of competition, involving storekeepers, street vendors, associations, unions, police, city hall regulators, city management, and city councilmen and their local bases. There are negotiations and races for power within the management of these spaces and the distribution of their territories.

In the center of these disputes is the game of clientelism, of protection markets and practices of extortion that allow in great measure distribution of the points of street sale: protection is needed to establish a point of sale, something like a license, an "informal business license," completely illegal, that requires payment of a quota for some guarantee of continuity of activity. These are unstable agreements and balances that can be undone by micro-situational politics and changes in function of political alliances between parties, government and city managers. The unions and associations of the street vendor are many, and are mobilized around the protocols of protection markets. This is what is at many times at the heart of negotiations, open or obscured, between these diverse actors. There is constant negotiations around the modus operandi of these political devices: procedures, money charged, criteria for the distribution of guarantees that benefit some and exclude others. There is also negotiation of tolerable levels of extortion—when these limits are surpassed, the conflict can take over the streets and be transformed into true battles. It is within these thresholds that the dispute is processed for appropriation of the overflow generated by street trade. As Freire points out:

> According to information from the vendors themselves, there are four syndicates in São Paulo alone that have different areas of control in the city and more than 160 vendors' associations, each that has its own specific means of activity and its own alliances and bases of support. These syndicates and associations deal directly with the city in situations of conflict, organizing demonstrations in cases of confrontation. They have started to act in the management of urban spaces were many vendors are concentrated, when not directly occupying control of the points. They negotiate also the limits tolerated in this market of protection to promote complaints against agents of public authority when extortion reaches very high levels.
>
> *(2008: 126)*

These games of power in the nucleus of an urban economy are entirely connected to globalized markets. This is the case in the city center, as well as in the various points of concentration of popular commerce in the peripheral regions. Here, the products circulate by means of difficult-to-maintain agreements between mafioso organizations, people linked to drug trafficking, poor traders, Korean intermediaries (and many others), along with city hall inspectors who attempt to validate official regulations, all of this is mixed in with pressure, corruption, and shady deals that can turn deadly. This is all within a gray zone of alliances, suspicious disputes or deals, all conducted through relations of force that unleash ever-present violence, either latent or overt, but that is potentially devastating. But it is exactly there that products of known, unknown, doubtful or simply illicit origin circulate, as well as the "overflow" of families doing piecework at home as they take advantage of extra time due to the discontinuous and uncertain rhythms of made-to-order production.

These games allow us to re-describe the lateral mobilities of the workers who transit the arteries of the "metropolitan bazaar," as well as the prosaic Doralice with whom I opened this chapter, an urban character, who, in her passages, allows us to see how this admixture of the illegal, informal and illicit is conjugated in the branches of the city. The fact is that individuals and families move about these tenuous borders of the legal and illegal, and they know well how to deal with the codes and rules on both sides, and how to play with the diverse identities that attend to these many universes that are superimposed and shuffled in life. They know, above all, how to exercise this special "art of circumvention" to prevent risks that are lodged in the folds of these porous borders: the always-present possibility of police violence, the extortion practices of city regulators, and the unstable agreements unraveling with black market entrepreneurs, not just in traffic of drugs.

In following the ways of people, goods, products and wealth circulating in the tenuous borders of the legal–illegal, I have demarcated some of the relations and social forms engendered in these folds of the legal and the illegal. In each situation, there is evidence of the dispute that dislocates, and makes and remakes the demarcation between the lawful and the unlawful, between justice and force, agreements and violence, order and its opposite. This is what is inscribed in the lateral mobilities of the urban workers who move within the borders of the legal and the illegal. This is what is explicit in the arenas of disputes and conflicts in the centers of popular trade, in the proper borders of the economy that are redefined in informal markets. These are the tracks to be followed if we want to understand the ways in which these vectors of globalization affect and redefine not only urban dynamics and social order, but senses of law, order and justice as well.

Notes

1 As discussed by Tarrius (2002), there would be no market nor trading relationships without cafés, bars, restaurants, nightclubs or games (official or clandestine), where information circulates, where there are the threads that form reciprocal engagements, information accords, and networks of confidence and reciprocity.
2 I owe this information to Helena Mena Barreto.

References

Freire, C. (2008) "Trabalho Informal e Redes de Subcontratação" [Informal Work and Sub-hiring Networks], São Paulo: Dissertação de mestrado [Master's Thesis], FFLCH-University of São Paulo.
——(2009) "Dinâmicas Urbanas e Mercado Informal: Das Calçadas às Lojas de Galeria" [Urban Dynamics and Informal Markets: From Sidewalks to Gallery Stores], São Paulo: Research Report, PPGS-University of São Paulo.
Geertz, C. (1979) "The Bazaar Economy in Cefrou," in C. Geertz, H. Geertz, and L. Rosen, eds, *Meaning and Social Order in Moroccan Society*, Cambridge: Cambridge University Press.
Kokoreff, M. (2004) "Trafics de drogue et criminalité organisée: une relation complexe" [Drug Trafficking and Organized Crime: A Complex Relation], *Criminologie* 7(1): 9–32.
Misse, M. (2006) *Crime e Violência no Brasil Contemporâneo* [Crime and Violence in Contemporary Brazil], Rio de Janeiro: Lumen Juris.
Palidda, S. (2002) "Milan global: entre affairisme et politiques sécuritaires" [Global Milan: Between Business and Security Politics], in M. Peraldi, ed., *La Fin des Norias? Réseaux Migrants dans les Économies Marchandes en Méditerranée*, Paris: Maisonneuve et Larose.
Peraldi, M. (1999) "Marseille: Réseaux migrants transfrontaliers, place marchande économie de bazar" [Marseille: Transborder Migrant Networks, Marketplaces and the Bazaar Economy], *Cultures & Conflits* (33–34): 51–67.
——(2002) *Cabas et containers: activités marchandes informelles et réseaux migrants transfrontaliers* [Bags and Containers: Informal Market Activities and Transborder Migrant Networks], Marseille: Maisonneuve et Larose.
——(2007) "Nouveaux aventuriers du nouveau capitalisme marchand. Essai d'anthropologie de l'éthique mercantile" [Adventurers of the New Mercantile Capitalism: An Essay in the

Anthropology of Mercantile Ethics], in F. Adelkhah and J-.F. Bayart, eds, *Les Voyage du développement: émigration, commerce et exil*, Paris: Karthala.

Pinheiro-Machado, R. (2008) "China–Paraguai–Brasil: Uma Rota para Pensar a Economia Informal" [China–Paraguay–Brazil: A Route to Discuss the Informal Economy], *Revista Brasileira de Ciencias Sociais* 23(67): 117–92.

Pliez, O. (2010) "Toutes les routes de la soie mènent à Yiwu (Chine): entrepreneurs et migrants musulmans dans un comptoir économique chinois" [All Silk Roads Lead to Yiwu (China): Entrepreneurs and Muslim Migrants at a Chinese Trading Post], *Espace Géographique* 2: 131–44.

Rabossi, F. (2005) "Dimensões da Espacialização das Trocas: A Propósito de Mesiteros e Sacoleiros em Cuidad del Este" [Dimensions of Exchange Spatialization: About *Mesiteros* and *Sacoleiros* in Ciudad del Este], *Revista do Centro de Educação e Letras* 6: 151–76.

Ruggiero, V. (2000) *Crime and Markets: Essays in Anti-Criminology*, Oxford: Oxford University Press.

Ruggiero, V. and N. South (1997) "The Late City as a Bazaar: Drug Markets, Illegal Enterprise and the Barricades," *British Journal of Sociology* 48(1): 54–70.

Tarrius, A. (2002) *La Mondialisation par le bas: les nouveaux nomades de l'économie souterraine* [Globalization From Below: The New Nomads of the Underground Economy], Paris: Balland.

——(2007) *La Remontée des Suds: afghans et marocains en Europe Méridionale* [The Rise of the South: Afghans and Morrocans in Southern Europe], Paris: L'Aube.

Part Two
Embodying globalization from below

Entrepreneurs, traders, peddlers

6

HONG KONG PETTY CAPITALISTS INVESTING IN CHINA

Risk tolerance, uncertain investment environments, success and failure

Alan Smart and Josephine Smart

Mr and Mrs Lee once operated a factory in Guangdong with a workforce that peaked at 50. When we first met them in 1983, they were self-employed, with no non-family full-time workers, producing brass pieces for electrical plugs, a small part of the complexly networked industrial landscape of Hong Kong. For the last few years, they have been once again self-employed, without paid employees, producing high quality bean products for local consumers. Throughout the 27 years that we have followed their lives, they have always been involved with investment plans, imagined, fulfilled and collapsed. Transnational investment allowed them to ramp up production and become petty capitalists, with hopes for wealth and success. Their ups and downs reflect related travails of Hong Kong's small and medium enterprises and what came to be known as the Guangdong model of development. In this chapter we draw on their life histories, contextualized by research with many others we've interviewed, to explore a pivotal but obscure figure of recent global transformations, the petty investor.

Petty investment is one of the most neglected dimensions of globalization from below. Traditional academic divisions of labor mean that those who study investment are unlikely to study migration, and vice versa. For example, in the 349-page *World Investment Report 2009* published by the United Nations Commission for Trade and Development, there are only two mentions of migration, and only one links it to investment: neglect encouraged by tendencies to dichotomize capital and labor. This assumption can be seen in arguments that the relationship between capital and labor is being transformed by globalization in ways that increase the bargaining strength of hypermobile capital against less mobile labor (Castells 1998; Harvey, 1989). In their formative discussion of transnationalism, Basch *et al.* (1994) see transnational investment and migration as distinct, if linked processes, and equate transnationalism with the social fields constructed and maintained by migrants. Their implicit assumption is that migration concerns the flow of labor, transnational investment, and the flow of capital.

Yet many of the Hong Kong entrepreneurs investing in China in the late 1980s had fewer assets than the average migrant to Canada or Australia (Smart and Smart 1998). Petty investors occupy a "liminal" space that is usually swept under the theoretical carpet. Marx told us, after all, that the petty bourgeois were not that significant because they were fated to be divided into one or the other of the polarizing classes of capitalism.

Hong Kong is a strategic site in which to examine the role of entrepreneurs with relatively modest assets engaged in cross-border direct investment. The transformation of its traditional colonial entrepôt role turned it first into a major manufacturing power-house and subsequently into the catalyst behind the capitalist explosion that has fueled the "rise of China." While large corporations were involved in both transformations, the role of small and medium enterprises was of particular significance.

How do these entrepreneurs fit with this book's emphasis on globalization from below or low-end globalization (Ribeiro 2009; Mathews 2007)? One could object that small and medium enterprises are not particularly "low-end" compared, for example, to shuttle traders, and that their actions are regional rather than global, and since the return of Hong Kong to Chinese sovereignty as a Special Administrative Region in 1997 not even transnational. However, a significant number of these smaller entrepreneurs like the Lees began with few economic resources and may end the same way. They are not what is usually imagined as the transnational investors of globalization from above. Furthermore, even after 1997 the Hong Kong/China border still operates much like a national border, particularly for movements from China to Hong Kong. While production is done in a compact geographical region, most of the products are meant for global markets; many products ending up in the markets described in other chapters in this volume. By describing the networks in which small and medium enterprises operate, greater light can be shed on the low-end retailing of Chinese goods.

The chapter first sketches key issues of transnational investment by petty capitalists. Following that, we sketch Hong Kong's role in the non-hegemonic world-system (Ribeiro 2009), up until the opening of China to foreign investment in 1979. Then we revisit our prior research on small-scale Hong Kong investors establishing factories in China, concentrating on investment. The next section includes new ethnographic material on how routinization of capitalist investment in China, particularly since accession to the WTO in 2001, and its adoption of more ambitious development goals, has marginalized small and medium investment from Hong Kong. Choices made by the Hong Kong Special Administrative Region government have reinforced the decline of the petty investor.

Petty capitalists and transnational investment

There is a substantial literature on the entrepreneurial activities of migrants in receiving countries (Portes *et al.* 1999; Waldinger *et al.* 1990; Zhou 1992). However, the main emphasis is on their *self-employment*, often as a result of the opportunities blocked to them due to racism or barriers from demands for local credentials or experience. In other work, we argued for attention to "petty capitalists," who we defined as "individuals or households who employ a small number of workers but are themselves actively involved in the labor process." This definition emphasized their ambiguous positioning between capital and labor, family and market, production and reproduction, market and community (Smart and Smart, 2005). We argued that the concept of "petty capitalist" is more useful to emphasize the meaningful experience of actors than terms such as "entrepreneur" or "family business." Concentrating on enterprises where proprietors are active in the labor process, even if only to the extent of producing prototypes or setting up equipment during product shifts, questions assumptions about boundaries between capital and labor. Productively engaged on the shop floor, the petty capitalist may be able to emphasize common purpose with workers, and has advantages in labor surveillance. Petty capitalists are intermediate, bounded by petty producers and subsistence producers on one side, and "real" capitalists on the other. This position is unstable: improved fortunes may lead to the shedding of the "petty" status, while a decline in fortunes may result in proletarianization or impoverishment. People's strategies and life trajectories move them back and forth between the categories. In most sectors, once the workforce exceeds a few dozen to 100, the capitalist is unlikely to be actively involved in production, leaving even shopfloor supervision to foremen. Even in smaller firms, once the second generation has taken over from the founder, the proprietor seems to be less likely to get his or her hands dirty.

Our emphasis on involvement in production as the defining characteristic of petty capitalists shifted attention away from their investment role. We correct this weakness here. A petty capitalist is involved in both self-employment and investment. On the investment side, an investor who does not hire labor but labors oneself or with family is a petty producer. One who does not invest in any significant amounts of production capital is self-employed, possibly a disguised employee working on a contract. A true petty capitalist is someone who hires some labor while also being engaged in production, but also invests working capital. It is the latter factor that defines the petty investor, which we limit here to what has been defined as "direct" investment, excluding passive portfolio investment.

Economic anthropologists understand that even petty production requires some investment in production capital, such as tools and raw materials. It is when analysts turn to globalization, or more specifically foreign investment, that petty investment shrinks from the stage. Small business is usually assumed to be local business, while business activities that operate regionally, nationally, or transnationally are seen as the province of increasingly larger enterprises. Historical evidence suggests that what Max Weber referred to as "pariah capitalists" (stigmatized ethnic minorities such as Jews) "played a crucial role in the development of trade, money management, and capital accumulation" (Reid 1997: 34). Where commerce, trade and money-lending were seen as corrupting, middlemen minorities could take advantage of neglected opportunities. While some enterprises were very wealthy, they have been outnumbered by larger numbers of small and medium enterprises. While large trading firms controlled the backbone of the network, there were opportunities for their relatives or townsmen in more marginal niches, such as the Chinese who operated small stores in poorly developed areas in Papua New Guinea, taking considerable risks trading in areas outside European influence (Wu 1982: 22).

The literature on return migration is relevant. Modernization theorists and other development proponents often argue that migration from poor rural areas to cities, and from poorer to richer countries, not only benefited individuals but also the sending areas. The benefits are not only remittances, which amounted to at least US$3 billion in 2009 and exceed the total value of foreign aid (*Economist* 2010), but also the transfer of knowledge and investment back home by return migrants. Development specialists ask how the investment impact of remittances and return migration can be facilitated and channeled into productive uses rather than those that encourage consumption and drive out local investments (Rhoades, 2002). James Watson, in a pioneering study of transnational networks linking emigrants from rural Hong Kong establishing or working in Chinese restaurants in Europe, concludes that the money sent back was usually invested in houses rather than productive enterprises. He suggests that they made a "clear distinction between *speculative investments* and *security investments*. While abroad even the most cautious villager may show an uncharacteristic flair for entrepreneurial activity and risk everything in hopes of making a quick fortune. When the emigrant returns home, he reverts to his former mode of behaviour and seeks to maximize his security by investment in the safest possible manner" (Watson 1975: 158). Productive investments in the village are made less likely by remittances that discourage work for low wages, while houses claim continuing membership and assert status. Similar patterns have been identified among rural Mexican emigrants but without agreement on the economic consequences (Cohen 1999, Cornelius *et al.* 2009, Kearney 1995, Massey *et al.* 2002, Rothstein 2007). A common finding is that although the majority of remittances are spent on consumption, a significant proportion is spent on productive investment, with positive effects on national economic output (Massey *et al.* 2002: 154).

Hong Kong as a hub of the non-hegemonic world-system

As a tiny free port with no significant natural resources other than an excellent harbour strategically located for the Chinese trade, Hong Kong has relied economically on transnational trade and industry. Before World War II, the British-controlled trading companies dominated trade. However, already before World War II, there was an internal split between the hegemonic and non-hegemonic world-systems. The laissez-faire policy was only retrospectively constructed as a framework that supported industrial expansion: previously it reflected policy bias against manufacturing that supported British merchant firms (Ngo 1999). Despite this, many smaller Chinese companies exploited opportunities to engage in what might be considered parts of what Ribeiro (2009) calls non-hegemonic globalization. The "South Sea" trade in dried seafood and birds' nests was organized through a cluster of family businesses on Hong Kong Island, and Hong Kong firms largely organized the export of labor from

China, and the facilitation of remittances and exports of speciality goods to the new Chinese communities in the Americas and elsewhere (Sinn 1997).

Hong Kong's role as a hub in the non-hegemonic system can be seen during the United States' and United Nations' embargoes on trade with China during the Korean War, 1950–1953. On July 2, 1955, Governor Grantham wrote to the Secretary of State for the Colonies that since 1950 Hong Kong had been called upon to "cut off, at its own expense, a major part of its own livelihood" and asked how anyone could expect "this dying city" to survive with its "swollen population and with a great part of its normal trade sacrificed for the good" (Zhang 2001: 133). Hong Kong's exports to China dropped from HK$234.8 million in January 1951 to HK$88.9 million in September 1951. Official trade dropped by 13 percent in 1952, and China's share of trade dropped from 56 percent in 1950 to 34 percent in 1952. By 1955, official trade with China was only 15 percent of Hong Kong's total (Zhang 2001). Hong Kong was still the People's Republic's most important trading partner in Asia and particularly crucial as a place where the embargo could be circumvented through smuggling. During this period, smuggling provided one of China's key ways to obtain foreign currency and scarce goods, but it continued afterward for other purposes. Throughout the Maoist period, legal trade with Hong Kong was an important source of hard currency, and provided Hong Kong with most of its food and water, as well as other goods. Emigration to Hong Kong, mostly illegal, also bolstered the social connections that would play a key role in the rapid growth of Hong Kong investment once the economic reforms in China began in 1979.

Hong Kong has been characterized by an industrial structure composed largely of many small companies. In 1977, 92.1 percent of the total manufacturing establishments and 40.2 percent of the employment in manufacturing employed fewer than 50 workers (Lin *et al.* 1980: 10; Hsia and Chau 1978: 12). The average number of employees per manufacturing enterprise dropped from 30.04 in 1959 to 27.65 in 1973 (Lin *et al.* 1980: 94) and again to 18.5 by 1984 (Hong Kong Government 1985: 323). A common pattern was that a partner or skilled worker in a firm set up his or her own factory, taking along a number of workers. The smallest businesses were either subcontractors or dependent on orders from import-export firms, and acted to buffer volatile market demand for large, well-established businesses (Chiu *et al.* 1997). Pragmatic attitudes by firms that have suffered from the fissioning process helped to produce this highly networked industrial landscape, since they are described as characteristically not "holding a grudge" but often accepting the situation by recruiting the new firm as a subcontractor during high market demand periods (Yeung 1998).

Recreation of the entrepreneurial stock and the preservation of an economy based on small and medium firms is related to a context where employees are provided few protections and where unions have been weak. Immigrants from China were more likely to become proprietors in the manufacturing sector than in commerce, partly because their backgrounds put them at a linguistic disadvantage in service sectors. Moving from employee to employer, however, requires access to assets such as capital and connections, and thus effective utilization of social networks is critical for those with small amounts of capital themselves (Chiu 1998). The type of products helped make enterprise fission and the reproduction of the small-scale character of industry possible. When little capital and much skilled labor is required, economies of scale have little significance and large and small manufacturers can operate side by side. Low capital-intensivity also facilitates changes of product lines according to market conditions, especially important in sectors where fashions change quickly. This was of greater importance for Hong Kong in the 1960s and 1970s than were low wages. Other countries could provide cheaper labor. Hong Kong's ability to switch products quickly and make profits on short production runs provided competitive advantage for new niche products. Since many of these niches became mass-market products such as plastic flowers, digital watches and electronic toys, ability to ramp up production through networking was crucial for benefiting from the high-margin periods of these product cycles. Success undermined itself by the late 1970s. Rapid growth increased wages and encouraged imitation by competitors. The opening of China provided a solution and prevented a shift towards more capital-intensive manufacturing within Hong Kong itself.

The Lees were in the bottom ranks of Hong Kong's subcontracting system in the 1980s, one step above those who did outsourced piecework, working in their homes assembling plastic flowers or stripping excess plastic from cheap molded toys (Chiu *et al.* 1997). The Lees occasionally paid neighbors to do piecework, but otherwise had no employees, only the help of their three children and two young relatives who lived with them due to problems in their own parents' household. They produced a specialized product: they cut copper rods into the round prongs at the end of electrical appliance cords to be inserted into power plugs. Completed orders of prongs went to other companies that assembled the full appliance. Initial investment was facilitated by loans from family and friends: business loans were rarely available for small businesses unless fully supported by collateral. The business operated in a separate outbuilding in a small housing compound in a Kowloon squatter area. They had two semi-automatic electrical cutting machines that only needed to be set up for a specific size and periodically reloaded. The family tried to keep the machines operating as close to 24 hours a day as possible. This generated a very irregular family schedule, with a late meal often taken at 2 a.m., and difficulty in getting the children to school on time. None of the children were successful students, limiting their opportunities as formal educational credentials have become increasingly important with Hong Kong's deindustrialization.

They were reluctant to move their operations to China in the 1980s, despite seeing cost advantages achieved by their friends and competitors, due in part to the wife's concern about the risk of her husband getting involved with a mistress there, a common social problem (Lang and Smart 2002). She also worried about the impact on their children, since either the business would be separated from their residence, or their children would follow them across the border and have to cope with the inferior mainland educational system. With both husband and wife actively involved in the business, separating enterprise and residence undermined their economic strategies, and would make it much more difficult to work such long hours without hired labor (Smart 1989). On the other hand, hiring labor was much more affordable in

China. This choice faced most manufacturers in Hong Kong by the late 1980s. A new investment landscape offered opportunities to move from self-employment to bigger enterprises, but posed risks.

The rise of Hong Kong petty investment in China, 1979–2001

Hong Kong petty capitalists who established factories in China in the first decade after China's economic reforms began in 1979 played important roles in generating the export-oriented manufacturing miracle that has transformed the world in a myriad of ways. More recently, as foreign investment in China has become more routinized, small and medium investors have been marginalized. Here we concentrate on how and why small and medium investors from Hong Kong became so important to China's miracle. Our past work has explored how petty capitalists operated in the pioneering phase of China's opening, the advantages created by their greater tolerance for risk and uncertain legal frameworks, and their use of social connections to facilitate operations in these contexts. After a brief summary, we concentrate on the petty investment dimension.

By the mid-1970s, low unemployment combined with high rents raised labor and other production costs above those of regional competitors. At about the same time, China's economic reforms started opening China to capitalist investment. Access to cheap labor and land across the border encouraged the transfer of the Hong Kong production system, rather than the alternative of upgrading technology and moving up the value chain (Smart 2001). In the early 1980s, wages in Dongguan in the Eastern Pearl River Delta were about one fifth to one sixth of that for equivalent work in Hong Kong (Lin 1997: 175). Foreign direct investment (FDI) utilized between 1979 and 1999 totaled US$307.6 billion, of which Hong Kong accounted for US$154.8 billion, half of the total, and Taiwan for US$23.86 billion (7.76 percent). Asia accounted for 76.79 percent of the accumulated total, compared to only 7 percent for the combined EU countries and 9 percent for the United States. FDI inflows soared after Deng Xiaoping's famous 1992 "southern tour" launched new reforms, expanding from US$11.01 billion in 1992 to US$45.46 billion in 1998 (Smart and Hsu 2005). It is harder to provide figures for the cumulative investment of small and medium enterprises, but their contribution was important, particularly in the first decade after opening (Smart and Smart 1991), because many Hong Kong petty capitalists were willing to take on greater risks in the pursuit of profits (Smart 1999).

In the first decade after 1979, the rules for doing business in China were far from clear and reliable. Small and medium Hong Kong enterprises were the first to commit themselves to the risks of investing (Lever-Tracy *et al.* 1996). They took advantage of pre-existing social connections, since many of them were first-generation migrants from China, establishing ties in native places they may not have ever visited (for second-generation migrants), but also by using these ties to find contacts in more suitably located sites (Smart and Smart 1991). Policies that allowed initiative on the part of local (township, village and county) officials made it possible to make deals quickly with often nominal attention to the formal rules of investment (Smart and

Smart 1993). One result has been that rather than factories being concentrated in existing cities or suburban areas, many factories were built in formerly rural townships, resulting in new factory towns scattered throughout the Pearl River Delta, particularly in the Eastern Delta near the border (Smart and Lin 2007).

Particularly before 1992, Hong Kong investments were generally smaller individually than Western investments, were typically negotiated at lower levels of the government hierarchy, and were more likely to concentrate on export-processing than on access to the domestic market (Smart and Smart 2001b). They tended to rely less on carefully negotiated contracts and more on personal ties and constructing trustworthy relationships. In the uncertain regulatory environment of the early years, such approaches allowed them to set up their enterprises more rapidly and with lower transaction costs. Guha and Ray (2001) have argued that most traditional FDI theory suffers from lumping together transnational corporations' (TNCs') FDI and those investments that come from expatriates. They argue that in low-wage countries, particularly those lacking transparent investment environments, expatriate investors have advantages over TNCs in labor-intensive manufacturing due to knowledge of both global markets and local conditions, languages and cultures. TNCs have competitive advantages due to their recognizable brand names and sophisticated technology. They tend to see FDI in emerging markets as a way of breaking into domestic markets that are closed to imports.

Critics have pointed out flaws in this synergy model. First, it tends to assume both the continuation of cultural commonalities and the power of shared identity to facilitate trustworthy business networks which can then operate efficiently with lower transaction costs. This culturalist position ignores internal differentiation among Chinese and takes identity as unproblematic (Hsing, 2002; Smart and Smart, 1998). Second, it assumes that even while social connections are used for business purposes, their basis in solidarity and commonality resolves problems of conflicting economic interests. Third, even if business ties are more easily constructed and maintained among co-ethnic Chinese, and even if they do generate effective and stable cooperation, the approach "risks oversocializing economic behavior that is rooted in business and technological considerations" and thus "assumes that social relationships determine economic transactions and outcomes" (Hsu and Saxenian, 2000: 1,994). While economic relationships are clearly socially and culturally embedded, markets and industries have their own dynamics that reward certain practices and drive others towards failure. Counter to synergy, in the last decade, the tensions that critics identify have come more to the fore and have sidelined small and medium Hong Kong investors who rely on brokerage between China and the rest of the global economy rather than on technological advantages. As China's export economy becomes more sophisticated, petty capitalists no longer have the resources needed as China tries to move towards high technology and the generation of their own brands and "national champions."

Huang has argued that the high levels of FDI recently achieved by China represent weaknesses more than they do strength (Huang 2003). FDI plays a large role in the Chinese economy not because all of the foreign firms are inherently superior "but because they are uniquely positioned to exploit many of the business opportunities in

China created by China's inefficient economic and financial institutions" (Huang 2001: 54). With a savings rate of 41.76 percent, China is not short of capital, but domestic private capital has been systematically disadvantaged. Domestic firms often need foreign partners to export, to obtain foreign currency, even to do business in other provinces. Despite these disadvantages, domestic private industry has expanded considerably in the last decade, increasingly displacing Hong Kong small and medium investors. Indeed, local investors have commented that wherever possible they try to cut Hong Kong middlemen out of the deal, conscious of the substantial profits that the Hong Kong investors have extracted in the past through their knowledge of and access to the West. As China becomes better integrated into the global economy, and its entrepreneurs more knowledgeable about the nature of global demands and capitalist markets, disintermediation (cutting out the intermediaries) is growing, at the expense of many smaller Hong Kong business operators.

Huang (2001) argues against positive evaluations of China's gradualist reform strategy by asserting that China's economy managed to grow in part as a result of luck: the nearby location of Hong Kong and Taiwan. Without its ties to ethnic Chinese capital, he says, "nonstate firms would have atrophied under the weight of the lending bias." The underdevelopment of the rule of law inherent in the gradualist strategy "would have deterred foreign investment if not for ethnic Chinese firms that possess relationship capital and cultural know-how that help foreign firms navigate China's murky business environment" (Huang, 2001: 62). Expatriate capital, then, took on a particularly crucial role in the early reform years.

The Lees' indecision about moving their operations across the border into Guangdong was eventually ended by the demands of the companies that they supplied. As almost all appliance manufacturers moved into Guangdong, they wanted their parts suppliers to be located near them, particularly given the problems of transport in the late 1980s and early 1990s (Yeung 1998). Either they moved to the same area as their main customers, or their customers would find new suppliers. Finally committing to the move in 1995, they also took the opportunity to hire a workforce, which peaked at about 50 employees, more available and much cheaper than it would have been in Hong Kong. They moved up the value chain, producing the entire plug assembly, which involved wiring, assembly and plastic molding in addition to the cutting of the copper rods. The cutting machinery was transferred from Hong Kong, rather than buying new numerically controlled machines, and still required regular setting up and supervision by Mr Lee. Required investment was financed with savings and loans from a number of kin. Expansion of their business was not simply a response to an opportunity, however, because the manufacturing ecosystem was not as fully developed in Guangdong as in Hong Kong. Manufacturers demanded more complete assemblies of components rather than the finely networked subcontracting practiced in Hong Kong. The Lees kept their younger children and dependents in Hong Kong, but two of the older ones that were failing in school went to work in the new China-based business. Mr Lee's mother took on supervisory responsibilities for the children who stayed in Hong Kong to go to school. Mrs Lee commuted between home and business once or more often each week, and became less actively involved with the business than she had been in Hong Kong. As she feared, this resulted in infidelity on the part of her husband, as he took part in the expatriate businessmen's networks, socializing in a context where their incomes made local "entertainment" affordable.

This section and the previous one summarized the "glory days" for smaller entrepreneurs in Hong Kong, when they first produced the "Hong Kong miracle" and then proceeded to help kick-start the rise of China, a phenomenon that has drawn global attention and the fear and loathing of many industries struggling to cope with the "China price." Next, we turn to the less triumphal tale of marginalization of small and medium enterprises, first in Hong Kong and subsequently in China.

The decline of Hong Kong petty investment from 2001

This section concentrates on processes contributing to the decline of the importance and success of smaller Hong Kong firms in cross-border investment. These processes include efforts in China to cut out the middlemen, preference in China for more technology-intensive investment, and actions of the Hong Kong government that have made cross-border initiatives more difficult than in the past.

The last decade has not been good for Hong Kong's small and medium firms. It started off catastrophically, as the handover on July 1, 1997 was followed the next day by the Thai baht crisis, the beginning of the protracted Asian Financial Crisis. The finance- and real-estate-based mode of growth that had become dominant since 1979 faced two major challenges. First, success itself generated huge increases in costs, particularly for residential and office rental costs and for the wages of professional and skilled staff (Tsang 1999: 44). Second, the Asian Financial Crisis cast doubts on the viability of reliance on wealth generated by serving as a regional hub: investment flows dropped sharply in the following years. Among the effects of the crisis on Hong Kong was a 50 percent reduction of real estate market values (from unprecedented peaks, however) that "cut at the heart of Hong Kong's internal 'growth' dynamics as this had developed since the opening of China" (Sum 2002: 80). Since so much of Hong Kong's economy, stock market and household economies relied on ever-increasing real estate prices, (Lui 1995), the sharp drop had immense multiplier effects, and generated deflation, sharp increases in unemployment, and decreases in economic growth.

Mutual interests linking the public sector and the dominant fraction of the private sector have produced a powerful dynamic where maintenance of profits and public budget surpluses has been unusually reliant on the real estate market. Between the 1984 signing of the Sino-British Agreement to return Hong Kong to Chinese sovereignty and the actual handover in 1997, the property market was buoyant, producing record real estate prices throughout the 1990s, peaking in 1997. These levels came to be seen as too high by the government, since they created costs of doing business in Hong Kong that were among the highest in the world, threatened Hong Kong's status as a regional financial center, and generated "unhealthy" speculation in ever-increasing housing prices. Real estate prices affected every aspect of Hong

Kong's society and economy, accelerating the transfer of manufacturing into China to take advantage of cheaper land as well as abundant low-wage labor, and convincing individuals that property investment rather than running a business was the way to get ahead.

Most interventions directed at helping Hong Kong out of the economic downturn from mid-1997 have done so through attempts to promote the property market (Fung and Forrest, 2002). In some ways, this might have been inevitable, given the centrality of real estate to Hong Kong's growth regime. For example, when the Administration bought US$15 billion worth of Hong Kong shares in order to prop up the stock market, 60 percent of these were property related, higher than the sector's weighting in the stock market (Sum 2002). A February 2001 survey, though, found that 75 percent of respondents believed that the government's housing policy mainly served developers rather than the poor, and 31.6 percent thought that policies were entirely for developers' benefit (Kong, 2001).

Consumer demand dropped sharply in Hong Kong after the property slump, contributing to serious deflation, the result of a higher level of consumer debt in Hong Kong than elsewhere in the region. Personal loans accounted for 55.8 percent of nominal GDP in Hong Kong in 1998, compared to 20.7 percent in South Korea, 33.6 percent in Singapore, and 40.9 percent in Taiwan. The ratio for Hong Kong had increased from 40.6 percent in 1995, and seems clearly associated with the escalation of housing prices until 1997. The average household in Hong Kong had total out-standing loans of HK$367,000 (Smart and Lee 2003). The effects were wide-ranging since small and medium firms tended to rely on the proprietor's real estate holding as collateral for loans needed to do business. With the slump, liquidity dried up rapidly. The inability of small and medium firms to access credit hampered economic recovery. Such domestic challenges combined with shifts in China's developmental strategies to create huge difficulties for Hong Kong petty investors.

The developmental regime of labor-intensive, export-oriented industrial development that was pioneered in Guangdong has already changed the world, as ubiquitous attention to the "China factor" in the business press indicates. Even advanced research and development are being transferred to China and India in order to save costs and take advantage of large numbers of lower-paid engineers and other highly qualified personnel. The transition path from labor-intensive manufacturing to sophisticated high-tech or advanced services, however, is complicated and requires restructuring in areas that have grown rapidly through export-oriented exploitation of cheap labor.

Guangdong prospered immensely by being the pioneer in absorbing foreign capital and allowing the exploitation of workers to produce exports to the West. The core of the Guangdong expansion was the Pearl River Delta, which had a population of just under 24 million in 2002, excluding unregistered migrants (on restrictions on internal migration, see Smart and Smart, 2001a). Its GDP grew from 11.92 billion yuan in 1980 to 941.88 billion in 2002. In relative terms, the Delta's proportion of the total GDP of China grew from 2.6 percent to 9 percent in the same period, while its share of exports grew by 2002 to an amazing 38.2 percent, largely through absorbing 27.3 percent of all the foreign capital invested in the PRC (Enright *et al.* 2005: 40)

What can be described as the Guangdong model was pioneered in the Pearl River Delta, relied on tactical alliances between local government and ethnic Chinese residing outside the PRC, and persistently pushed the limits of what was acceptable to the Chinese government (Smart and Lin 2007). However, this development strategy may have reached its limits in Guangdong itself. While similar forms of production are being transferred to less developed parts of China, and will continue, the richer parts of Guangdong are increasingly struggling to find new paths to maintain their rapid economic growth. Limits to this development model have created challenges for Hong Kong's small and medium entrepreneurs. New developmental regimes are being explored in Guangdong and China more generally that leave little room for the kinds of contributions that they have made in the past. Rather than relying on technologically unsophisticated foreign investors, China has become much more interested in fostering its own industrial national champions, preferably producing high-tech products (Thun 2004). Foreign investors are now prized primarily for the technology that they are willing to transfer. While Hong Kong entrepreneurs facilitated the mobilization and exploitation of China's advantages in cheap labor and land, generating greatly needed hard currencies through their networks and knowledge that allowed China to access export markets, these advantages are now less valued. While there is no real shortage of labor, supplies of very cheap labor have tightened significantly after decades of rapid growth, and as economic expansion moves inward so that migrants are able to find wage employment much closer to home. Paying higher wages can easily resolve the labor shortage for factories in Guangdong, but with labor-intensive production, this threatens their competitive position. As Guangdong has become richer, it has much less need for foreign investment in technologically unsophisticated sectors, and the negative externalities associated with such industries have grown. Pollution, food safety scares, international concern about hazardous products bearing "made in China" labels, alternative uses for land such as real estate developments, a desire to be seen as moving more quickly up the ladder of technological sophistication: all of these factors make the kind of foreign investment that created the Guangdong miracle less desirable at present than in the past.

Hong Kong entrepreneurs benefited from being early pioneers prepared to accept risks large Western corporations were reluctant to commit to, particularly before the negotiations for China's accession to the WTO helped to routinize the rules of the game for foreign investors. As early pioneers were joined by better capitalized and better connected Western corporations, the competitive position became less advantageous for small and medium enterprises.

The Lees suffered from their reluctance to move into China. Their commitment in 1995 seemed to be just about the time that the tables turned against smaller Hong Kong investors. The deal that they could negotiate was not particularly advantageous, and by 1998 they had had to downsize production dramatically, sell their apartment in Hong Kong, and move into a cramped apartment above their factory in China.

The youngest child stayed in Hong Kong with the grandmother, but the ones that had not already moved to China to work dropped out of school around this time and joined their parents at the factory. By 2002, the factory was closed, the property was lost, and they moved back to Hong Kong, declared bankruptcy, and moved into subsidized public housing. Another attempt to establish a factory in Guangdong in a more remote village where Mrs Lee's family came from collapsed relatively quickly with no profits and the loss of money lent by Mr Lee's mother.

After working for wages for several years at a wholesale outlet, the Lees again undertook an entrepreneurial endeavor in 2006. This time, however, their enterprise was based back in Hong Kong, wholesaling tofu/bean curd products and bean sprouts. They were also back to self-employment, with both of them working full-time without any employees. They found that their customers were greatly concerned about the safety of food products that had been sourced in China. They found one tofu producer operating in Hong Kong, who could charge a much higher price for these goods than China-produced ones, and copied this approach. However, the problems of producing at competitive prices in Hong Kong remain. Their current efforts involve establishing a bean sprout operation in Mrs Lee's native village in order to retain control over the entire food supply chain. Although they would not be able to market these goods as Hong Kong products, which provides a major advantage in the context of the high level of worry about Chinese food safety practices, the hope is that the trust-based relationships that they are developing with their customers could allow them to provide a higher level of security over the quality of their goods. This would at least increase the reliability of their market, if not increase the price premium. By 2009, they had started to expand their scale somewhat. They employed two drivers and one full-time employee. They were renting a small apartment near their business so it could be operated 24/7 without having to sleep in the office as they had done earlier. This is a small example of a modest revival of food-related production within Hong Kong, based on a strong consumer perception about the greater safety of Hong Kong products. This trend started in Hong Kong well before the widespread global worries about the safety of Chinese products that exploded onto the headlines of newspapers in 2007, sparked by the tainted pet food case. The growing trend towards marketing products as "not from China" (Carey 2007) is opening up a new range of opportunities for entrepreneurs everywhere, as is the environmental concern for local products.

Conclusion

While this chapter has identified many remarkable achievements for Hong Kong's petty investors, the trajectory in the last decade can be seen as very discouraging. The experiences of the Lees, while certainly not representative, indicate the suffering caused by increasing barriers to small and medium business people created in the last decade in both Hong Kong and China. Within China, some of these barriers are simply the enforcement of rules on labor and the environment that were overlooked in the past, but others result from deliberate industrial strategies. In Hong Kong, petty capitalists have been affected by efforts to revive the property market and encourage the financial sector which have tended to increase their costs of business. Belated efforts to improve the welfare state, such as the mandatory provident scheme, have also been increasing the costs for small business. Seen from another perspective, however, their story is one of impressive persistence despite setbacks and failures. The prospects for Hong Kong's petty capitalists as a whole are uncertain. It may be that the period in which their particular merits were crucial to the success of the development strategies of both Hong Kong and Guangdong is not only over, but unlikely to return.

The broader lessons of this chapter concern the situations in which petty investors can prosper and those in which the vistas of opportunity diminish. Although the recent financial crisis has encouraged skepticism about theories of risk management, the conventional idea is that rewards are inversely related to risks. When the risk is low, rates of return should be relatively low, whereas riskier investment scenarios demand a premium for the risk that investors take on. Petty investors, who cannot wait for the long term but require that their investment generates a short-term return in order to support themselves and their family, have fewer options. Low-risk investments are unlikely to generate enough income for them, particularly if the barrier to entry is low, since many others may adopt the same approach. High-risk strategies, particularly those with substantial degrees of uncertainty or personal risk for managers in large corporations, such as in situations where bribes must be paid or where the legal framework is unclear, may create niches for smaller investors. Such opportunities may particularly apply when there are sharp edges between radically different ways of doing things, or where transactions across a social or symbolic boundary may generate stigma (e.g. vice industries or usury in medieval Europe). In such situations, when social connections provide mechanisms to reduce barriers to entry, petty investors with the right social contacts may have significant opportunities to pioneer the new niche before the large players move in. Cross-border trade and production may be particularly prone to create such opportunities, as a number of chapters in this volume attest. But these rich prospects are not likely to last, and latecomers like the Lees may find that their gambles fail to pay off. However, even early entrants are more likely to fail in these circumstances, although the phenomenon of failure is given much less attention than is success (Smart and Smart 2000). The role of Hong Kong petty investors in fostering the rise of China shows their potential global significance, but our account should also suggest that the windows of opportunity for their involvement can be fleeting and reliant on distinctive conditions.

References

Basch, L., N. G. Schiller and C. S. Blanc (1994) *Nations Unbound: Transnational Projects, Postcolonial Predicaments and Deterritorialized Nation-States*, London: Routledge.
Carey, J. (2007, July 30) "Not Made in China," *Business Week*, 41–43.
Castells, M. (1998) *End of Millenium: The Information Age*, vol. 3, Oxford: Blackwell Publishers.
Chiu, C. C. H. (1998) *Small Family Business in Hong Kong: Accumulation and Accommodation*, Hong Kong: Chinese University Press.

Chiu, S. W. K., K. C. Ho, and T. L. Lui (1997) *City-States in the Global Economy: Industrial Restructuring in Hong Kong and Singapore*, Boulder, CO: Westview.

Cohen, J. H. (1999) *Cooperation and Community: Economy and Society in Oaxaca*, Austin, TX: University of Texas Press.

Cornelius, W., D. Fitzgerald, and S. Borges (eds) (2009) *Four Generations of Nortenos: New Research from the Cradle of Mexican Migration*, San Diego: Center for Comparative Immigration Studies.

Economist (2010) "Remittances." May 1: 97.

Enright, M., E. Scott, and K. Chang (2005) *Regional Powerhouse: The Greater Pearl River Delta and the Rise of China*, Singapore: Wiley.

Fung, K. K. and R. Forrest (2002) "Institutional Mediation: The Hong Kong Residential Housing Market and the Asian Financial Crisis," *Housing Studies* 17(2): 189–207.

Guha, A. S. and A. Ray (2001) "Expatriate vs. Multinational Investment: A Comparative Analysis of their Roles in Chinese and Indian Development," in T. N. Srinivasan, ed., *Trade, Finance and Investment in South Asia*, New Delhi: Social Science Press.

Harvey, D. (1989) *The Condition of Postmodernity*, Oxford: Basil Blackwell.

Hong Kong Government (1985) *Hong Kong Annual Report*, Hong Kong: Government Printer.

Hsia, R. and L. Chau (1978) *Industrialisation, Employment and Income Distribution*, London: Croom Helm.

Hsing, Y. T. (2002) "Ethnic Identity and Business Solidarity: Chinese Capitalism Revisited," in L. J. C. Ma and C. Cartier, eds, *The Chinese Diaspora: Space, Place, Mobility, and Identity*, Lanham: Rowman and Littlefield, 221–35.

Hsu, J. Y. and A. Saxenian (2000). "The Limits of Guanxi Capitalism: Transnational Collaboration between Taiwan and the USA," *Environment and Planning A* 32: 1,991–2,005.

Huang, Y. (2001). "Internal and External Reforms: Experiences and Lessons from China," *Cato Journal* 21(1): 43–64.

——(2003) *Selling China: Foreign Direct Investment During the Reform Era*, Cambridge, UK: Cambridge University Press.

Kearney, M. (1995) "The Local and the Global: The Anthropology of Globalization and Transnationalism," *Annual Review of Anthropology* 24: 547–65.

Kong, L. (2001) "Housing Scheme Rethink Urged," *South China Morning Post,* 27 February.

Lang, G. and J. Smart (2002) "Industrialization, Migration and the 'Second-Wife' in South China," *International Migration Review* 36(2): 546–70.

Lever-Tracy, C., D. Ip, and N. Tracy (1996) *The Chinese Diaspora and Mainland China: An Emerging Economic Synergy*, Houndsmill: Macmillan Press.

Lin, G. C. S. (1997) *Red Capitalism in South China Growth and Development of the Pearl River Delta*, Vancouver: University of British Columbia Press.

Lin, T. B., V. Mok, and Y. P. Ho (1980) *Manufactured Exports and Employment in Hong Kong*, Hong Kong: Chinese University Press.

Lui, T. (1995). "Coping Strategies in a Booming Market: Family Wealth and Housing in Hong Kong," in R. Forrest and A. Murie, eds., *Housing and Family Wealth: Comparative International Perspectives*, London: Routledge, 108–32.

Massey, D., J. Durand, and N. J. Malone (2002) *Beyond Smoke and Mirrors: Mexican Immigration in an Era of Economic Integration*, New York: Russell Sage Foundation.

Mathews, G. (2007) "Chungking Mansions: A Center of 'Low-End Globalization'," *Ethnology* XLVI(2): 169–83.

Ngo, T. W. (1999) "Industrial History and the Artifice of Laissez-Faire Colonialism," in T. W. Ngo, ed., *Hong Kong's History: State and Society under Colonial Rule*, London: Routledge, 119–40.

Portes, A., L. E. Guarnizo, and P. Landolt (1999) "The Study of Transnationalism: Pitfalls and Promise of an Emergent Research Field," *Ethnic and Racial Studies* 22(2): 217–37.

Reid, Anthony (1997) "Entrepreneurial Minorities, Nationalism, and the State," in Daniel Chirot and Anthony Reid, eds., *Essential Outsiders: Chinese and Jews in the Modern*

Transformation of Southeast Asia and Central Europe, Seattle: University of Washington Press, 1997, 33–71.

Rhoades, R. (2002). "European Cyclical Migration and Economic Development: The Case of Southern Spain," in G. Gmelch and W. Zenner, eds, *Urban Life*, Long Grove, IL: Waveland Press, 253–64.

Ribeiro, G. L. (2009) "Non-Hegemonic Globalizations: Alter-native Transnational Processes and Agents," *Anthropological Theory* 9(3): 297–329.

Rothstein, F. (2007) *Globalization in Rural Mexico: Three Decades of Change*, Austin, TX: University of Texas Press.

Sinn, E. (1997) "Xin Xi Guxiang: A Study of Regional Associations as a Bonding Mechanism in the Chinese Diaspora: The Hong Kong Experience," *Modern Asian Studies* 31(2): 375–97.

Smart, A. (1989) "Resistance to Relocation in a Hong Kong Squatter Area Market," in G. Clark, ed., *Traders Against the State*, Boulder, CO: Westview Press, 119–38.

——(1999) "Flexible Accumulation Across the Hong Kong Border: Petty Capitalists as Pioneers of Globalized Accumulation," *Urban Anthropology* 28(3/4): 373–406.

——(2001) "Unruly Places: Urban Governance and the Persistence of Illegality in Hong Kong's Urban Squatter Areas," *American Anthropologist* 103(1), 30–44.

Smart, A. and J. Y. Hsu (2005) "The Chinese Diaspora, Foreign Investment and Economic Development in China," in R. C. Keith, ed., *China as a Rising World Power and its Response to 'Globalization,'* London: Routledge.

Smart, A. and J. Lee (2003) "Financialization and the Role of Real Estate in Hong Kong's Regime of Accumulation," *Economic Geography* 79(2): 153–71.

Smart, A. and G. Lin (2007). "Local Capitalisms, Local Citizenship and Translocality: Rescaling from Below in the Pearl River Delta Region, China," *International Journal of Urban and Regional Research* 31(2): 280–302.

Smart, A. and J. Smart (1998) "Transnational Social Networks and Negotiated Identities in Interactions between Hong Kong and China," in M. P. Smith and L. E. Guarnizo, eds, *Transnationalism from Below*, New Brunswick: Transaction Publishers, 103–29.

——(2000) "Failures and Strategies of Hong Kong Firms in China: An Ethnographic Perspective," in H. W. C. Yeung and K. Olds, eds, *The Globalisation of Chinese Business Firms*, London: Macmillan, 244–71.

——(2001a) "Local Citizenship: Welfare Reform, Urban/Rural Status, and Exclusion in China," *Environment and Planning A* 33: 1853–69.

——(2001b). "Personal Relations and Divergent Economies: A Case Study of Hong Kong Investment in South China," in S. Low, ed., *Theorizing the City: The New Urban Anthropology Reader*, New Brunswick, NJ: Rutgers University Press, 169–200.

Smart, A. and J. Smart (eds) (2005) *Petty Capitalists and Globalization: Flexibility, Entrepreneurship and Economic Development*, Albany, NY: SUNY Press.

Smart, J. and A. Smart (1991) "Personal Relations and Divergent Economies: A Case Study of Hong Kong Investment in China," *International Journal of Urban and Regional Research* 15(2): 216–33.

——(1993) "Obligation and Control: Employment of Kin in Capitalist Labor Management in China," *Critique of Anthropology* 13(1): 7–31.

Sum, N. L. (2002) "Globalization and Hong Kong's Entrepreneurial City Strategies: Contested Visions and the Remaking of City Governance in (Post-)Crisis Hong Kong," in J. R. Lang, ed., *The New Chinese City: Globalization and Market Reform*, Malden: Blackwell Publishers.

Thun, E. (2004) "Industrial Policy, Chinese-Style: FDI, Regulation, and Dreams of National Champions in the Auto Sector," *Journal of East Asian Studies* 4: 453–89.

Tsang, S. K. (1999) "The Hong Kong Economy: Opportunities out of Crisis?", *Journal of Contemporary China* 8(20): 29–45.

Waldinger, R., H. Aldrich, and R. Ward (1990) *Ethnic Entrepreneurs*, Newbury Park, CA: Sage.

Watson, J. L. (1975) *Emigration and the Chinese lineage: The 'Mans' in Hong Kong and London*, Berkeley: University of California Press.

Wu, D. (1982) *The Chinese in Papua New Guinea: 1880–1980*, Hong Kong: Chinese University Press.

Yeung, H. W. C. (1998) *Transnational Corporations and Business Networks: Hong Kong Firms in the ASEAN Region*, London: Routledge.

Zhang, S. G. (2001) *Economic Cold War: America's Embargo against China and the Sino-Soviet Alliance 1949–1963*, Washington: Woodrow Wilson Centre Press.

Zhou, M. (1992) *Chinatown*, Philadelphia: Temple University Press.

7

FROM SECONDHAND CLOTHING TO COSMETICS

How Philippine–Hong Kong entrepreneurs fill gaps in cross-border trade

B. Lynne Milgram

Introduction

Since the 1970s, in the Philippines, as throughout regions of the global south, structural adjustment policies and the reduction of state responsibility have left many people little choice but to find alternative types of work to meet their subsistence needs (Balisacan 1995; Chant 1996). Women, in particular, continue to leave the Philippines to find better paying employment across the globe in contract wage labor and as domestic helpers and nurses (Chant and McIlwaine 1995). Looking for work options within the Philippines, some women who have access to sufficient capital have built on their customary roles as household financial managers and as the country's foremost public marketers to forge innovative avenues of transnational work trading a variety of goods, such as used clothing, cosmetics and health supplements, between the Philippines and nearby Hong Kong (Milgram 2001, 2004, 2008). For most of these women, labor mobility through such "informal" initiatives is a strategy of dire necessity enabling household survival.[1] By building on past work experience and personal networks, and applying their actions to cross-border opportunities, Filipina entrepreneurs link institutions and sectors of societies not previously connected, or link them in different ways in order to realize their rights as citizens to viable work.

In this chapter, I use Filipina women's innovative initiatives in two branches of Hong Kong–Philippine trade—importing secondhand clothing and importing cosmetics and health supplements—to suggest that through these enterprises, women unsettle dominant notions of legal/illegal work and challenge the state to expand its parameters of citizenship rights to include their trade. I focus particularly on women traders in Baguio City, in the northern Philippines, whose self-made occupations and citizenship claims are often marginalized in the Philippine national agenda. To contest their exclusion from the government's vision of appropriate employment and modernity, these Filipina entrepreneurs continue to devise "pragmatic sideroads" (Stoller 2002: 40) through which they more integrally embed their already viable trade into the urban economy. Given the ongoing government debates about the legality of their cross-border businesses, however, these women's entrepreneurial flexibility encompasses substantial risks along with its opportunities.

The risk in the secondhand clothing industry is anchored in the Philippine Republic Act (Government of the Philippines 1966), which continues to prohibit the importation of used clothing into the Philippines for commercial resale.[2] This national government decree, originally imposed as a protectionist measure to support the Philippine textile and garment industries, remains today as an anomaly among the government's broader neoliberal policies. Once used clothing has been imported into the country, it can be legally sold by licensed retailers and even by itinerant street vendors (Milgram 2008). The precarious positioning of the used-clothing trade in the Philippines is augmented by the Hong Kong government's ongoing clampdowns on the city warehouses in which Filipina traders conduct business (Li 2006). Filipina women entering Hong Kong as tourists are not authorized to engage in income-generating work in the city.

Because of such threats to the used-clothing industry, some entrepreneurs are supplementing this trade with that of alternative commodities such as health supplements and cosmetics—brand-name products that are very popular in the Philippines. Although there is no official import ban on these goods, entrepreneurs maximize profits by using shipping methods that stretch the loopholes in allowable customs exemptions, thereby enabling them to avoid paying import duties. In securing their Hong Kong–Philippine trade route through which to transport secondhand clothing, these women entrepreneurs can then use this same route to import different goods to meet shifting market demands. As Urry (2007: 52) argues with regard to such new "mobility systems" of trade, "the key is not the things themselves" that circulate, but rather the "structured routeways through which people, objects and information are circulated." The on-the-ground details of Baguio City entrepreneurs' micro cross-sector trade apply a face to these routeways, a face that has generally been missing in much of the literature on macro mobility-scapes.

Acting at the margins of visibility, Philippine–Hong Kong entrepreneurs thus challenge the state's rule over its territory, most often expressed in the form of control over people's movements and over the goods that occupy, use and cross national spaces (Abraham and Schendel 2005: 14). By engaging in capitalist trade through personalized channels, these women, in effect, materialize a "non-hegemonic grassroots" form of globalization (Ribeiro 2009: 298, 324). Their "brokerage practices" (Ribeiro 2009: 324), however small-scale, thus enable these women to make variable connections between interdependent systems of the formal/informal and legal/illegal.

In earlier research, I outlined the various capacities in which women work in the secondhand clothing industry, as small-, medium- or large-scale entrepreneurs, within the Philippines and between the Philippines and Hong Kong (Milgram 2004, 2005, 2008). In this chapter, I explore how the increased risks that have arisen in this industry especially since 2007 have challenged the viability of this once-lucrative business while simultaneously providing entrepreneurs with new trade opportunities (e.g. same routes, new products). To situate the ways in which Filipina traders activate livelihood options, I review some of the literature analyzing the intersection of legal/illegal work and cultural citizenship. By focusing on women's pioneering business practices between Hong Kong and the Philippines, I highlight the tactics traders use to move marginal activities into mainstream arenas and explore the extent to which traders' actions may have the power to subvert national political and economic agendas.

Legal and illegal practices and cultural citizenship

The disjuncture between state laws, market practice and the experiential reality of entrepreneurs engaged in self-employed transnational trade make visible various understandings of legality and illegality. Cross-border informal sector enterprises such as importing banned secondhand clothing or importing grooming products without paying the required customs duty are illegal because they defy the rules of formal political authority, but these actions are acceptable and "licit" to traders who feel it is their right as Philippine citizens to be able to earn an integral living through their personal labor, resources and ingenuity. I suggest, like Abraham and Schendel (2005: 4), that rather than considering the state the sole authority as to whether a trade is legal or illegal, "we build upon a distinction between what states consider to be legitimate ('legal') and what people involved in such transnational enterprises consider to be legitimate ('licit')." As this research argues, "There is a qualitative difference of scale and intent between the activities of internationally organized criminal gangs or networks and the scores of micro-practices that, while often illegal in a formal sense, are not driven by a organizational logic or a unified purpose" to break national laws (Abraham and Schendel 2005: 4). Philippine–Hong Kong entrepreneurs, like the traders discussed by Gauthier in this volume, thus emerge as "ant traders" (Abraham and Schendel 2005: 4) engaged in a small-scale trade to enable themselves and their families to survive.

Constructing a sharp dichotomy between legal and illegal practice in such micro-transnational flows fails to capture the complexity of people's livelihoods that emerge simultaneously as legal/illegal and as formal/informal (Abraham and Schendel 2005: 4–5). Current scholarship argues that licit and illicit practices coexist in social and economic life and are together imbricated in state processes, since states themselves do not always uphold the law (Andreas 2000; Heyman and Smart 1999: 10–11). As Heyman and Smart maintain (1999: 11), "legality and illegality are […] simultaneously black and white and shades of gray." These circumstances reflect the Baguio City situation where infractions to such importing laws are variably tolerated and punished (Milgram 2008), since the Philippine government has failed to institute the basic "political and economic foundations required even by a minimalist role of the state in economic transformation" (Hutchcroft 1998: 28–29).

A pivotal feature of Philippine–Hong Kong entrepreneurs' work is that while operating within an informal economic sphere, traders simultaneously depend on and engage with formal sectors (e.g. for the procurement and distribution of goods). Individuals can thus be "physically present, but legally absent"; they can also be "physically absent" (e.g. conducting business from the Philippines) but economically present by fulfilling their family and community obligations, such as providing employment and paying rent in Hong Kong (Coutin 2007: 9, 11). Like female Caribbean inter-island "suitcase" traders (Brown-Giaude 2011; Trotz 2006), Filipina entrepreneurs' cross-border trade challenges old hierarchies of socioeconomic and political inclusion and exclusion.

In a similar light, recent scholarship exploring contemporary experiences of citizenship argues that citizenship encompasses not just a political position but also an engaged arena of both cultural performance and contest. Holston (1999: 169; 2008) identifies the circumstances giving rise to this dual process:

> Although in theory full access to rights depends on [national] membership, in practice that which constitutes citizenship substantively (rights and duties) is often independent of its formal status. Indeed, it is often inaccessible to those who are formal citizens (e.g., the native poor), yet available to those who are not (e.g., [well-off] legally resident 'aliens').

In the Philippines, this difference between formal and substantive citizenship is, in part, mapped along the formal–informal economic divide. Despite a nationalist rhetoric that guarantees all Philippine citizens basic rights, in practice, the livelihoods of informal sector workers, such as self-employed Hong Kong–Philippine entrepreneurs, place them outside national notions of modernity and progress, privileging instead citizens associated with formal-sector work and the vision of appropriate development (Mills 2012).

Because the clandestine nature of Filipinas' cross-border work precludes them from publicly protesting for their cause, entrepreneurs advocate through subtle not-so-visible channels such as building individual networks in both the Philippines and Hong Kong and personally lobbying government officials behind the scenes. Filipinas' cross-border trade then still operates in a peripheral zone of value, and so entrepreneurs must pursue such multiple channels of "insurgent citizenship" (Holston 2008) in order to best accommodate their livelihoods as the following account of traders' advocacy demonstrates.

The Philippine trade in secondhand clothing[3]

Secondhand clothing worldwide has shifted from its humble origin as an inexpensive functional commodity fulfilling the clothing needs of the poor, to a fashionable and inexpensive product that people actively pursue across class and space (Palmer and Clark 2005; Ramirez 2009; Subido 2003). In the Philippines, the used-clothing industry is known locally as *ukay-ukay* (to dig) or *wagwag* (to shake and sell or buy), terms that graphically capture the experience of shopping for secondhand clothing. The dramatic increase in the north's export of used clothing to countries such as the Philippines began in the mid to late 1980s fueled by a surplus of these goods in the north and the economic liberalization of southern economies that enabled more people to enter the market as consumers of imported products generally (Hansen 2000: 11–12). Charting the international trade of secondhand clothing, Karen Tranberg Hansen (2000: 99–126) shows that the bulk of used clothes that enter the north's export trade to regions such as Africa, Asia and Latin America originate in donations to charitable organizations; these garments are then channeled to different European and Asian centers for collection, packing and redistribution. This northern-based flow of used clothing to the Philippines is dominated by tightly controlled trading cartels that operate in the textile market in the Santa Cruz area of Manila. New entrepreneurs looking to directly engage in this Manila-based trade have been unable to penetrate these long-standing networks. Filipina traders are thus commonly confined to work as retailers for the wholesale goods the Santa Cruz marketers offer them.

The Hong Kong–Philippine branch of the used-clothing trade developed gradually since the 1970s, along with Hong Kong's rapid economic growth (Smart and Lee 2003). The rise of Hong Kong's own middle and upper classes, their new purchasing power and awareness of changing global fashion trends created local sources of used clothing. The widespread practice for Hong Kong working couples to hire Filipina nannies to care for their children (Constable 1997; Parreñas 2001) provided Filipina caregivers with opportunities to purchase small amounts of used clothing from charitable organizations such as the Salvation Army and to obtain used clothing as gifts from employers, all of which they would periodically mail home to Philippine family members. These Filipina nannies thus provided Filipina entrepreneurs with kin networks that could facilitate the latter's access to this geographically proximate business frontier. The Hong Kong–Philippine branch of the used-clothing industry thus presented feasible opportunities for female entrepreneurs looking to enter this business or to expand their existing operations through more direct access to used-clothing supplies.

FIGURE 7.1 Shoppers in Baguio City. Photo by B. Lynne Milgram. Reproduced with permission

These two sectors of the secondhand clothing trade in the Philippines are identified by the manner in which their respective goods are packaged. Secondhand clothing arriving in the Philippines through the northern-based channel bound for the Santa Cruz Manila wholesale market is packaged in 45 kilo compressed bales that contain a single garment type, such as men's boxer shorts, women's skirts, boys' T-shirts, men's pants or household linens and blankets. Clothing that is sourced in and shipped from Hong Kong is packaged in standard-size *balikbayan* boxes (72 × 42 × 48 cm) that contain assorted types of garments for both men and women as well as special boxes of assorted handbags, shoes or children's wear.[4] Both boxes and bales of secondhand clothing are priced according to the quality of the goods they contain—A, B or C grade clothing (see Milgram 2004).

Baguio City, the most highly industrialized center in the northern Philippines has, since the mid 1980s, emerged as the center for the retail and wholesale sales of secondhand clothing (Abaño 2010: A1, 6; Cabreza 2001, 2006; Cimatu 2002). Innovative Baguio City used-clothing entrepreneurs with capital to invest started their businesses in the 1980s by purchasing bales of secondhand clothing from the aforementioned suppliers based in Manila's Santa Cruz wholesale textile market. Consumers enthusiastically embraced the introduction of high-fashion, good-quality and low-priced used clothes, combining these with nationally manufactured ready-to-wear garments; these pioneering used-clothing traders were thus able to earn substantial profits (Almendral 2004; Sanidad 2001). From the mid-1990s, building on their early business success and seeking more direct access to used-clothing stock, Baguio City entrepreneurs forged international linkages with suppliers in Hong Kong, thereby bypassing Manila-based intermediaries. Hong Kong's geographical proximity to the Philippines and the city's economic wealth facilitated these women's business expansion into the used-clothing trade. Filipina traders took advantage of the accessibility of Hong Kong: a two-hour flight from Manila, the ability to secure a two-week tourist visa beforehand or at the airport, and having personal connections with family members already working in the city.

Filipina used-clothing entrepreneurs make frequent trips to Hong Kong throughout the year and, by repeatedly renewing their tourist permits, they can remain in the city for periods of approximately two months. During these visits, traders purchase used clothing and arrange to rent warehouse space in which to sort, pack and ship garments back to the Philippines. Most of these cross-border entrepreneurs engage in both wholesale and retail sales. They supply their own retail used-clothing stores in Baguio City—stores that are usually managed by family members—and wholesale boxes of used clothes to other stores in Baguio City and Manila as well as in urban centers throughout the northern, southern and central Philippines.

Philippine–Hong Kong entrepreneurs nurture personal networks by drawing the majority of their employees from family and community members. They hire Filipina women who work in Hong Kong as domestic helpers and want to earn extra income on their day off and they bring family members from the Philippines to Hong Kong, paying their travel expenses between the two locales. Independent traders who are part of the diasporic South Asian community living in Hong Kong with residency

FIGURE 7.2 Filipina woman in Hong Kong warehouse. Photo by B. Lynne Milgram. Reproduced with permission

permits they attained under British Commonwealth rights before the 1997 handover of Hong Kong to China, also play a prominent intermediary role between Filipina traders and Hong Kong sources of used clothes. South Asian entrepreneurs with Hong Kong resident status can legally register their businesses and thus access used clothes sold in volume by charitable organizations such as the Salvation Army. The Salvation Army currently sells used clothes, in bulk, only to their client list of government-registered businesses. As Filipina entrepreneurs are technically visiting Hong Kong on tourist visas, they do not have the legal status to purchase goods offered by organizations that maintain access restrictions, such as the Salvation Army. Filipina traders thus arrange sourcing and shipping partnerships with Hong Kong-based and English-speaking South Asian businessmen.

Such business partnerships commonly entail Filipina entrepreneurs to sublease warehouse space from South Asian leaseholders, but the rent is not payable in cash. Rather, the agreement is rooted on the exchange of services. Filipina traders verbally agree to purchase all of their stock of used clothing from that assembled by their South Asian business partner. In return for free use of the latter's warehouse space to sort and pack their goods, Filipina entrepreneurs also agree to ship their boxes of used clothes to the Philippines in the shipping containers that South Asian businessmen hire to transport their own clothing shipments. Filipina entrepreneurs root their actions in Philippine customary practice that supports women's roles in public financial arenas. Hence, although South Asian traders hold stronger positions given their residency status, any exclusion of Filipinas from particular spheres of opportunity in Hong Kong tends to be based more on issues of legal status rather than on issues of gender difference.

Since 2000, due to the growing popularity of used clothing in the Philippines, entrepreneurs have steadily increased the volume of goods they export from Hong Kong, resulting in keen competition to obtain sufficient quantities of good-quality stock. Filipina traders thus find it increasingly difficult to fill the number of boxes of fashionable clothing they need from the volume of secondhand garments they purchase from their business partners. As Caroline Bannug,[5] 44 years old and a long-time trader, explains: "From every truckload [mini-van] of used clothing we purchase, we must pack 30 to 32 boxes of medium to good quality garments to meet our costs. If we only pack 28 boxes, we lose money, and this now occurs more often." Karen Talag, 48 years old and a trader in business since 1999, continues:

> The quality of goods we currently receive from our *suki* (favored supplier) is often poor and deliveries commonly contain large percentages of *besura* (unusable garments) that we throw in the trash. If we pack boxes of used clothes that contain poor-quality garments, we will betray the trust of our buyers in the Philippines and ultimately lose their loyalty. Since 2005, more Philippine imports of clothing from China means more competition for our goods, so this is another reason we have to pack high-quality goods while still keeping prices competitive [see Comanda 2009].

Renewed challenges, new realignments

In earlier research (Milgram 2008: 28–29) I demonstrated that in response to such business problems with their South Asian partners, some successful Filipina traders were able to directly negotiate rental leases with Hong Kong landlords and make purchasing agreements with independent, local Chinese used-clothing collectors, both of which gave these Filipina entrepreneurs more control over their businesses. Since late 2006, however, renewed efforts by the Hong Kong government to restrict enterprises operated by Filipinas not holding registered business licenses has resulted in an increase in warehouse raids, confiscation of goods and the deportation of Filipina workers (*Designing Hong Kong Newsletter* 2008). This has jeopardized entrepreneurs' profits, their independence and the security of the Filipinos whom they employ. Secondhand clothing traders such as Susan Tabay, 46 years old, who has been in business since 2001, explain that the growing demand for used clothing means that more local Hong Kong businesses are collecting these goods by placing brightly colored collection boxes, both authorized and unauthorized, near the city's dense apartment complexes. Susan suggests that, "The Hong Kong police can easily follow any of these local collectors to our warehouses as the collectors make daily clothing deliveries to us. Once the police know the floor on which our unmarked premises are located, they can return to raid us at any time." Indeed, three of the warehouses I had visited in 2006 were subsequently raided in early 2007. Cecille Talag, 26 years old, was present at the time of an early 2007 raid and describes her experience:

> When the police arrive, they first check our passports and our return tickets. We are trained to explain that we are not in business but just visiting and that

we have purchased these clothes as gifts for Philippine family members. Our Filipina employers, who are not always here, give us [formal-looking but not legal] receipts for the clothes we pack. In the past, if we had the correct documents, the police would leave. But now, although we have the proper identification, our goods are confiscated, the warehouse is locked up such that we cannot reenter and we [the packers] are detained at airport immigration until we can secure a flight home. We just pay a rebooking fee on our return ticket.

Another Filipina packer, Sarah Buduhan, 24 years old, who was deported after a raid on the warehouse in which she had worked, explains that in some cases Filipina packers are detained in jail. In such instances, when Filipina entrepreneurs hold partnerships with South Asian dealers, the latter sends his lawyer to represent the detained Filipinas until they are sentenced to detention, usually a three- to six-month term before being deported.

In addition, because Filipina women working as used-clothing traders in Hong Kong do not have legally registered Hong Kong businesses, they must negotiate personal arrangements with Philippine customs brokers to complete the export–import documents in a way that enables the safe shipment of their goods. Filipina entrepreneurs pay Philippine customs duties on their imported shipments but the duty they pay is not assessed on used clothing, but rather on different, legally permitted goods, since traders do not accurately declare the content of their shipments. If their shipping containers are held at Philippine customs due to spot checks, traders must trust the advice and the connections of their brokers to secure the release of their detained goods. As substantial capital is invested in these boxes of used clothing, when entrepreneurs lose one shipping container, which occurs at least once a year, this loss threatens their already tenuous business positions (see Cabuag 2010: A1, A6; Garcia 2006; Julian 2006; Salaverria 2006). Filipina entrepreneurs rarely recover confiscated shipments, and if they succeed, it is only after generous under-the-table "gifts" to customs officials. Such circumstances make visible how licit and illicit practices collide in everyday practice (Heyman and Smart 1999: 10–11).

In response to the ongoing risks of their trade, Baguio City used-clothing entrepreneurs continue to formally lobby government officials to lift the restrictions on this industry. Traders have successfully enlisted Baguio City councilors, some of whom have family members also engaged in this business, to use the influence of their office to support their cause across government levels. Some councilors, for example, have actively lobbied to open the debates about the illegality of importing used clothing in light of the substantial employment it provides throughout the Philippines (City of Baguio 2006; Opiña and Olson 2006). In addition to supplying needed local jobs, entrepreneurs argue that the customs duties they pay (albeit misdeclared) contribute to government income, that their trade offers consumers the option to purchase inexpensive good quality clothing and that this service is already integrated into the country's urban economy. Through their collective efforts to realize their aims, Filipina entrepreneurs, in effect, become "political actors"; indeed, politicians eager for votes may "become spokespersons for these social agents" as they advocate for such "illicit" trades (Ribeiro 2009: 321) as occurred with Baguio City councilors serving in the 2007–2010 municipal administration. However, some of the gains traders achieved in the late 1990s and early 2000s were lost in the 2007 and 2010 elections when supportive government officials were not re-elected to office (See 2001a, 2001b). Traders assert, however, that they will continue their advocacy. Paradoxically, if the used-clothing trade is, in fact, legalized, increased competition could mean lower profits for those currently successful traders given that more women may decide to enter this business.

To date, the used-clothing trade in the Philippines remains unauthorized. Most entrepreneurs continue to navigate extended periods of tolerance interspersed with stretches of harassment and intimidation. The increased risks in the industry have led a number of Philippine–Hong Kong entrepreneurs to apply their knowledge of transnational trade to related business opportunities in which they can engage more on their own terms.

Transforming trade: used clothing, cosmetics and moneychanging

Jane Talango, 38 years old, explains the circumstances that have encouraged her to alter her work. Jane started her retail used-clothing enterprise in Baguio City in 1994 and began traveling to Hong Kong in 1998. Fluctuating local sales and the growing insecurity in this Hong Kong–Philippine trade, however, encouraged her to develop alternative options (Cruz 2002; Lacorte 2005; *Sun Star Baguio* 2009). Jane explains:

> Every year I would lose some of my stock when my [shipping] containers were seized at Philippine customs and now that our Hong Kong business locations are raided more often, our South Asian partners have moved their warehouses farther out of the city—often to GI [galvanized iron] sheds located in isolated rural areas. This increases our travel time and the expense of transporting the clothing to and from the warehouses. It is really a scary business, good profits, but risky. So in 2007, I decided to try something new.

For her first alternative venture, Jane established a business as a moneychanger—a career shift that other former used-clothing traders have similarly made, using their contacts in the used-clothing industry. Jane was able to rent her sister's stall that formerly sold Baguio City crafts and knitted products and which is fortuitously located in an aisle of the Baguio City Public Market where other moneychangers conduct business. Jane rented out her street-based used-clothing retail store to another trader in order to take over her sister's premises. When she was engaged in the used-clothing trade full-time and needed to exchange Philippine pesos for Hong Kong dollars, Jane often used the market moneychangers because they do not require clients to supply government-issued identification documents in order to complete transactions. Jane thus had a personal connection with her *suki,* who holds a license from the Philippine Central

FIGURE 7.3 Store within Baguio City Public Market. Photo by B. Lynne Milgram. Reproduced with permission

Bank to engage in foreign exchange and who agreed to sub-contract or sponsor Jane as a "commissioner" in this work. Most moneychangers operate their businesses without a permit from the Philippine Central Bank but as Patricia Banga, 55 years old, explains: "If our businesses are really illegal why do the banks send us customers when they cannot complete some types of transactions and why then are we not visited by the authorities? We are in this side aisle of the Baguio City Public Market, but we all have our small signs advertising our services and everyone knows where we are located—even newly arrived tourists seem to find us right away."

Moneychangers, like Jane, explain that they learn about foreign exchange by watching television and Internet market reports:

> I watch market analysts compute US dollars to pesos to Hong Kong dollars etc. I watch Bloomberg Channel Asia and I am always scanning the Internet news to learn how the stock market will affect currency rates. World events such as earthquakes and economic problems like those now being experienced in Greece or the Toyota problem in Japan can cause the dollar, the yen, or the euro to change daily. Our profit on each transaction is less than ten percent so I lose easily if I do not keep track of shifts in currency exchange rates.

Jane had a strong customer base from the beginning of her business, drawing her clients from the women with whom she worked in the secondhand clothing trade, both large-scale traders and women who periodically travel between the Philippines and Hong Kong to pack clothes or to make their own small export-bound purchases. By mid-2009, when we met, Jane had reduced the number of trips she makes to Hong Kong, to develop instead, a niche business that gives special exchange rates to her best clients, those who are still fully engaged in this trade. Jane's other clients, like those of most moneychangers, are contract workers visiting from Hong Kong, Australia, Singapore and the Middle East, seamen, tourists and Filipinos who are traveling abroad. Although Filipinos can easily transfer funds to Hong Kong via Western Union, for example, Patricia explains that many clients still prefer to use a moneychanger on the "black market" as they do not need to show identification, fill out forms, pay a remittance fee, or answer questions about the source of the funds. Patricia notes: "You just show your money and we exchange it right away." As Julie Batton, 42 years old, another moneychanger who formerly traded secondhand clothes, told me, "We are primarily in competition with one another for business, not Western Union or the banks; but as we sell the same product—money—and as our rates are almost the same, we depend upon our earlier business networks to provide us with loyal returning clients."

When entrepreneurs such as Jane, Julie and Patricia found themselves decreasing their direct engagement in the used-clothing trade, they looked for another business they could combine with moneychanging to diversify their operations. During their business trips to Hong Kong, when they were unable to purchase the volume of used clothing they required to make a profit, some entrepreneurs started parallel businesses purchasing cosmetics, personal grooming products and health supplements (vitamins) marketable in the Philippines. These goods include brand names such as Jurgens, Nivea, Bath and Body Works, Ponds, Gillette, health supplements, herbal teas and non-allergenic soaps. Filipina entrepreneurs making this career shift, as with money-changing, can easily do so as they use some of the same Hong Kong–Philippine "routeways" (Urry 2007: 52) they established to purchase and ship secondhand clothing to now buy and transport beauty and health products. While continuing to trade secondhand clothing (albeit in smaller quantities), some entrepreneurs have collectively rented smaller spaces in Hong Kong in which to pack their new commodities in the same standard-size *balikbayan* boxes in which they pack used clothes, but they ship their goods individually through independent door-to-door delivery services (e.g. Federal Express). Traders' clients come from the general Baguio City population but are primarily women and particularly students who attend the city's numerous universities—many of the same people who would be shopping for used clothing.

Jane also draws on her Hong Kong networks—domestic helpers and used-clothing packers working in Hong Kong—to secure these new goods for her when she cannot travel personally to Hong Kong. Jane pays a small fee to her contacts to purchase specific products from Hong Kong's discount stores, pack the goods in *balikbayan* boxes and mail them to the Philippines via door-to-door delivery services. As individually shipped *balikbayan* boxes customarily contain the personal belongings of or gifts from overseas Filipino contract workers (OFWs), they are not usually subject to customs duty. Traders like Jane and her fellow businesswomen also avoid paying import duty on these goods by addressing the boxes to different family members and friends and by spacing out the timing of their deliveries—a shipping technique that small-scale used-clothing entrepreneurs also use (see Milgram 2004).

In addition, Julie sources products through her American relatives:

> I ask my friends and relatives living in the US to buy certain products for me when they see these goods on sale at home. I also order products on-line when I discover that they are discounted. I pay with my credit card and I have the goods shipped to my American relatives. They accumulate these items until they can fill a *balikbayan* box that they then ship to me through a door-to-door service. The shipping cost is $75.00, more expensive than Hong Kong shipping, but I do not pay duty as my relatives declare the box contents as gifts. Many Filipinos with relatives or friends living abroad regularly receive *balikbayan* boxes and thus customs agents are used to clearing such goods.

Julie identifies another periodic source for her stock. Overseas contract Filipino workers returning on home visits are, by custom, expected to bring *balikbayan* boxes of gifts to friends and relatives (see Release 2009). If these OFWs have extra cosmetics, for example, they bring them to Julie to sell, or if Baguio City residents receive cosmetics or vitamins as gifts that they do not use, Julie will purchase these products: "This alternative source of products helps me maintain variety in my stock to differentiate my products from those of my competitors." Patricia outlines a similar alternative micro-routeway through which to add cosmetics and health products to her stock of used clothing: "When I was in Hong Kong buying used clothing, I established contacts with cosmetics suppliers and learned the locations of the best bargains to enable me to have other traders subsequently do my purchasing for me [...]. With text and e-mail communication, now I travel less frequently to Hong Kong to purchase these goods but I first had to know the pathways to them." Access to and knowledge of new communication technologies thus emerges as a powerful tool that enables these Filipina entrepreneurs to reconfigure their labor from hands-on purchases to those effected through digital networks—actions that stretch beyond national borders, thereby bypassing some constraints of state control (Ignacio 2005; Urry 2007: 53).

Entrepreneurs like Jane, Julie and Patricia explain that they apply their past experience in the used-clothing trade to their cosmetic and vitamin businesses, in effect similarly determining aspects of regional consumption (Brown-Giaude 2011; Freeman 2007). "It is all about the body," Julie notes: "what we wear, how we groom ourselves and how we keep our bodies healthy—these issues frame what we buy. People are more health-conscious today, as well as wanting to look fashionable while finding a bargain."

Patricia explains that much like the used-clothing trade, each entrepreneur is *kanya kanya* (independent) in most aspects of business. As entrepreneurs sell similar products, they focus on nurturing client loyalty by offering discounts or a lay-away plan and ensuring the high quality of the goods they sell (e.g. reliable product expiry dates). Jane maintains, "My goods are not like *pandesal* (popular white flour buns) that you can sell every day." Most Filipina entrepreneurs confirm that in their new businesses they need to stock the most popular brands, know their customers' tastes, and gain the latter's confidence. At the same time, while consumers are generally aware that Philippine–Hong Kong entrepreneurs may have obtained their goods through legally questionable means, they welcome the fact that the products are less expensive, not usually taxed and have been personally vetted by their *suki* trader.

While the competition among sellers is keen, cooperation occurs on an informal basis. For example, Patricia explains: "If a customer asks for a product which I do not have but which I know my neighbor has, I get the product from her, add a small markup, and sell it. In this way, we each profit." Patricia relates that she has friends who import beauty products in bulk that they sell in duty-free shopping zones (former US army bases). Patricia's friends sell her small amounts of selected products or of slow-selling goods that they wish to clear. Jane has entered into a similar sub-contracting arrangement with one of her customers, Carol. Each week, Carol purchases from Jane, a variety of lotions, shampoos, soaps and health supplements that she subsequently sells to her fellow office workers. Jane gives Carol a discount that provides her with a small profit. Although the alternative trade in beauty and health products generally remains small-scale, augmenting moneychanging or importing used clothing, it provides entrepreneurs with a less risky work option.

Conclusion

By fashioning personalized pathways through which to realize new work options, Philippine–Hong Kong entrepreneurs confront, challenge and at times overcome barriers to their claims for viable livelihoods as Philippine citizens. They maintain continuity with their originally established routeways by sourcing and marketing their goods through well-worn channels that utilize kin and community networks and customary credit relations (Davis 1973). In so doing, these entrepreneurs interconnect "fragmented global spaces" (Ribeiro 2009: 320)—they gain access to the resources they consider crucial for their well-being, the information they require about their rights, labor laws, and collective action, and they use this knowledge to challenge employers or government systems (Mills 2008), both in visible and in not-so-visible ways. Their mobility across socioeconomic and technological sectors thus enables these female entrepreneurs to be no longer marginal to, victimized or left behind by global capitalism, but to be among its vibrant participants.

Yet, while entrepreneurs' actions have indeed crafted a "contemporary global nomadic trade" (Ribeiro 2009: 321), enabling some women to realize the gendered and class flexibility they desire, there remain limits to their new-found work potential and rights. Filipina women's tourist status in Hong Kong and the ongoing, yet out-dated Philippine Presidential Decree upholding the illegality of importing used clothing into the country, constrain their livelihoods and their ability to enact change. Unlike most activist tactics that require public attention for their causes, Hong Kong–Philippine traders straddling legal/illegal spheres require invisibility to succeed. Although entrepreneurs access formal government channels to argue their cause when applicable (engaging in letter-writing campaigns and personal political lobbying), most of their actions are confined to less obviously detectable avenues such as negotiating personalized (albeit illegal) agreements to secure the export and import of their goods and using new mobile technologies to facilitate purchasing and shipping. Such work conditions highlight the simultaneous creative and repressive manifestations of traders' socioeconomic mobility and citizenship claims. While the economic opportunities of contemporary globalization facilitate entrepreneurs' freer and broader movement, this potential is counterbalanced by restrictive state measures in which "political rationality and cultural mechanisms continue to deploy, discipline, regulate, or civilize subjects in place or on the move" (Ong 1999: 19). Hence, Filipina traders seeking to contest patterns of socioeconomic inclusion and exclusion have little choice but to carve out their own particularized domain by continuing to negotiate symbolic trade-offs and realignments within the (il)licit parameters of their work.

This ambiguity in Filipina entrepreneurs' cross-border enterprises underscores the close relationship between legal and illegal practice. Traders do not regard their trade of used clothing and cosmetics as smuggling; rather, they claim that their businesses represent their right to make an integral living through their personal ingenuity, networks and hard work (Browne 2004). Traders' actions, such as those of Jane Talango, Julie Batton and Patricia Banga, as we have seen, thus question naturalized distinctions between illegal and legal work that do not consider broader socio-economic, political and civil rights contexts. To this end, Abraham and Schendel (2005: 25, 31) suggest applying the concept of "social legitimacy or licitness" to actions such as those of Filipina entrepreneurs, and positioning this understanding against "political legitimacy or legality" as defined by the state. The range and com-plexity of the routes through which Filipina entrepreneurs pursue their livelihoods foregrounds the usefulness of conceptualizing "multiple kinds of criminal space" (Abraham and Schendel 2005: 31)—everyday "niches that escape state control" (Ribeiro 2009: 321) but do not necessarily imply any illegal intent. In this light, although Filipinas' informal Hong Kong trade remains on the edge of what is commonly thought of as acceptable economic practice, these traders' advocacy has brought their so-called marginal pursuits closer to the center, thereby helping to realize some of the citizenship rights these women warrant and demand.

Acknowledgments

Field research for this chapter has been conducted in the Philippines over several periods from 2003 to 2011 and in Hong Kong in 2006 and 2008. Financial support for this research has been provided by the Social Sciences and Humanities Research Council of Canada (SSHRC), Standard Research Grants (2000–2003, 2004–2007, 2008–2011) and by OCAD University, Faculty Research Grants. In the Philippines, I am affiliated with the Cordillera Studies Center, University of the Philippines Baguio, Baguio City. I thank my colleagues at CSC for their generous support of my research and I thank my Research Assistants, Aileen Dao-ines and Analyn Amores-Salvador, for their insightful guidance. To the many people in the Philippines and in Hong Kong who answered my numerous questions about this trade, I owe a debt of gratitude. I also wish to thank the volume editors for their thoughtful comments on earlier drafts of this chapter.

Notes

1 Filipina entrepreneurs' self-constructed and independent cross-border trade between Hong Kong and the Philippines is considered by the state as operating within an "informal sector." Lindell (2010) argues that this highly contested term generally refers to a heterogeneous group of activities and employment relationships that share common characteristics, most notably, the lack of legal recognition, regulation or state protection.
2 Although, in theory, the importation of used clothing into the Philippines is illegal, the on-the-ground parameters of this trade continue to be negotiated and debated at different levels of business and government. The Philippine Republic Act No. 4653 (Government of the Philippines, 1966) states that it is "unlawful" to import "textile articles commonly known as used clothing and rags." The Central Bank Circular No. 1060 (Bangko Sentral Ng Pilipinas, 1985) and the subsequent Presidential Decree No. 2033 (Government of the Philippines, 1986) both outlined some exceptions to the laws banning the commercial importation of used clothing although maintaining the overall restriction.
3 This section draws on and expands basic background research on the secondhand clothing industry documented in an earlier publication (Milgram 2008).
4 *Balikbayan* is the pan-Philippine term used to identify Overseas Filipino Workers (OFWs). The term is also applied to the boxes that OFWs use to transport their personal belongings and gifts back to the Philippines. As these boxes commonly contain Filipinos' personal possessions, they are not subject to import duty. The size of the box corresponds to that allowed by airlines for standard check-in luggage.
5 All personal names of people are pseudonyms.

References

Abaño, I. B. (2010) "'Ukay-Ukay' Capital of the Country," *Business Mirror* 5: 269, September 19.
Abraham, I. and W. van Schendel (2005) "Introduction: The Making of Illicitness," in W. van Schendel and I. Abraham, eds, *Illicit Flows and Criminal Things: States, Borders, and the Other Side of Globalization*, Bloomington: University of Indiana Press, 1–37.

Almendral, A. (2004) "Clothes to Dig For," *Filipinas* (July): 16–18.

Andreas, P. (2000) *Border Games: Policing the U.S.-Mexico Divide*, Ithaca: Cornell University Press.

Balisacan, A. (1995) "Anatomy of Poverty during Adjustment: The Case of the Philippines," *Economic Development and Cultural Change* 44(1): 33–62.

Bangko Sentral Ng Pilipinas (1985) *Central Bank Circular No. 1060*, Manila, PH: Bangko Sentral Ng Pilipinas, May 22.

Brown-Giaude, W. (2011) *Higglers in Kingston: Women's Informal work in Jamaica*. Nashville: Vanderbilt University Press.

Browne, K. (2004) *Creole Economics: Caribbean Cunning Under the French Flag*, Austin: University of Texas Press.

Cabreza, V. (2001) "Baguio Means Berries, Veggies and 'Ukay-Ukay,'" *Philippine Daily Inquirer* B2, August 12.

——(2006) "Baguio Now a Brand," *Philippine Daily Inquirer* B1, June 19.

Cabuag, V. G. 2010. "'Ukay-Ukay': The Price of Prohibition," *Business Mirror* 5: 269, September 19.

Chant, S. (1996) "Women's Roles in Recession and Economic Restructuring in Mexico and the Philippines," *Geoforum* 27 (3): 297–327.

Chant, S. and C. McIlwaine. (1995) *Women of a Lesser Cost: Female Labour, Foreign Exchange & Philippine Development*, London: Pluto Press.

Cimatu, F. (2002) "'Wagwag' Tourism," *Philippine Daily Inquirer* A14, February 10.

City of Baguio, City Council (2006) Resolution Number 127, May 22.

Comanda, R. (2009) "The Ukay-Ukay Trade Could Be Entering a Slump," *Sun Star Baguio* 7, January 7.

Constable, N. (1997) *Maid to Order in Hong Kong: Stories of Filipina Workers*, Ithaca: Cornell University Press.

Coutin, S. (2007) *Nations of Emigrants: Shifting Boundaries of Citizenship in El Salvador and the United States*, Ithaca: Cornell University Press.

Cruz, C. (2002) "Contraband Entry through Wagwagan Alarms Mayor," *Sun Star Baguio* A1, January 20.

Davis, W. (1973) *Social Relations in a Philippine Market: Self-Interest and Subjectivity*, Berkeley: University of California Press.

Designing Hong Kong Newsletter (2008) "Expand the Review on Hawker Licensing Policy," June 10. http://www.designinghongkong.com/cms/ (accessed June 14, 2008).

Freeman, C. (2007) "The Reputation of Neoliberalism," *American Ethnologist* 34(2): 252–67.

Garcia, C. (2006) "Customs Probes 'Ukay-Ukay' Smuggling," *Manila Standard* B4, April 25.

Government of the Philippines (1966) *Republic Act No. 4653*, Manila, PH: Government of the Philippines (General Auditing Office, Department of Finance), June 17.

——(1986) *Presidential Decree No. 2033*, Manila, PH: Government of the Philippines, February 6.

Hansen, K. T. (2000) *Salaula: The World of Secondhand Clothing and Zambia*, Chicago: University of Chicago Press.

Heyman, J. M. and A. Smart (1999) "States and Illegal Practices: An Overview," in J. M. Heyman, ed., *States and Illegal Practices*, Oxford: Berg, 1–24.

Holston, J. (1999) "Spaces of Insurgent Citizenship," in J. Holston, ed., *Cities and Citizenship*, Durham: Duke University Press, 155–173.

——(2008) *Insurgent Citizenship: Disjunctures of Democracy and Modernity in Brazil*, Princeton: Princeton University Press.

Hutchcroft, P. (1998) "Sustaining Economic and Political Reform: The Challenges Ahead," in D. Timberman, ed., *The Philippines: New Directions in Domestic Policy and Foreign Relations*, New York: Asia Society, 23–47.

Ignacio, E. (2005) *Building Diaspora: Filipino Cultural Community Formation on the Internet*, New Brunswick: Rutgers University Press.

Julian, P. (2006) "This 'Ukay-Ukay' Shipment Didn't Make It to the Stores," *Philippine Daily Inquirer* A8, June 19.

Lacorte, G. (2005) "'Ukay-Ukay' Seen Losing Sales to Brand-New Items," *Philippine Daily Inquirer* B3, January 29.

Li, F. (2006) "Collection Cages Set to be Removed," *South China Morning Post* 14, June 27.

Lindell, I. (2010) "Introduction: The Changing Politics of Informality—Collective Organizing, Alliances and Scales of Engagement," in I. Lindell, ed., *Africa's Informal Workers: Collective Agency, Alliances and Transnational Organizing in Urban Africa*, London: Zed Books, 1–30.

Milgram, B. L. (2001) "Situating Handicraft Market Women in Ifugao, Upland Philippines: A Case for Multiplicity," in L. Seligman, ed., *Women Traders in Cross-Cultural Perspective: Mediating Identities, Marketing Wares*, Stanford: Stanford University Press, 129–59.

——(2004) "Refashioning Commodities: Women and the Sourcing of Secondhand Clothing in the Philippines," *Anthropologica* 46(2): 189–202.

——(2005) "Ukay-Ukay Chic: Tales of Secondhand Clothing Fashion and Trade in the Philippine Cordillera," in A. Palmer and H. Clark, eds, *Old Clothes, New Looks: Secondhand Fashion*, Oxford and New York: Berg, 135–53.

——(2008) "Activating Frontier Livelihoods: Women and the Transnational Secondhand Clothing Trade Between the Philippines and Hong Kong," *Urban Anthropology and Studies of Cultural Systems and World Economic Development* 37(1): 5–47.

——(2009) "Negotiating Urban Activism: Women, Vending and the Transformation of Streetscapes in the Urban Philippines," in M. Butcher and S. Velayutham, eds, *Dissent and Cultural Resistance in Asia's Cities*, London: Routledge, 110–27.

Mills, M. B. (2012) "Thai Mobilities and Cultural Citizenship," *Critical Asian Studies* 44(1): 85–112.

Ong, A. (1999) *Flexible Citizenship: The Cultural Logics of Transnationality*, Durham: Duke University Press.

Opiña, R. and E. Olson (2006) "Exclude Ukay-Ukay in Anti-Smuggling Bill," *Sun Star Baguio Weekend* 1: 11, May 21.

Palmer, A. and H. Clark (2005) *Old Clothes, New Looks: Second Hand Fashion*, Oxford: Berg.

Parreñas, R. S. (2001) *Servants of Globalization: Women, Migration and Domestic Work*, Stanford: University of California Press.

Ramirez, J. (2009) "The A-Z of Baguio 'Ukay' Shopping," *Philippine Daily Inquirer* F1: 3, April 24.

Release, I. (2009) "OFWs are RP's Top Remitters," *Sun Star Baguio* 6, June 26.

Ribeiro, G. L. (2009) "Non-Hegemonic Globalizations: Alter-native Transnational Processes and Agents," *Anthropological Theory* 9(3): 297–329.

Salaverria, L. (2006) "Customs Seizes P19-M Cargo in Metro, N. Luzon," *Philippine Daily Inquirer* A19, June 24.

Sanidad, P. (2001) "From Skyscraper to 'Wagwag,'" *Baguio Midland Courier* 3: 35, December 9.

See, D. (2001a) "Wagwag Businesses Given a Chance to Secure Permits," *Baguio Midland Courier* 4, October 7.

——(2001b) "City Padlocks Wagwag Shops," *Baguio Midland Courier* 2, November 18.

Smart, A. and J. Lee (2003) "Financialization and the Role of Real Estate in Hong Kong's Regime of Accumulation," *Economic Geography* 79(1): 153–71.

Subido, Paulo (2003) "A Guide to the Ukay-Ukay Safari," *The Philippine Star* H2, April 11.

Stoller, P. (2002) *Money Has No Smell: The Africanization of New York City*, Chicago: University of Chicago Press.

Sun Star Baguio (2009) "The Ukay-Ukay Trade is Now in a Slump," *Sun Star Baguio* 7 , January 7.

Trotz, D. A. (2006) "Rethinking the Caribbean Transnational Connections: Conceptual Itineraries," *Global Networks* 6(1): 41–59.

Urry, John (2007) *Mobilities*, Cambridge: Polity.

8

MEXICAN "ANT TRADERS" IN THE EL PASO/CIUDAD JUÁREZ BORDER REGION

Tensions between globalization, securitization and new mobility regimes

Mélissa Gauthier

This chapter is about the alternative routes to economic participation that emerge in the nooks and crannies of globalization. Around all Mexico's border-crossing points, there is an impressive system of smuggling from the United States called *fayuca hormiga* which means "ant trade." Based on ethnographic fieldwork conducted in the El Paso/ Ciudad Juárez border region, this chapter focuses on Mexican *fayuqueros* or "ant traders" whose livelihood involves the smuggling of used clothing across the Mexican border for resale on the other side. It explores how people involved with "globalization from below" in the northern Mexican borderlands experience the new context of increased cross-border securitization.

The first section considers the continuing and changing role of state borders in the wake of new security and trade agreements and the increasing global mobility of persons, objects and information. As Heyman (2004: 321) points out, "NAFTA has increased border traffic more than fourfold. At the same time, national security concerns favor more thorough and effective inspections, with attention to a wider range of putatively risky people and items." The second section describes the activities of non-hegemonic economic globalization as practiced in the El Paso/Ciudad Juárez border region. The third section explains how the Mexican government is "modernizing" its ports of entry along the border by implementing new security measures (like a new border inspection system called SIAVE, a Spanish acronym for "system of vehicle control") aimed at intercepting the flow of contraband. The final section discusses some of the potential effects of these new security measures on the ability of Mexican *fayuqueros* to move things across the Mexican border while avoiding customs.

The border's economic underworld

All international borders represent lucrative zones of exchange and trade, often illicit and clandestine. As Grimson (2002: 154) suggests, in every border region there are people "who live off crossing the border." In the border areas between Mercosur states, people who perform this activity are known as *pasadores* ("couriers") or *paseras* (literally "ferrywomen") (Grimson 2002: 154). Other terms used elsewhere to refer to people engaged in similar activities across international borders are "tourist traders" (Hann and Hann 1992), "shuttle traders" (Yükseker 2004; Holtom 2003), "suitcase traders" (Freeman 2001), "ant traders" (Cichocki *et al.* 2001; Gauthier 2010) or "baggers" (Ribeiro 2009).

Their cross-border activities are examples of economic practices that are current worldwide and are part of what Ribeiro (2009) calls "economic globalization from below" or "non-hegemonic economic globalization" because the activities involved "defy the economic establishment everywhere on the local, regional, national, inter-national and transnational levels" (Ribeiro 2009: 313). As a result, states and major corporations are inclined to consider activities within this form of non-hegemonic economic globalization as illegal, a threat to national and global economies. Although these activities are illegal because they resist the norms and rules of formal political authority, they are usually quite acceptable in the eyes of those most closely involved, and they can even have widespread social legitimacy (Schendel and Abraham 2005; Heyman and Smart 1999; Flynn 1997).

The perspective of these agents of grassroots globalization has too often been neglected in studies which favored perspectives 'from above', ones that overstress "the influence of corporate capitalism in defining the state and its limits" (Donnan and Wilson 1999: 90). James Scott (1985) is well-known for uncovering less visible, "everyday forms of peasant resistance"—foot dragging, dissimulation, desertion, false compliance, pilfering, feigned ignorance, slander, arson, sabotage—by "viewing things from below" (see Lahusen 1989). Non-hegemonic economic practices are "everyday forms of resistance" of a sort. That is, they reflect the attempts of common people to avoid the control of authorities. Yet the main motive of these agents of "economic globalization from below" is economic survival, not political defiance. As Ribeiro (2009: 313) points out, those who participate within this parallel global economy do not intend to destroy capitalism but to benefit from it. In that sense their everyday motivations and actions are more accurately described by what Campbell and Heyman (2007) refer to as "slantwise" behavior. By "slantwise" they mean "actions that are undertaken by actors in order to achieve their own ends and that, although they do not necessarily involve intentional political resistance, frustrate state interests" (Campbell 2009: 12).

This chapter attempts to shed light on the border's economic underworld, the one in which nation states' normative and regulating powers are contested by people who make a living by crossing state lines. By focusing on the perspective of the participants in these non-hegemonic economic practices, I want to distance myself from state-centric analyses of border economics which are grounded by rigid definitions of what is legal and illegal and rarely take into account the people who actually participate in informal and illicit economies. According to Galemba (2008: 20), what is needed is "a more ethnographically informed approach to understand how such individuals shaped, and were shaped by, their experiences in an economy often simultaneously formal, informal, legal, and illegal." Ethnographic studies of economic globalization from below in different regions of the world can help us better understand how the formal/informal, licit/illicit, legal/illegal often come together in actual practices at and across state borders (Galemba 2008; Nordstrom 2000).

Anthropologists interested in the phenomenon of cross-border small-scale trading have played a major role in analyzing the double-faced nature of borders as both economic opportunities and barriers for small-time traders. On the one hand, people who make money from the illicit economy of the international border are directly dependent on the very existence of the international border. On the other hand, they constantly fight against the very thing that ensures their livelihoods (Kloppers 2004: 142). For these people the international border is at the same time a basis for and a menace to their working lives. "Without borders they would not exist, so they would never call for 'an end to borders.' Still, an undue 'hardening' of the border demands more sophisticated methods of smuggling, and this could also be their downfall. In other words they do want state borders but they want them on their own terms" (Grimson 2002: 168).

In recent years, there has been a renewed discourse about borders following the events of 9/11 and the prominence of the securitization discourse. In the 1990s, it was commonplace to describe globalization as auguring a new borderless and deterritorialized world, one in which the ability of states to regulate activities within and across their borders was undermined. Yet territorial borders did not become uniformly eroded in the new world orders that emerged under neoliberal globalization, and in many cases, the securitization of international borders has intensified. The processes of globalization and securitization are drawing anthropologists' attention to reconfigurations of state borders analyzed in light of their "selective permeability and differential filtering effects" (Anderson 2001: 3; see also Ferrer-Gallardo 2008: 303). Pallitto and Heyman (2008: 327) conceptualize this problem as "a tension between securitization and neoliberalist globalization, which operate both to enable and to restrict movement. While the nationalistic imperative of border security urges restriction, globalization demands unrestricted movement of economic actors." As Donnan and Wilson (2010: 6) suggest, "this variable experience of borders as structures of state power is clearly one that has always been a potential result of crossing borders, but there is also clearly a new emphasis on the role of borders in enhancing certain forms of movement, but restricting others, in the post-9/11 world." Along these lines, this chapter explores how people involved with "economic globalization from below" in the northern Mexican borderlands experience the new context of increased cross-border securitization. In the following pages, I will describe the activities of non-hegemonic economic globalization as practiced in the El Paso/Ciudad Juárez border region.

Trade over the El Paso/Ciudad Juárez border

The border between Mexico and the United States is a classic setting for smuggling (Heyman 1994: 54), and much has been written about the traffic in illegal drugs and undocumented migrants from Mexico to the United States. In contrast, the traffic in contraband merchandise from the United States to Mexico has received little attention in the academic literature. In addition to firearms and ammunition, a wide range of prohibited items from the United States is smuggled into Mexico including electronic goods, used cars and tires, American alcoholic products and even frozen chickens (O'Day and López 2001: 237). Another popular item smuggled into Mexico is secondhand clothing from the United States.

Secondhand clothing is retailed in stores and warehouses along the American side of the border and brought into Mexico where its import for resale is prohibited. According to the administrator of border customs at an international bridge in Reynosa, used clothing is one of the leading contraband products they seize. The situation can be compared to drugs going north (Bogan 2005). There are many cases of "documented smuggling," in other words, the passing off of wearable used clothes as "mutilated rags" to customs officials at the Mexican ports of entry, thereby avoiding the need for impossible-to-obtain licenses and high tariffs (Malkin 2003). This form of "documented" contraband is controlled by large-scale smuggling operations that use falsified documents and phantom companies in order to ship large volumes (e.g. 65-foot tractor trailers) of secondhand clothing into the interior of Mexico. However, the most common way of bringing used clothing into Mexico for resale remains small-time smuggling conducted by inhabitants of the area who make frequent trips to the United States and carry used clothing over the border in a car trunk or a suitcase.

This impressive system of smuggling from the United States, which also often requires some bribery of Mexican customs officers, is called *fayuca hormiga*, or "ant trade." "The evocative Spanish expression '*hormiga*' (on a small scale, literally antlike) signifies the energetic, industrious habits" (Campbell 2005) of those who perform this activity, which involves the carrying of small quantities of goods by the same person repeatedly in order to sell them for a profit on the other side of the border (see also Cichocki *et al.* 2001: 56). In other words, it is both characterized by the high frequency of cross-border movement and low volume of product carried per trip. Participants in *fayuca* are called *fayuqueros* and include working-class professional traders, middle- and upper-class visitors to the United States, and returning migrant workers and families. The work of a *fayuquero* is gender-neutral—both women and men buy used goods in El Paso and resell them in Juárez (Staudt 1998: 75).

Mexican "ant traders" have various options for purchasing used clothing in downtown El Paso including Goodwill and other thrift stores, flea markets, yard sales and "clothing by the pound" stores. In addition, most US border towns like El Paso have companies that specialize in selling discarded clothing in bulk to customers from Mexico. There is an army of "ant traders" feeding the market for recycled and refurbished clothing in Ciudad Juárez which represents a dynamic sector of employment and a major source of provisioning for Mexican border consumers. While some used-clothing vendors sell their merchandise directly in front of their houses or in the streets, others manage to get a stall at one of the numerous Juárez street markets called *tianguis*.

The first time I met her, Rosa was rummaging carefully through the racks at Ropa por Libra—"Clothing by the Pound," the downtown El Paso store she has visited nearly every week, for the past 20 years. The 53-year-old woman, who is from the neighboring Mexican city of Ciudad Juárez, studied a children's shirt carefully, inspected and rejected a blouse, then took a pair of men's trousers and finding no stains or rips whatsoever, nodded her head in satisfaction. A few moments later, she took a small bundle of clothing and tossed it onto a scale at the counter. So goes a typical transaction at Ropa por Libra, an El Paso institution that has counterparts in other American border cities. Rosa was planning to cross back over the Rio Grande and wash and iron the clothes she bought in order to resell them. She hoped to make a little profit on each sale; with the proceeds, she would be back at Ropa por Libra the following week.

A few days after our first encounter in El Paso, Rosa was busy tending her clothing stand in a *tianguis* that pops up around a dusty field in an unpaved Juárez neighborhood every Friday. Rosa was a *tianguista*, i.e. a mobile vendor who always follows the same weekly itinerary that takes her to several neighborhoods on the outskirts of Ciudad Juárez where bundles of metal joists are momentarily converted into a maze of temporary stands. Rosa had a different *colonia* to visit every day of the week: Monday, Francisco Sarabia; Wednesday, Navarro; Thursday, Arroyo de las Víboras; Friday, Fronteriza Alta; Saturday and Sunday, Fronteriza Baja. Tuesday was Rosa's only day off, the one she usually spent shopping "on the other side" of the border in El Paso.

The soccer field that anchors the *tianguis* is filled with piles of brush mixed with trash, and the swamp onto which the market has expanded is a de facto garbage dump. The plastic roofs of the *tianguis* begin to appear at their roving destination around 7:00 am. The sound systems are cranked up and the local instant Walmart is open for business. It took me a while to find Rosa when I visited her at the *tianguis* for the first time. She was hidden under a loosely tied plastic tarp that sheltered her from the sun and the blowing dust of the dry spring season. Some of her clothes were stacked in neat piles on a long wooden table, with the prettiest things hanging from the roof of the moveable booth neatly displayed on metal hooks.

Rosa sat behind the table also filled with dusty plastic toys, hair accessories and flip-flops, dangling her feet, smiling halfheartedly. She had also brought back Asian-imported "*fayuca*" from her last cross-border sourcing trip across the Rio Grande. El Paso Street is home to a large number of "Dollar Stores" (variously named "Family Dollar," "General Dollar," "99¢," "Señor Dollar," etc.) all oriented to the cross-border market. "Los Chinos," as these shops mostly owned by Korean merchants are locally called, sell a full range of general merchandise including packaged food, vitamins, cosmetics, clothing, kitchen wares, household items, floral supplies and even cheap goods bearing Mexican icons but which are manufactured in China or Vietnam (Ruiz 2005).

A daily parade of Mexican shoppers and *fayuqueras*, sometimes also called *chiveras*, or goatherds, crosses the Rio Grande to buy low-priced goods in great quantities from El Paso downtown merchants. The easiest way for most Juárez residents like Rosa to cross the border is to walk across the downtown bridge into El Paso—the pedestrian line generally moves pretty fast—pass through the customs hall and wave their border crossing card (BCC) also known as a "laser visa." Walking between the two downtowns takes her only a few minutes. The main shopping zone for Mexican cross-border pedestrians is the south end of downtown, where the Santa Fe International Bridge ends and becomes El Paso Street. The concentration of stores in the southern section of downtown, particularly the streets nearest the Santa Fe International Bridge reflects the restricted spatial mobility of the customers: many Mexicans shoppers like Rosa walk to the shops closest to the border and must carry their purchases home.

On their way back to Juárez, they lug their best finds to the international bridges and sneak them across the border in zippered carry bags, backpacks and suitcases. Most of the time, "ant traders" simply trust their luck in going through the Mexican ports of entry. For many years, their entrance to Mexico via the international bridges has been screened through a red light/green light random system of car and pedestrian inspection operated by Mexican customs (*Policía Fiscal*). On crossing the bridge into Mexico, drivers can choose to pass by customs in the lanes that say, "Nothing to Declare" or, conversely, in the "To Declare" lanes, which are normally deserted. In each of the "Nothing to Declare" lanes, there is an automated selection mechanism, i.e. a traffic light. Similarly, when crossing the border on foot, people can be asked to push the button on a solitary "stoplight." A green light means an automatic customs clearance, i.e. the driver or pedestrian may proceed through the customs facilities without inspection. A red light, on the contrary, indicates that the person's vehicle or luggage will be inspected. Much pressure was brought to bear against this measure by El Paso downtown merchants, so that red lights became fewer and farther between, and people passed through relatively easily day after day.

The fact that Mexican customs authorities increased the proportion of green lights in the past is a very good illustration of the tension between trade and security at the border. According to Mexican customs authorities in Juárez, the proportion of red lights is said to represent only 5 percent compared to 95 percent of green lights (Batista 2003). As a result, the work of *fayuquero* has been made easier by the fact that the Mexican customs system relies on random checks, meaning that only about one in 10 or 20 vehicles are checked—if they trigger the red inspection light upon crossing (Payan 2006: 877). According to the federal Attorney General's Office, Mexico checks only 10 percent of the 230,000 vehicles that cross the border each day (a more thorough inspection is conducted 30 kilometers or so south of the border). Some extremely busy border crossings like Ciudad Juárez and Tijuana, with thousands of pedestrians and vehicles crossing back and forth every day, randomly select people to push the button. Mexican customs officials can decide who must push the button at their own discretion. Many "ant traders" I have interviewed mentioned the randomness of Mexico's border inspection system when asked to explain their willingness to "take a chance" at the Mexican ports of entry.

Although on one hand the probability they have of getting a green light is relatively high, on the other hand their chances of having to pay informally for their used-clothing imports in the form of bribes to the Mexican customs agents are also high. In Spanish, bribes are referred to as "*la mordida*" (literally, "the bite"). The *mordida* system is a deep-rooted, traditional way of getting around and through the system in

Mexico. Paying *mordidas* is often considered as the most efficient—or the only—way of getting things across the Mexican border. Many "ant traders" I have talked to said they have been harassed by Mexican customs agents or Federal Preventive Police officers and have been asked for bribes. Some of them talked their way out of the situation, others paid *mordidas*, and still others were stalled at the bridge until relatives brought money so they could pass. Overall, Mexican *fayuqueros* think of themselves as open targets for bribery and other forms of extortion when they re-enter Mexican territory.

Sneaking used clothing across the Mexican border is a real cat-and-mouse game involving various "tricks of the trade." As Oscar Martínez (1994: 314) has noted, "Over time, the only changes in the contraband game have been in the volume of the merchandise making its way from one country to the other and in the strategies invented to circumvent the law." In the past, Mexican women used to smuggle used clothing across the border by doing consecutive round-trips by foot across the Santa Fe Bridge while wearing several layers of clothing. In recent times, "the special challenge *fayuqueras* face involves posing as shoppers rather than as traders" (Staudt 1998: 78). Their major strategy consists in taking a small quantity of merchandise on each trip, while claiming that they are goods for personal use. In order to avoid the customs agents' attention on their way back home, they must try to minimize the size of their bags or make more frequent trips. People returning to Juárez by walking over the Santa Fe Bridge who are unable to pass through can also choose to turn back, re-enter the United States and try again via the other bridge.

Another trick that was very popular among *fayuqueras* like Rosa was catching rides with men who earned their livelihood smuggling used cars known as *"chuecos"* (a Spanish adjective for crooked) into Mexico. These men can buy up to five cars in Texas and drive them across the border every week (Zarembo 1999). They offered women free rides across the border because Mexican customs officials are usually less suspicious towards drivers with passengers on board. The most experienced drivers are apparently able to tailgate the car in front of them in order to sidestep the red light/green light inspection system. Some "ant traders" driving across the border fold all the garments and place them in clothes baskets that they transport in the trunk of their car so as to suggest a trip to the laundromat in El Paso should they be stopped for inspection. They carry soap and bleach and put fabric softener sheets between the clothes to mask the smell of mothballed used clothes and to give them a scent of freshness which can make the authorities believe that the garments have indeed just been washed. Once again, making two or three trips to transport several hundred pounds of clothing helps them minimize the risk of losing their entire stock if they are caught.

Other people who also make a living from the "ant trade" are known as *pasadores* ("couriers"). The *pasadores* are hired by used-clothing traders who do not want to risk crossing with their merchandise on their own. They smuggle clothes into Mexico for around US$20 each trip. The *pasadores* are almost all men, who act as packers, loaders and drivers. They gravitate to the most frequented used-clothing warehouses in El Paso, where they load their mini-vans with used clothing. Their cargo of used clothing can weigh as much as half a ton. The mini-vans used by the *pasadores* usually have border plates, tinted windows and back seats removed to make room for more clothing. They also have reinforced suspensions so that they do not look overloaded. It is estimated that around ten mini-vans transport used clothing across the border on a daily basis (Minjáres 2003).

The *pasadores* have arrangements with Mexican customs officials that allow them to smuggle large volumes of used clothing on a daily basis. The Spanish term *arreglo* is used to designate this kind of understanding or arrangement that can be reached between the authorities and the law breaker. It generally involves the transfer of a sum of money from one party to another (O'Day and Lopez 2001: 240). However, the *arreglo* only ensure the passing of the *pasadores* through the Mexican customs facilities with their goods. People who import large volumes of secondhand clothing back to Mexico for resale may face other forms of extortion and corruption once they have re-entered Mexican territory. As the following example shows, they always run the risk of being stopped by the Federal Preventive Police (*Policia Federal Preventiva*) or the municipal police once in Juárez.

I have spent a significant amount of time in the course of my fieldwork at the largest used-clothing outlet in El Paso helping some informants in the sorting process. Inside the massive building, people crawled over mounds of clothes dumped across a concrete floor as Spanish music played on the radio. Everywhere there were clothes from many periods and all seasons, in every permutation of style. In the background, unopened, half-ton bales were stacked to the rafters as if they were bales of hay. In the center, high-volume buyers were surrounded by thousand-pound bales of clothes that they bought for approximately US$300 apiece. Among them was a woman named Paty who purchased some US$3,000 worth of clothes every week. She came to the warehouse twice a week in order to sort something like a dozen bales of used clothes.

As a result of the large volume of clothes she processed on a weekly basis, Paty needed the help of at least four professional sorters or *surtidoras* to assist her in the sorting process, which is largely manual and very labor intensive. These women were daily commuter workers from Juárez who crossed the border into El Paso legally with a laser visa to "work" informally at various used-clothing warehouses, where they were paid by high-volume buyers like Paty. All around them, in huge mounds, were piles upon piles of used clothes that reached up to the sky. As they chatted, they kept sorting the clothing at a furious pace. Their main task was to dig out the clothes from the compressed bales and inspect them in order to separate goods that were torn or stained from the wearable goods. Paty set aside some of the prettier items for her own market stall. She also prepared special orders (*pedidos*) for some of her privileged long-time buyers coming to the "opening day."

The sales event took place once a week at the market stall owned by Paty in an area of downtown Juárez called "*las segundas*." This expression is commonly used to designate markets dedicated to secondhand goods. The "segundas" area contains several hundred semi-permanent and permanent stalls open seven days a week that specialize in used clothing, catering to the local population. The "opening day" was

the moment for Paty to sell back her large used-clothing imports to her regular customers who came with a view to buy in order to resell. Every Tuesday morning
around 8:00, the place was abuzz with activity. Radio music and cries by vendors,
"¿Qué va a llevar?" (What will you take?), increased the noise level. When a new
arrival was uncovered for resale, its opening was much like the hustle and bustle of
holiday shopping. The concern with newness and choice was perceptible around the
crowd of customers fighting for the best items and selecting particular pieces to resell.
Paty's sister-in-law, who also set up a stand in a *tianguis*, came to see her every week
to pick up the unsold clothing that had been displayed on hangers for too long.
Paty's business profited from a brisk turnover of American used clothing.

Large importers of used clothing like Paty are the main source of provisioning for a
significant number of secondhand traders who also sell in street markets. In 2007, the
Municipal Commerce Office (*Dirección de Comercio Municipal*) of Ciudad Juárez estimated the number of registered street markets at 226, with some 6,500 traders, of
which four in ten sold secondhand goods. The majority of the city's secondhand
traders or *segunderos* sold clothing and appliances (Nájera 2007). Those who do not
go shopping in El Paso like Rosa can count on the "opening day" to fill their own
market stalls or home-based businesses week after week. Paty and all her crew were
always extremely busy in El Paso on the eve of the opening day.

Paty also hired someone to transport her weekly cargo of used clothing into
Mexico. His job was to carry out up to five passages across the border at the wheel of
Paty's mini-van to the market in downtown Juárez. Prior to each passage, Paty called
her contact from the custom services with her mobile phone. If for some reason
she could not reach him, she would ride around the international bridges hoping to
be able to locate him. Paty paid him bribes as high as 600 pesos for each passage
of used clothing. Yet paying the bribes to her contact from the Mexican customs
provided no absolute guarantee of safe passage.

The deal Paty had with the Juárez customs official did not protect her from
the federal police officers once in Juárez. Paty's driver was stopped by the Federal
Preventive Police (*Policia Federal Preventiva*) one afternoon on his way back to the
market in Juárez. He was told to contact Paty, who immediately went to his rescue.
The federal police officers asked her to pay a bribe of 10,000 pesos (US$1,000). Paty
had no other choice. She not only felt responsible for her employee, but also, failure
to pay the *mordida* would have meant that her entire cargo of used clothing and her
mini-van would have been confiscated. The next morning, everybody at the
"opening day" agreed with Paty on the fact that she had been treated unfairly by the
Federal Preventive Police. Paty's contact from the customs was also extremely upset
when he learned what happened to her with the federal police officers that day. He
immediately instructed her to use a different car for transporting her merchandise
across the border in an attempt to divert the PFP officers' attention. Paty does not
like to use her other car because it is much smaller than the mini-van and does
not have a reinforced suspension. As this example demonstrates, for smugglers, "the
issue is avoidance, trickery, evasion, and 'slantwise behavior'" (Campbell 2009: 12;
see also Campbell and Heyman: 2007).

This kind of cross-border strategy used by Mexican *fayuqueros* and *pasadores* in order to evade customs control officials might be undermined by new security measures aimed at helping Mexican authorities detect drug money, weapons and other contraband that are smuggled into Mexico from the United States. In efforts to inspect and regulate the flow of traffic going south, Mexico is putting in place new technology such as vehicle scales, cameras and vehicle access gates at ports of entry along its border with the United States. The next section describes the new border inspection system called SIAVE (a Spanish acronym for "system of vehicle control") which represents a major shift in the way the country is dealing with incoming traffic from the US.

Mexico's new border inspection system

The Mexican government's demonstration of authority at the place of entry into Mexico has generally been regarded as minimal and disorganized in contrast with the obvious show of force that the US government exercises at the place of entry into the United States (Heyman 2010: 30). The administrator for Mexican customs in Tijuana describes SIAVE as "a modern system that brings Mexican border crossings into the modern age" (Holguin 2009). As he explained, "before we had this program, it was just a random system; there was no electronic record about the cars." According to the administrator, one of the goals of the new border inspection system is to avoid the traffic of illegal items into Mexico by having a better control of the risk from suspicious vehicles at the border (Navarro 2009).

The new system of vehicle control (SIAVE) is based on a screening process very similar to the one existing at American ports of entry. It will record the plate numbers, and type, model, brand and weight of each vehicle, along with an image of the passengers in each one. The SIAVE process begins with two cameras that read license plate numbers of vehicles entering Mexico. Vehicles are then weighed on scales, and finally head to the scanner for the vehicle profile. A light will indicate if the vehicle needs to go to a secondary inspection; otherwise, a gate will go up to let the car go through. By weighing cars to see whether they are unusually heavy, and by running license plate numbers through a database of suspicious vehicles, the government hopes to catch more hidden contraband (Olson 2009).

The new system, intended to work at all Mexico border crossings, started operating in Ciudad Juárez at the beginning of 2010 (García 2010). This new system is just one part of the government's efforts to upgrade ports of entry into Mexico. According to the Mexican customs administrator at the San Luis port of entry in Sonora, next year ports will be equipped with X-ray machines that will allow for "nonintrusive inspections," and will also eventually get dogs trained to detect contraband. Aside from that, pedestrian lanes will also be furnished with X-ray equipment to detect the contents of backpacks (Neyoy 2009).

The customs overhaul is not all about new technology or data gathering, but also includes a change in agents hoping to catch tax-evaders as well as fight organized crime operations. In August 2009, Mexico's customs function was taken over by a new agency, OCE (*Operadores de Comercio Exterior.* Foreign Commerce Operators) after the prior agency was found to be heavily involved with organized crime. Within a few days, 700 customs officers where suddenly fired all over Mexico and quickly replaced by 1,400 newly hired agents who had undergone months of training and background checks to ensure they had no criminal records. The number of agents assigned to Juárez border ports of entry increased significantly from 45 to 126. In addition, the local administrator for Mexican customs in Juárez announced the adoption of a new job rotation policy to ensure that the new officials were frequently going to be assigned new tasks or locations. According to him, "all these changes comply with a program of modernization of the country's entire custom system" (García 2009).

The recent intensification in the level of border control exercised by the Mexican government at the place of entry into Mexico is directly linked to the problem of narco-violence afflicting Mexico and its northern border regions. El Paso/Juárez ports of entry are considered the nerve center of the arms trade and the narco-money laundering that fuel Mexico's drug cartel wars (Esquivel 2010). President Felipe Calderón, for instance, has characterized the stream of smuggled weapons as one of the most significant threats to security in his country (McKinley 2009). According to the attorney-general of Arizona, "the characteristic of the arms trade is it's a parade of ants—it's not any one big dealer, it's lots of individuals," he said. "That makes it very hard to detect because it's often below the radar" (Ayres 2009).

The most common way of smuggling firearms and narco-dollars into Mexico is repeated trips across the border of one to three guns and moderate sums of money "referred to in border parlance as the ant (*hormiga*) run" (Esquivel 2010). According to a US Customs and Border Protection officer, this process involves people who live in Ciudad Juárez but cross the border daily to work or shop in El Paso and who are recruited and paid by members of Mexican drug cartels to introduce moderate sums of money ranging between 5,000 and 10,000 dollars and weapon parts on their way back to Mexico in their backpacks, purses, shopping bags, etc. (Esquivel 2010). According to the officer, the only way to find the drug money and the firearms that are introduced on the Mexican territory through Ciudad Juárez would be the systematic inspection of all pedestrians entering Mexico through the international bridges, something that might be facilitated by the imminent installation of X-ray equipment in pedestrian lines to detect the contents of backpacks (Neyoy 2009).

While Mexican authorities say they are confident that the inspections will enhance their ability to spot traffickers, some experts are much more skeptical about their chances of slowing the weapons supply (Marosi 2009). According to a gun trafficking expert with the Mexican think tank collective for the Analysis of Security and Democracy, gunrunners easily smuggle thousands of weapons in small numbers at a time, taking them apart and hiding them in suitcases or even televisions and DVD players. These weapons wouldn't necessarily be detected by weight. In addition, "if the car has no criminal record, and is apparently legal, it will not necessarily be stopped and checked," she said (Olson 2009).

Moreover, the new infrastructure has already created concern in the business community that the new inspection procedures will have an additional economic impact on already-long border crossing wait times when it comes to entering Mexico (Navarro 2009). During the system's initial test phase, some Mexican border-crossers have complained of long delays upon returning to Mexico. With traffic backups awaiting them on the way back home, "there's going to be no incentive for consumers from Mexico to come across," according to Juan Carlos Escamilla, the mayor of San Luis, Arizona. Economics are a serious concern in American border communities like San Luis given that this city's sole source of tax revenue is sales tax money, which is largely generated by consumers from Mexico who cross the border (Neyoy 2009). "We are not opposed to homeland security, we are not opposed to national security," he said. "But we are opposed to the burden on our community." This kind of reaction towards the new technology that is being implemented by Mexican customs authorities clearly illustrates the tension between trade and security at the border.

Discussion

At the moment, it remains difficult to foresee the extent to which the cross-border mobility of Mexican *fayuqueros* can be affected by the implementation of new security policies at the Mexican ports of entry. A system like SIAVE in which vehicles are weighed, checked against an official weight table and diverted to secondary inspection if they exceed a pre-set weight parameter can without doubt interfere with the cross-border activities of large importers of used clothing like Paty. In a similar way, the installation of X-ray equipment in pedestrian lines to detect the contents of backpacks and suitcases could be highly detrimental to small-scale cross-border traders like Rosa.

In an interview given by the administrator for Mexican customs in Tijuana one year after the implementation of SIAVE, the official revealed that the new border inspection system was being very successful with regard to the smuggling of pirated and consumer goods that affects the activities of established merchants—with an average of MXN$4 million worth of goods seized every month. According to the official, this represents a 15 percent increase that can be directly attributed to SIAVE (Juárez 2010). In fact, the new border inspection system seems to be much more effective in catching motorists carrying consumer goods like used clothing than in stopping the flow of illegal weapons.

In a paper commissioned in the course of a joint project on US–Mexico security cooperation coordinated by the Mexico Institute at the Woodrow Wilson Center and the Trans-Border Institute at the University of San Diego, Douglas Farah (2010: 17) provides some interesting evidence about the system's limited impact on detecting weapons. According to the author, the most telling information came from Mexican border authorities who are monitoring an important border crossing area where two gamma-ray machines were installed in 2009 for non-intrusive inspections of southbound vehicles. By their admission, Mexican officials acknowledged that the system has led to no bulk cash seizures and had a limited impact on detecting weapons in that area since it was installed in November 2009. "We really cannot say SIAVE has helped us at all with bulk cash," said one Mexican official (Farah 2010: 17).

The situation seems to be similar in Ciudad Juárez, where not a single firearm has been confiscated in the first half of 2010 according to statistics provided by the administrator for Mexican customs in Juárez (Diario de Juárez, 2010). Moreover, the fact of replacing all the customs agents does not seem to have resolved the problem of corruption. Indeed, corruption allegations involving payoffs to OCE agents were already coming out in the local newspapers less than a year after their arrival in the area of Ciudad Juárez. The new Mexican customs personnel reported pressures by organized crime for the introduction of firearms and other merchandise into the interior of Mexico (*Diario de Juárez*, 2010). The local smuggling scene and corruption allegations against Mexican customs authorities are the focus of intensive coverage by local newspapers.

In the course of my fieldwork, the cross-border activities of some of my informants were affected on several occasions due to the coverage of corruption in the local press (Gauthier 2010). Every time information regarding the possibly illegal behavior of customs agents starts to circulate in the media, the *fayuqueros* can expect to be given a very hard time by Mexican customs authorities anxious to safeguard their image. In the following weeks, one can hear the refrain, "*Ya no hay pasada!*" (There is no more passing). Or alternatively, "*Ya no hay arreglo.*" (Basically, the fix isn't in, there is no arrangement). Within a month, however, things are usually back to normal along the border as the public's attention begins to focus on other matters.

Interestingly, most people I have talked to in these circumstances agreed on the fact that the customs authorities could not prevent them from introducing their merchandise across the Mexican ports of entry indefinitely. Moreover, many of them were extremely confident about their capacity to continue to operate in the future with the complicity of corrupt officials by maintaining or building new alliances with them through the *mordida* system. As Martínez (1994: 53) points out, "while government intervention is expected for the purpose of enforcing national tariff laws or keeping out undesirable products, borderlanders also expect officials to be flexible and tolerant, allowing a certain amount of illegal traffic to go on in order to maintain the delicate interdependence between the two sides of the border."

Overall, Mexican *fayuqueros* "have interests that run counter to those of the 'ordinary' traders, in that they need a flexible border with low levels of control" (Grimson 2002: 154). The new border inspection system's effectiveness remains to be seen and further research is needed in order to more fully understand the tension between "smart and secure borders" and low-end globalization in the northern Mexican borderlands. Yet, there is already some evidence about the system's limited impact on detecting weapons and narco-dollars. Because those market flows are rooted in the unique economic integration of the border region, they remain the most convincing evidence that the new border-security policies are unsuccessful. It is not immediately evident that technology can resolve the tension between the imperatives of securitization and globalization along the US–Mexico border. On one hand, the implementation of new security measures aimed at helping Mexican authorities detect drug money, weapons and other contraband that are smuggled into Mexico from the United States reflects "the concern of the state to demonstrate its ability to safeguard its territory and citizens from external and internal threats" (Donnan and Wilson 2010: 16). On the other hand, the needs to check cars must be balanced with the imperative to keep traffic flowing and not cause backups that have a significant economic impact. According to Farah (2010: 10), "that tension, between security concerns and trade concerns, is one that will likely grow in coming years as traffic grows."

This chapter has described the tug-of-war between such illicit networks, which are culturally and socioeconomically part of the borderland economy, and increased border-security policies. The economic activities of cross-border traders described in this chapter are supported by a variety of mechanisms including trust within networks and reliance on corrupt officials and institutions (Smart 1988, Heyman and Smart 1999). This chapter shows how top-down security policies often overlook the complex net of loyalties and interests in which smugglers, sellers and law-enforcement agents are entrenched. By detailing the strategies that Mexican *fayuqueros* must use on a daily basis to subvert the ever-tightening border control that they are facing when they re-enter Mexico, this chapter illustrates the limits of increased border securitization and commodity controls in practice.

References

Anderson, J. (2001) *Theorizing State Borders: 'Politics/Economics' and Democracy in Capitalism*, CIBR/WP01-1, Belfast: CIBR Working Papers in Border Studies.

Ayres, C. (2009) "US Cracks Down on Sinaloa Drug Cartel as Mexico Sends in the Army," *The Times*, February 27.

Batista, H. P. (2003) "Extreman Fiscales Revisión en Puentes" [Mexican Customs Officers Maximize Inspections on Bridges], *El Diario de Juárez*, November 27.

Bogan, J. (2005) "Illegal Resale Trade in Mexico Offers *Ropa Usada* for Dirt Cheap Prices," *San Antonio Express-News*, August 22.

Campbell, H. (2005) "Chicano Lite: Mexican-American Consumer Culture on the Border," *Journal of Consumer Culture* 5(2): 207–33.

——(2009) *Drug War Zone: Frontline Dispatches from the Streets of El Paso and Juárez*, Austin: University of Texas Press.

Campbell, H. and J. Heyman (2007) "Slantwise: Beyond Domination and Resistance on the Border," *Journal of Contemporary Ethnography* 36(1): 3–30.

Cichocki, B., M. Menkiszak, K. Pelczyńska-Nałęcz, and A. Wilk (2001) *The Kaliningrad Oblast in the Context of EU Enlargement*, CES Studies 2. Warsaw: Centre for Eastern Studies.

Donnan, H. and T. Wilson (eds) (1999) *Borders: Frontiers of Identity, Nation and State*, Oxford: Berg.

——(2010) *Borderlands: Ethnographic Approaches to Security, Power and Identity*, Lanham, MD: University Press of America.

Diario de Juárez (2010) "Aduanales Corruptos Dejan que Juárez se Inunde de Armas" [Corrupt Mexican Customs Officers allow Juárez to be Flooded with Weapons], *El Diario de Juárez*, June 24.

Esquivel, J. (2010) "El Paso–Juárez: El Tráfico de la Muerte" [El Paso–Juárez: The Trafficking of Death], *Proceso*, February 8.

Farah, D. (2010) *Money Laundering and Bulk Cash Smuggling: Challenges for the Merida Initiative*, Woodrow Wilson International Center for Scholars, Working Paper Series on US–Mexico Security Cooperation, May.

Ferrer-Gallardo, X. (2008) "The Spanish–Moroccan Border Complex: Processes of Geopolitical, Functional and Symbolic Rebordering," *Political Geography* 27: 301–21.

Flynn, D. (1997) "'We are the Border': Identity, Exchange, and the State along the Bénin–Nigeria Border," *American Ethnologist* 24(2): 311–30.

Freeman, C. (2001) "Is Local: Global as Feminine: Masculine? Rethinking the Gender of Globalization," *Signs: Journal of Women in Culture and Society* 26(4): 1007–37.

Galemba, R. (2008) "Informal and Illicit Entrepreneurs: Fighting for a Place in the Neoliberal Economic Order," *Anthropology of Work Review* 29(2): 19–25.

García, S. J. (2009) "Aduana no se Militariza Aclara Administrador" [Customs Not Militarizing, Says Mexican Customs' Deputy Administrator] *El Mexicano*, August 18.

——(2010) "Fotografían Autos al Entrar al País" [Cars Photographed Upon Entering the Country], *El Mexicano*, March 2.

Gauthier, M. (2010) "Researching the Border's Economic Underworld: The *Fayuca Hormiga* Trade in the US–Mexico Borderlands," in H. Donnan and T. M. Wilson, eds, *Borderlands: Ethnographic Approaches to Security, Power and Identity*, Lanham, MD: University Press of America, 53–72.

Grimson, A. (2002) "Hygiene Wars on the Mercosur Border: Local and National Agency in Uruguaiana (Brazil) and Paso de los Libres (Argentina)," *Identities: Global Studies in Culture and Power* 9(2): 151–72.

Hann, C. and I. Hann (1992) "Samovars and Sex on Turkey's Russian Markets," *Anthropology Today* 8(4): 3–6.

Heyman, J. (1994) "The Mexico–United States Border in Anthropology: A Critique and Reformulation," *Journal of Political Ecology* 1: 43–66.

——(2004) "Ports of Entry as Nodes in the World System," *Identities: Global Studies in Culture and Power* 11(3): 303–27.

——(2010) "US–Mexico Border Cultures and the Challenge of Asymmetrical Interpenetration," in H. Donnan and T. Wilson, eds, *Borderlands: Ethnographic Approaches to Security, Power and Identity*, Lanham, MD: University Press of America, 21–34.

Heyman, J. and A. Smart (1999) "States and Illegal Practices: An Overview," in J. Heyman, ed., *States and Illegal Practices*, Oxford: Berg.

Holguin, R. (2009) "Mexico Makes Significant Border Changes," *KABC-TV Los Angeles*, December 3.

Holtom, P. (2003) "Coping with the Future of the Small-Scale Cross-Border Traders in Kaliningrad's Borderlands," in H. M. Birckenbach and C. Wellmann, eds., *The Kaliningrad Challenge: Options and Recommendations*, Münster: Kieler Schriften zur Friedenswissenschaft, Bd. 10, (Kiel Peace Research Series 10), LIT Verlag.

Juárez, U. E. (2010) "Decomisa Aduana 4 mdp de Mercancía Mensualmente" [Mexican Customs Seize MX$4 Million Worth of Merchandise Monthly], *El Mexicano*, October 28.

Kloppers, R. (2004) *Border Crossings: Life in the Mozambique/South Africa Borderland*, PhD Dissertation, University of Pretoria.

Lahusen, S. (1989) "Everyday Peasant Resistance 'Seen From Below': the Anthropological Approach of James C. Scott," *JASO* 20(2): 173–79.

Malkin, E. (2003) "Mexico Making Headway on Smuggling," *New York Times*, June 5.

Marosi, R. (2009) "Mexico Tightens Security at U.S. Border Crossings," *Los Angeles Times*, November 24.

Martínez, J. O. (1994) *Border People: Life and Society in the U.S.–Mexico Borderlands*, Tucson: University of Arizona Press.

McKinley, C. J. (2009) "U.S. Is Arms Bazaar for Mexican Cartels," *New York Times*, February 26.

Minjáres, G. (2003) "Fayuquean 5 Toneladas de Ropa Cada Día" [They Smuggle Five Tons of Used Clothing Daily], *El Diario de Juárez*, November 24.

Nájera, H. (2007) "En la Frontera Norte, el Primer Mundo se Vive con Artículos de Segunda" [On the Border, The First World Lives on Second Hand Goods], *El Diario de Juárez*, June 18.

Navarro, T. (2009) "Mexico's New Border Inspection System Has Business Leaders Worried," *San Diego News Network*, November 27.

Neyoy, C. (2009) "Upcoming Border System Draws Concerns," *Yuma Sun*, October 31.

Nordstrom, C. (2000) "Shadows and Sovereigns," *Theory, Culture & Society* 17(4): 35–54.

O'Day, P. and A. Lopez (2001) "Organizing the Underground NAFTA: *Fayuqueros* and *el arreglo*," *Journal of Contemporary Criminal Justice* 17(3): 232–42.

Olson, A. (2009) "Entry to Mexico Toughens: Mexican Customs Changes Tactics as Way to Stop Guns," *El Paso Times*, April 1.

Pallitto, R. and J. Heyman (2008) "Theorizing Cross-Border Mobility: Surveillance, Security and Identity," *Surveillance & Society* 5(3): 315–33.

Payan, T. (2006) "The Drug War and the U.S.–Mexico Border: The State of Affairs," *South Atlantic Quarterly* 105(4): 863–80.

Ribeiro, G. L. (2009) "Non-Hegemonic Globalizations. Alter-native Transnational Processes and Agents," *Anthropological Theory* 9(3): 297–329.

Ruiz, C. (2005) "Chinos Venden a la Virgen y a Juan Diego en un Dólar" [Chinese Sell the Virgin and Juan Diego for $1], *Periodico Norte de Ciudad Juárez*, August 7.

Schendel, W. van and I. Abraham (eds) (2005) *Illicit Flows and Criminal Things: States, Borders and the Other Side of Globalization*, Bloomington: Indiana University Press.

Scott, J. (1985) *Weapons of the Weak: Everyday Forms of Peasant Resistance*, New Haven: Yale University Press.

Smart, A. (1988) "The Informal Regulation of Illegal Economic Activities: Comparisons Between the Squatter Property Market and Organized Crime," *International Journal of the Sociology of Law* 16: 91–101.

Staudt, K. (1998) *Free Trade? Informal Economies at the U.S.–Mexico Border*, Philadelphia: Temple University Press.

Yükseker, D. (2004) "Trust and Gender in a Transnational Market: The Public Culture of Laleli, Istanbul," *Public Culture* 16(1): 47–65.

Zarembo, A. (1999) "Mexico's Hot 'Chocolates': One Governor Cracks Down on Cars Smuggled from the United States," *Newsweek International*, August.

9

AFRICAN TRADERS IN GUANGZHOU

Routes, reasons, profits, dreams

Yang Yang

In mid-July 2009, a local Guangzhou police station was surrounded by more than 100 African protesters. An African man had previously been in an illegal money exchange store during a police raid, and without a legal visa document, he fled and jumped from the window and subsequently died. The African community was furious over the man's death, and over the frequent immigration raids that led to his death; they took the dead man's body to the police station, expressing their anger and demands for justice. The event brought worldwide media attention to the existence of a large African population in southern China who live at the margins of the law trading goods between China and Africa.

In the past decade, tens of thousands of African traders have arrived in Guangzhou, the major city of China's "world factory" of Guangdong Province. It is estimated that in 2009 there were about 20,000 Africans living long-term in Guangzhou and thousands more visiting the city regularly (*South China Morning Post* 2009). They gather around several major wholesale markets near the old railway station in the city and purchase Chinese manufactured goods in bulk for shipment back to Africa, particularly West Africa. Many traders manage to open their own shops and become middlemen in this lucrative global business. Due to their large African population, districts of Guangzhou such as Sanyuanli and Xiaobei have become known as "Chocolate City," "Little Africa," and "Guangzhou's Harlem."

Large proportions of the goods vended in these districts are illegally brought into traders' home countries. Nigeria, where many African traders in Guangzhou come from, banned the importation of textile products in 2002 to block foreign competition (BBC 2002), but textiles remain one of the most common items among traders, who bribe customs officials in Nigeria to bring their goods into the country. Even if they are brought through home customs legally, they are typically related to illegal or semi-legal business activities such as counterfeiting, smuggling, and underground banking. Reliable and smooth handling of the goods and money is therefore possible only through personal networks. Nonetheless, traders often find themselves facing bankruptcy not just because of bad business management, but often because of China's visa policy and local corruption.

Based on extended fieldwork in Guangzhou, this chapter explores the routes, livelihoods, and motivations of African traders in southern China through their individual stories. It discusses the organization of the market as well as individual economic activities reflecting economic globalization from below, where traders with relatively small capital can potentially become upwardly mobile by taking advantage of the infrastructural advancements made possible in the modern age of globalization, such as fast international transportation, convenient communication, mass manufacturing, and brand recognition, for short-term gains.

The trading activities of the Africans in Guangzhou represent an economic "underworld," a world that is not only untraceable through customs or by economic surveys, but is also rapidly proliferating throughout the developing world; it represents, in short, a key site of "globalization from below." Numerous papers have been published on Chinese investment and interests in African countries (Alden 2007; Mohan and Power 2009; Prah 2007; Rotberg 2008; Tull 2006; Waldron 2008), but only a little research has thus far been conducted concerning Africans in China. Bodomo (2010) has explored through surveys the demographic profiles of the African population in Guangzhou. He proposes that the traders serve as bridges between the Chinese and Africans, which the authorities in China should recognize in order to make more business-friendly policies. Li *et al.* (2009) have also gathered information through survey, and argue that an ethnic enclave has formed in Guangzhou, resulting in racial conflicts and social instability. They argue from the perspective of the local community, leaving aside any discussion of how this trade is significant in the larger picture of China–Africa connection and globalization processes. However, the African traders, Chinese local residents, Chinese factory owners, and the governments of the nations involved obviously have very different visions of what the future should look like. In this chapter, more ethnographic in focus than the work cited above, I discuss the lives, livelihoods, and views of African traders in Guangzhou, a group whose voices have generally, as of yet, been unheard.

There are number of books exploring African diaspora communities working in the informal economy. MacGaffey and Bazenguissa-Ganga (2000) discuss the stories of Congolese traders in Paris. Some of these traders are undocumented migrants, while others are students who failed academically; still others are former government employees, whose opportunities for achieving better lives are hindered by their societies back home. In selling forged passports and smuggling goods, these traders represent a "second economy" which is legally, spatially, and institutionally marginalized; the disorder of their community is essentially a form of resistance for the disempowered, they claim (MacGaffey and Bazenguissa-Ganga 2000: 171). Stoller (2002) discusses West African street vendors, often Muslims, from Senegal, Mali, Niger, and Gambia, earning a living in New York City selling African masks, drums, patterned cloth, and African music tapes. He describes the reproduction of West African-style markets in America and the socio-economic problems that many traders have to face while trying to support their relatives back home.

This chapter parallels these earlier studies, but focuses on the role of African traders in the informal economy in China, which is now one of the world's newer sites for cheap and counterfeit manufactured goods. It is the source of many of the products discussed in other chapters of the book. China's position in the world-system is ambiguous—while China is the world's second largest economy, it is also still a developing country. China is largely ethnically homogeneous; its strict immigration policy makes it hard for foreigners, especially those from the developing world, to obtain Chinese visas. Linguistically, the local people speak very little English, and virtually no French or Arabic or other languages spoken by these traders, and very few traders speak Chinese. I have heard many accounts of fraud made possible through the language barriers experienced by most Africans in Guangzhou. Almost every trader avoids using the official Chinese banks because of the complex and bureaucratic money exchange protocols. Instead, they look to underground banks, at the risk of being caught in a police raid. Despite all these difficulties, China still attracts numerous West African traders, for reasons that are distinctively different from the cases of Congolese in France or West African Muslims in New York. They only want to make money in China and very few would like to live in China, a sentiment often shared freely and openly by African traders.

Having been the norm of business for millenia before the industrial revolution, individual traders remain an important conduit between buyers and producers throughout much of the developing world. This is especially true between China and Africa, where the African traders are today's Arabs on the new "Silk Road" (see Pliez's chapter in this volume), with cotton or synthetic clothes instead of silk, and freight services in place of camels. The African traders are essentially middlemen, who come to the source of their goods, the Chinese producers; they are competing with Chinese and African retailers back in their home countries to get their textiles and electronic goods to market at the lowest possible prices.

The African and Latin American consumers who eventually buy these products cannot afford the goods produced by the core countries that so many seek. South China, as a major generator of cheap and low-quality and often copied goods, serves as a source for these goods flowing from the semi-periphery to the periphery (Mathews 2011: 209). Chungking Mansions in Hong Kong (see Mathews' chapter 4) is one of the many markets like Guangzhou's Sanyuanli, where traders from less developed districts buy Chinese counterfeits. Compared to the African markets in China, there is less state control over Chungking Mansions; in Chinese markets, efforts at state control are frequent; but like Chungking Mansions these markets in China involve traders of various cultural backgrounds pursuing their economic interests, transcending all potential religious and racial conflicts.

The globalization from below practiced in these markets is non-hegemonic, in the sense that it does not aim to combat or to destroy legal businesses and laws within different societies. The practitioners of this form of globalization from below pursue a similar dream of becoming rich and having a better living just like the CEOs of multinational corporations. In places like Sanyuanli and Xiaobei, these traders are given the opportunity to take their share of the economic prosperity of the world. As Ribeiro

(2009: 325) argues, these transnational grassroot traders integrate into the global economy through "blurring borders, creating transfrontier social spaces, and linking different global fragmented spaces." Through this non-hegemonic process of globalization, they are able to gain upward mobility and economic survival, albeit through contesting and circumventing in multiple countries laws and regulations (Falk 1999; Li *et al.* 2009; Mathews 2007, 2011).

These traders are engaged in globalization from below through channels of the informal economy. As opposed to the formal economy, the informal economy is defined as the transaction of goods or services outside national economic calculation, in three ways: 1) international customs calculations are ignored; 2) transactions go unreported; and 3) the added value is not discovered (Schneider and Enste 2003: 9). Some economic anthropologists also refer to the informal economy as the "anti-economy" (Halperin and Sturdevant 1990: 324), either deviating from the mainstream economy (such as smuggling or drug-dealing) or operating in parallel to the mainstream economy (such as street vending and small household businesses). By these definitions, the structure of the informal economy in different countries is invariably dependent on the laws and regulations of these countries. In fact many small businesses across the world today are not fully compliant with the law, and in this sense the labeling of some economic activity as "underground" or "informal" may be misleading (see Morales 2007: 266).

The informal sectors of many countries of the world are growing larger in an age of globalization, which is especially true in developing countries where a greater part of people's economic activities is hidden from the official record. Schneider and Enste (2003: 29–42) analyzed the size of the shadow economy in 76 countries and found that the percentage of the informal "shadow" economy in gross national product (GNP) is more than 30 percent in Africa, Latin America, and most of Asia, while Organisation for Economic Co-operation and Development (OECD) countries have the lowest percentage, at 12 percent. China and sub-Saharan African countries have a large proportion of their economies in the shadow economy, which has been an important contributor to the Chinese economic miracle since the 1980s in Guangzhou, Wenzhou, Xiamen, Beijing, Qingdao, Jinan, and other cities (Hsu 2009: 6). In many sub-Saharan African countries, the informal economy is one of the major ways to deal with poverty and is an important source of employment for young people (Lachaud 1990).

This chapter, in describing the lives and livelihoods of African traders in south China, portrays the African diaspora involved in China's informal economy in particular, in the context of China being economically open, but politically closed to foreign traders. Through the flow of goods and people between China and the African continent, we can understand what globalization means for these petty entrepreneurs, who trade in places where they are cultural outsiders and where they continually risk running afoul of foreign law in their course of business.

African traders: who they are and where they come from

The China–Africa trade relation was established as the People's Republic of China (PRC) government was founded. From 1949 to 1977, the relationship was political as China assisted Africa with food, money, living necessities, and military training to fight against colonialism and hegemony (Li, 2008: 23–25). After the 1978 Reforms, more emphasis had been put on economic cooperation: China seeks to obtain from African countries raw materials such as crude oil, iron, cotton, and diamonds; African imports from China include electrical appliances, textiles, machinery, chemicals, and so on (Ampiah and Naidu, 2008: 7–8; Li, 2008: 31). It was also after the Reform that China embraced a more liberal economy and its manufacturing industry became increasingly privatized and deregulated. Guangzhou became known as the "world's factory" as the private manufacturers flourished in southern China, where cheap goods are produced with low labor costs. Around the same time, market demand in the populous regions of West Africa underwent a rapid expansion. For instance, the Nigerian markets rely heavily on imports, earning Nigeria a reputation as the "cargo economy"—"ships laden with containers docking at Nigeria's ports and returning almost empty to their places of origin, as Nigeria does not have much to export" (Ogunsano, 2008: 198). On the other hand the country has fragile and malformed democratic institutions, where individual life and property cannot be ensured with safety, particularly from Nigeria's corrupt government (Alden, 2007: 68; Ogunsano, 2008: 196). Such a situation has deepened the local market's dependency on foreign imported goods, especially from China.

In the 1980s and the 1990s, African merchants flocked to the bi-annual Canton Fair in Guangzhou. The Canton Fair was started in 1957, and has since become the largest international trade fair in China. It is one of the preeminent expo events where Chinese manufactured goods are displayed and ordered for export to different corners of the world. The African markets found their inexpensive "gold mine in the east" here. In the late 1990s, many more individual dealers traveled from sub-Saharan countries to Guangzhou to order goods outside of organized fairs and events.

These individual traders differ from those Canton Fair businessmen from international firms in the sense that they do not own or represent any companies back in their countries, nor do they have funds for placing substantial orders. Instead of attending the trade fair held in officially built expo halls, these traders gather around the old railway station where shops are sublet to Chinese and African migrants, who are more likely to sell fake goods and participate in semi-legal activities. Instead of getting an official invitation letter to stay in China for three months, these traders find ways to buy invitation letters from Chinese suppliers they do not even know and, if they need to, overstay their visas. Instead of staying in nice hotels, these traders find free accommodation through networks or stay at specially discounted rooms in cheap hostels. Instead of having institutional guarantees and certificates, these traders may have nothing more than an oral promise or a hand-written receipt that is kept off the books. At the center of the "world's factory," Guangzhou, these African traders use the tools of globalization—fast transnational transportation and extremely convenient communication via mobile phone—to potentially build, with little start-up capital, entrepreneurial enterprises cutting across continents.

The traders in Guangzhou today come from Nigeria, Ghana, Mali, Cameroon, Senegal, Kenya, and Tanzania, among other countries. The majority are Nigerian Igbo, who are mainly Christians from Nigeria's eastern regions. Compared to other

Africans, these Igbo usually stay for longer periods in China and sometimes manage to open multiple shops in China, earning a reputation of being "very good at business." My Igbo friends said that they had to be good at business to survive, "If you want to know about Igbo, you need to know the history of the Biafran War": a Nigerian ethnic war in the late 1960s that resulted in the mass expropriations of Igbo wealth and property. "We became the poorest ethnic group in Nigeria, and we could not enter good entry-level jobs because we were discriminated against. So Igbo had to stand on their own feet and make profits from whatever possible means," one trader in Guangzhou said. Here is the story of another trader:

> Eric, who now owns two clothing shops in Guangzhou and Lagos, is one of the many traders who has started his business from scratch in China. When he was a 15-year-old boy in the Imo state of Nigeria, his family contacted a local clothes shop. They reached an agreement to let Eric become an apprentice in the shop. In the following nine years, Eric worked as a shop assistant while he learned about the textile market and sale techniques. He, as an apprentice, would only receive food, accommodation, and pocket money, but at the end of his apprenticeship Eric's master rewarded him with a small fortune in money, enough for him to buy a flight ticket to China and to rent a shop front there. By that time Eric had already heard about the "gold rush" in China, so he bought a flight ticket to Beijing, where he met some other African traders who told him of better opportunities in the south, in Guangzhou. With the money he was given by his master, he became successful by buying clothes from Chinese local factories and selling to other African traders in Guangzhou and also to Nigerian consumers in his Lagos shop.

Eric is among the fortunate traders who became successful with their previous experience as merchants in Africa. Some of them come from middle-class family backgrounds and have attended universities back in their home countries. I know several traders with bachelor degrees such as business management, electrical engineering, biochemistry, and even philosophy. Like college graduates in general, they do not find book knowledge useful in actual trading and have to find consultants in Guangzhou. Eric offers consultancy services to his peer traders new to China, for an undisclosed commission. He told me that even so, some traders were not willing to come back to China because they expected a better profession than that of a low-end trader. Eric sneered at these people, "The job market in Africa is bad. There is a better chance of getting money in China."

There are also many traders from relatively lower-middle class family backgrounds. They had to make harder efforts to find their way to China. Jeff's story is typical:

> Jeff was sent to become an apprentice in a clothing shop when he was 13 years old. He served his master for nine years before his master let him go with an amount of money sufficient to come to China. He bought a one-way ticket to Hong Kong three years ago and then crossed the border to Guangzhou. By then, he did not

have enough money left over to start a shop or buy much inventory. So he talked to a few people like himself and found employment in a Ghanaian logistics shop, where he became a laborer, transporting bulks of goods for freight or shipping. He worked for two years and, together with previous savings, he accumulated enough to open a shop. He is now married to a local Chinese woman and both work in the shop selling clothes and offering consultancy services to short-term traders.

Less fortunate traders end up losing all their money; my estimate is that about half of the African traders who come to Guangzhou lose all their money, often money that their relatives invested with them. Desperate traders sometimes make a scene at the market after losing money. Eric's new Nigerian neighbor on the same market floor once started a fistfight with Eric. It turned out that the man, without knowledge of how to run a clothing business, had no customers for two months and was about to go broke; he blamed the surrounding shops for "stealing his customers." It proved to be an ineffective tactic, because after that incident no Africans would talk to him. A month later, his shop was closed. It was said that this man and his Chinese wife from Hebei had to return to Nigeria.

Most Africans I know seek to use the money they earn from their China trade to open shops in their homelands. There are a few others who have an ambition to invest in political campaigns in Africa with the hope of becoming politicians so that they could move up the social hierarchy much faster than they could through trading. Several traders who used to be soccer players in Nigeria participated in soccer matches in Guangzhou and Dongguan, with the hope of being noticed by scouts from the United States or Europe. Meanwhile, they also trade to accumulate capital for themselves and their relatives. Few African traders, however, view China as a home. "China is not my place. I come here just to make money. Nothing else. Once I get the money I want, I will leave."

The markets

Within and around Guangzhou, I conducted three months of fieldwork, concentrating in the Sanyuanli (三元里), Xiaobei (小北), and Foshan (佛山) districts.

These three districts house the majority of the African population in Guangdong province and are distinctly different from neighboring communities. Sanyuanli, where I spent most of my time researching, is a Nigerian- and Ghanaian-based market and has a large population of long-term African middlemen who sell goods to traders coming from West Africa. Xiaobei is mainly populated by Muslims and is a more expensive market, with more short-term traders from Islamic areas in Africa and the Middle East, such as Mali, Senegal, Guinea, Northern Nigeria, Yemen, and Jordan. Foshan is a neighboring city of Guangzhou, but its cheap rents and convenient transportation links with the above two trade areas make it a major African residential area, especially for traders who can't afford hotels or don't hold valid visas.

FIGURE 9.1 Fieldwork location. Map by Yang Yang. Reproduced with permission

There are two kinds of markets in Guangzhou that African merchants go to: "African markets," where there is a high percentage of African-owned shops, and Chinese wholesale markets, where stores are managed by Chinese locals. The former are a popular trade destination, particularly for short-term traders from Africa, because they can easily find business consultants and shop assistants who speak fluent Igbo, French, and Arabic, as well as English. As discussed later, there are also many informal agencies in these markets that facilitate the needs of African traders in terms of finance and living. The latter mainly accommodate Chinese buyers and there is much less accommodating of African traders. The language spoken in these markets is Chinese and there are no money exchange stalls for traders who only carry US currency, the standard currency taken out of Africa. Africans who go to these Chinese markets are usually either big clients who can afford to hire Chinese interpreters or "localized Africans" who have stayed for a lengthy period in China and often have shops/companies in the African market targeting short-term traders.

Sanyuanli, with approximately 20 percent of its shops managed by Africans, is a typical "African market" in Guangzhou. There are several trade buildings hosting a variety of small shops selling different kinds of products, as summarized in Table 9.1.

The African shops are not much different from the Chinese shops in terms of appearance. The clothes stores are stuffed with stocks of shirts piled up waist high. At the storefront, people affix steel chains to the ceiling to hang colorful shirt samples as displays. The clothes on display change almost on a daily basis and one can always sense the invisible hand of the market, as styles change to accommodate the desires of

TABLE 9.1 Trade buildings and goods in Sanyuanli

Buildings/centers	Trade goods
Tangqi (唐旗), Canaan (迦南), Old Tian (天恩), New Tian (新天恩), Baile (柏樂)	Clothes, handbags, shoes, electronics
Meibo (美博)	Cosmetic products, perfume
Ziyuangang (梓元崗)	Leather products, backpacks, handbags

customers—the middlemen in Guangzhou, and behind them, the retail customers back in Africa. In the Tangqi building, the African shop owners and shop assistants generally occupy the public resting area and corridors as they pile up clothing stocks that they can no longer fit in their small shops.

The African shops and the Chinese shops are distinctly different in one important respect: while many Chinese rent stores directly from the administrative department of the market, the Africans almost always get sublets. One can easily observe this by looking at the business license papers on the wall of these shops. To find a shop to start a business, some African traders find Chinese networks and some contract the services of real estate agencies or just look around for street advertisements. The Chinese use sublets too, but for Africans it is out of necessity rather than choice, unless they have Chinese wives or business partners. This is because for them, it is always best to avoid formally registering anything with their passports, thus avoiding *mafan* (trouble). The word *mafan* is probably the most popular Mandarin word among Africans in China, except perhaps *wo ai ni* (I love you). In one trader's opinion, "They [the police] require everything to be registered with my passport. When I check into a hotel, the staff needs to scan my passport. When I find a house to live, they need my passport. When I rent a shop, they want my passport. You Chinese are *mafan*. So many Chinese in my country [Nigeria] and we never give them *mafan*." *Mafan* in the context of registering means that their information can be easily traced by the Chinese police in case their visa expires, making it harder for these traders to return to China.

The existence of underground banks is a consequence of traders seeking to avoid having to present their passports to the authorities. The illegal money exchange stores are operated by Chinese who deal with the business community very discreetly. In Xiaobei, where police control is stricter, money exchange services are available by telephoned request and the business environment is a restaurant or café, where the police are less likely to raid. In Sanyuanli, on the other hand, the money exchange providers take up the disguise of a clothes shop to blend into the market. Nevertheless, it is still easy to tell them apart from bona fide clothes shops, in that these shops never actually sell any clothes. A typical underground bank in Sanyuanli often looks like a clothes shop that is about to go out of business: there are just a few jackets or shirts hanging on the wall and there is no inventory in the shop. The interior space is divided into two by a transverse thin wall with a small door. In front of the wall, there is a writing table where the shop owner sits and drinks tea. African traders come by and walk directly to the room behind the thin wall where no one catches the sight of their transaction.

FIGURE 9.2 African shops in Sanyuanli. Photo by Yang Yang. Reproduced with permission

The Chinese government forbids currency exchange outside of legal banks, which are usually government owned. It is a common irony to see an official notice saying "No illegal money exchange activity!" right next to these illegal banks. These underground bankers are only very rarely harassed by the authorities, with many of them having personal connections within the government banks. These banks make a profit by exploiting the exchange rate differential between the buying rate offered to their clients, from whom they buy at a deep discount, and the selling rate offered by the banks that they exchange with, to whom they sell at a more modest discount. The foreign traders still go to these banks because they do not want to go through the process of presenting passports. Newcomers may be curious about the credibility of these underground banks, because there is no security watching the door and there is no guarantee that the large amounts of RMB notes are authentic. But my African informants have never heard of a single case of money fraud at the money exchange. A trader explained, "They don't need to cheat. If they cheat, they don't have business anymore. It's not worth it." Other than immigration raids targeting visa overstayers, the market remains a peaceful and secure location for money transactions.

Money transfer services, on the other hand, are offered by the African logistics companies rather than by the Chinese underground banks. The firms also offer "customs clearance" services, which involve clearing the customs barriers for imported goods in West Africa. Although customs brokerage is a licensed profession in many countries, the ones in the African markets in China are illegal. My informants said that their method of clearing the barriers was to bribe customs officials. The logistics firms transport money, goods, samples, and sometimes gifts for mostly African clients. Since they are handling large sums of cash and goods, and crossing national borders, every logistics company has to be trustworthy and have diverse networks in the airlines and freight industries, including connections with many flight attendants, who can provide their personal luggage quotas during each flight and use it to transport goods between the two continents. The goods are charged by the kilo at a fixed rate. On the leaflets of the logistics companies that send goods to Nigeria, the kilo rates usually have several price ranges: for container, for air cargo, and for contraband goods and banned goods. The last price range includes fees to pay off the customs in Nigerian ports of entry.

African entrepreneurship in China

The most frequently traded clothes in the African market are made of cotton, from farms located in various northern Chinese provinces. The clothes factories in the Yangtze River Delta and Pearl River Delta buy the cloth and apply various fashion designs; these clothes are then sold through agencies at wholesale markets. Retailers from all over China and West African countries come to the wholesale markets and purchase clothing of various designs in bulk. The Africans, who have their own stores in Guangzhou, then divide the clothing into smaller shares to sell to short-term African traders, as in the case of the Sanyuanli market. The traders then ship the goods they bought by air and sea back home, where they sell the goods in their family-run stores or to other African local retailers.

"Money is the priority here." I was told by a trader. "You need to be smart and be aware of those who approach you. They always want something from you. You make sure you get something from them too." To become a successful entrepreneur, an African trader has to learn how to be street-smart while doing business in China.

An African trader needs to understand three things when participating in the industry. First, there is a tremendous profit margin on a single piece of clothing from the moment it is produced in the factory until purchased at a commercial retailer. Every market participant tries to earn a share by squeezing themselves somewhere into the supply chain. Clothes traders clearly benefit from buying and selling textile goods, but there is also a large subsidiary industry that relies on them, like the underground banking and logistics industries, which all add to the final cost of a piece of clothing. It is amazing how many interest groups can take profit from this process. Even an interpreter can increase the cost of the product. As I accompanied my informants to a wholesale market and helped them with translation, many wholesalers would first ask me, "Do you charge a commission?" Then I realized that it is very common for an English interpreter to charge, typically 0.5 percent of a transaction, to help conduct business smoothly. Just by adding more positive adjectives to the translation, an interpreter can influence the decision-making of the buyer.

Second, any price fluctuation in the supply chain can make a huge difference, and such fluctuations are closely linked to ongoing political and social issues. In 2010, the price for raw cotton material sharply increased, reaching the highest price of the last 15 years. It is reported that cotton prices increased by 20 percent during the Mid Autumn Festival in 2010, on September 22–24 that year (Cotton China 2010). African traders could pay some RMB 25 for a shirt of average workmanship in 2008, but now most shirts cost over RMB 30 per piece. The profit loss is very significant for traders, as they buy tens of thousands of pieces. A trader told me that since he had only about RMB 20,000, he ended up buying much less than he had come to expect from his experiences a year earlier:

> I had to pay much more for each shirt. Do you know what that means to me? I will have to sell at higher prices and people may not buy from me. They will go to shops that offer lower prices because they have cheaper stocks or they have connections with factories. Maybe somewhere the cotton farmers decided not to plant cotton anymore and go to work in the city, but this is bad for me and my clients. Now even the value of the RMB is so high, my money will be gone soon. I need to do something. I must find cheaper sources, or I will go to cheaper countries like India.

Third, fashion matters. It is risky for a trader to purchase large quantities of clothes within a short period, because he may have no buyers at all when fashions in Africa change. Compared to electronics and mobile phones, the clothing business is much more fickle in terms of style. The fashion in the Sanyuanli clothing market changes on a weekly basis; one can simply observe the different arrangement of clothes on display on the shop fronts to understand the changing fashions of distant sub-Saharan markets. The clothes sold from China and African local fashion trends have a mutual influence. An African trader said, "I ask my brothers in Nigeria to tell me what design is popular there. But sometimes when every trader sells certain kinds of clothes from here, it will form a trend in Nigeria." African shop owners in this sense are better positioned that their Chinese competitors not only because they share a common language with their African clients, but also because they can better understand fashion trends back home.

The stories of African traders in China often involve the contesting legal boundaries both in China and Africa. As mentioned above, many traders overstay their visas in order to gain more time for doing business. To avoid showing their passports to the authorities, they go to underground banks. In the case of the textile trade to Nigeria, bringing Chinese manufactured clothes into the country is forbidden, but the majority of Igbo traders are engaged in the clothing business and almost everyone find ways to smuggle the goods back into Nigeria. In the African market, everyone is aware of the semi-legality of their activities and that they need to do all they can to appear trustworthy and reliable, while at the same time, using deceit as much as they can to gain more profits.

The first key to success is networking. The business generally relies on trustworthy networks and credible employees. By knowing the right people, a trader can know where to find a certain product, which factory to contact, how to find the cheapest cargo service, whom to share a freight container with, and so on. Many African traders first came to China along with friends who had prior experience doing business in China; at the very least, they had talked to such people. Cliff, who used to be a soccer player in Nigeria, told me how he found his way to becoming a trader through networks. To quote from my fieldnotes:

> Cliff was enthusiastic about playing football and played for a club back in Imo Nigeria from his early adulthood. The job was not well paid and he, like his peers, wanted to go to Europe or North America to play professionally. Some friends in the club shared with him the story of making money in China, but he thought it was too far away. Later his soccer team went to Singapore to play and he lived there for a few months. Cliff worked as a part-time laborer at the port where he again saw containers of Chinese manufactured goods and decided that it would be good for him to go to China. He talked to sailors and friends who went to China many times and built up a few contacts; then he headed to Hong Kong where he met more friends and traveled to Guangzhou with them. He stayed at a friend's house at night and worked as a laborer at a Nigerian shop during the day. Eventually, he was able to open his own cargo firm, using his connections at the container companies and ports. Now Cliff hires new laborers for his firm and has opened a warehouse in Nigeria, where his family sells goods.

Traders who have excellent social skills often have similar stories to Cliff's, but there are also other ways to expand networks. The most popular social locations for Africans in China are the churches and amateur soccer clubs. In Xiaobei, Muslim traders often go to the Xiaodongying Mosque. Catholics go to the Shishi church. The Mosques and Catholic churches in Guangzhou are usually approved by the local government, while the Protestant churches are often not recognized by the Chinese government, and operate underground. There are several local soccer teams, each organized usually according to the nationality of the players. Regular soccer "world cups" are held in both Guangzhou and Dongguan, where teams of nationals from Nigeria, Ghana, Cameroon, Brazil, Japan, Korea, and France join the games. The churches sometimes also organize friendly matches during weekends. Traders' presence at these religious/sport activities enhances their credibility among peers and their ability to make connections.

These networks can also be bought through "consultancy" services, often advertised on the name cards of African shop owners. Eric is one of the many African business consultants in Guangzhou. When the economy is bad for buying products for his own store, Eric turns to offering consultancy services for newcomers. The summer is a trade season when many short-term traders come to China and Eric is often busy picking up his "friends" from the airport or train station to show them around Guangzhou. He offers information on sourcing, and in case his clients need to leave China before the goods are ready, he will help with quality checks and shipment. Eric told me that consultancy brings in most of his income during summer. "I gain from charging for the service and also from the Chinese factories. They know very well that they need to pay me a percentage of commission. If they don't, I won't bring them business next time. After all, it's fierce competition."

Playing tricks and avoiding being cheated are important to street-smart entrepreneurs. "I prefer to call it business management," a trader said. "I've studied in business school. Many big companies cheat by getting away with not paying some taxes, or underpaying the employees, or exaggerating profits to increase stock value. We cheat in similar ways." They "manage the business" in a down-to-earth sort of style: freeloading bus rides, reporting their goods as something else at customs, pretending to be short of money while bargaining, and delaying picking up goods so that they could use the supplying factory for temporary storage. However, these tricks do not generally jeopardize the economic well-being of those upon which they are employed, so they are more or less accepted.

Counterfeiting, on the other hand, involves contesting the boundary between legal and illegal, order and disorder. It is common for an African trader to send an original samples of products through a logistics company to Guangzhou, where local factories then manufacture thousands of copies of it. These samples are often European or American branded lighting systems, auto parts, computer components, electronic audio systems, shirts, and jeans. I saw a photo of an African trader leaning against a German construction scraper and at the bottom of the photo was written: "I want two of this machine made in China." It is also common for traders to download clothes patterns online, or travel to Hong Kong where they can buy several brand-name shirts, and then mass produce them in Guangzhou. It is not difficult to find Chinese private factories that copy everything from glasses frames to electric generators. China is one of the few places in the world with a highly productive manufacturing sector at a low cost combined with a general absence of intellectual property protection; and African traders are well aware of this.

The issue of the morality of bringing in large quantities of copied goods into Africa is complicated for many traders. In Sanyuanli and Xiaobei, everyone knows the goods on display are counterfeit. They understand well that they are cheating the capitalist system by taking advantage of technologies and designs that large corporations have spent billions investing in. They accept the fact that the influx of Chinese manufactured products may hurt the African local manufacturing industries, but still, most claim that "what I do is good for Africa." A trader said,

> Not many people in my country can afford original products from Europe and America. There is no way we can produce things in Nigeria as cheaply as China can. We come to China because it is cheaper than everywhere else. Because of the goods I take back, African people can buy more variety of things at lower prices. For a long time, we could only get second-hand 'dumped goods' from Europe and we are sick of that. We want something better and I am bringing Africans something better.

China is embarrassed by its involvement and complicity with African migrants in profiting from the production of what is probably the largest amount of fake goods in the world, which undermines its effort to build up the images of its cities as being developed and global. Between the 2008 Beijing Olympics and 2010 Asian Games in Guangzhou, frequent police raids have occurred both in African markets and the traders' residential districts. Since then, the African traders have had to become street-smart in dealing with the Chinese police too. It is said that even for Africans who hold legal visas and licenses, everyone must look out for themselves because "the police with 'mufti' [undercover police] sometimes just arrest anyone with black skin," causing chaos in the market. If an undercover policeman is by himself, the traders have learned to pay a bribe to get away. In case of serious raids, the traders pay the security guards to leak information about when the raid will happen and everyone will rapidly close their shops and hide for several hours. African traders must also learn the quickest routes of escape from each market building and the best locations for hiding.

In late July 2010, another African protest took place in Tangqi. It was one of many demonstrations that were not reported in Chinese mass media since the July 2009 incident. A group of undercover police ran into Tangqi and several other market buildings nearby to arrest traders with expired visas. With the help of a market security guard, they caught a Nigerian man, beat him up, and sent him to detention. African shop owners were outraged at the security unit of the building for helping the police; they shut all African shops and stood in the corridor, loudly chanting protests. The "peace maker," an African senior responsible for solving disputes, sought a meeting with the building manager. He said, "Our people try to do business here and we never get involved with drug problems or other crimes. The market should be a peaceful place for trading and the security should ensure that. Why did they sell us out? Why do the police only target Africans but not also other foreigners in China?" The protest ended as the traders organized among themselves and negotiated with the manager, who eventually dismissed the head of the security unit. Everyone knew that in the future they had to protect themselves and act "smarter" through networks rather than rely on the security guards for protection against police.

Conclusion

In the course of my research, Eric and Jeff and many other shop owners pondered whether they should close their businesses in Guangzhou and leave for other countries, because "China is only for business, but it is not good for living." Compared to developed regions in Europe and North America and East Asia, China lacks a secure investing and living environment for these traders. Nonetheless, the availability of cheap contraband products is something the traders cannot find in developed countries. As labor costs continue to rise in China, these traders may migrate to cheaper manufacturing centers in Southeast Asia that may eventually come to substitute for China in manufacturing cheap, perhaps counterfeit "first world products" for Africa. These countries too may provide a good place for business, but not for making a life. Between the lure of life in the developed world, and profits in the less developed world, China is where these traders remain for now.

FIGURE 9.3 A protest scene in Sanyuanli. Photo by Yang Yang. Reproduced with permission

The world's wealth distribution is becoming progressively more imbalanced in an age of neoliberal globalization. In countries in sub-Saharan Africa, it is the common people who are punished for the failings of their governments. Coming to China is a window to a better future for many African traders, who, although often among the better-off in their home countries, sense that they can prosper only by leaving their home countries. Coming to China provides a potential channel for these people to gain a share of the world's economic prosperity, and perhaps also benefit their fellow citizens back home—although how much they aid and how much they hurt their fellow citizens through their provision of cheap, short-lived goods remains an open question.

The African traders in south China embody self-interested efforts to bring globalization to those who lack the money to afford globalization as conventionally defined, through "economic globalization from below." As described in this chapter, this is a bittersweet process. While they are able to adopt street-smart strategies to overcome various obstacles, they face state and social condemnation. As a result, most African traders do not plan to ever settle down in the hostile environment of China. For now, given the lure of profit, China is able to attract these traders, but the future of such trade is becoming more uncertain. Today, "going to China" remains a golden opportunity for many young apprentices back in Africa, a ticket to potential personal wealth and to societal globalization for those areas of the world that have been thus far largely shut out.

References

Alden, C. (2007) *China in Africa*, London; New York: Zed Books.

Ampiah, K. and S. Naidu (2008) "Introduction: Africa and China in the Post-Cold-War Era," in S. Naidu and K. Ampiah, eds, *Crouching Tiger, Hidden Dragon? Africa and China*, Scottsville, South Africa: University of KwaZulu-Natal Press, 3–19.

Bodomo, A. (2010) "The African Trading Community in Guangzhou: An Emerging Bridge for Africa-China Relations," *China Quarterly* 203: 693–707.

British Broadcasting Corporation (BBC) (2002) "Nigeria Bans Textile Imports," http://news.bbc.co.uk/2/hi/business/2296025.stm (accessed October 28, 2010).

Cotton China (2010) http://www.cottonchina.org/news/pubzmb.php?articleid=104164&news time=2010-10-09 (accessed October 9 2010).

Falk, R. (1999) *Predatory Globalization: A Critique*, Cambridge: Polity Press; Blackwell.

Halperin, R. and S. Sturdevant (1990) "A Cross-Cultural Treatment of the Informal Economy," in E. Smith, ed., *Perspectives on the Informal Economy: Monographs in Economic Anthropology No 8*: Lanham, Maryland: University Press of America, 321–41.

Hsu, S. (2009) "Introduction," in J. Li and S. Hsu, eds, *Informal Finance in China: American and Chinese Perspectives*, Oxford: Oxford University Press, 3–11.

Lachaud, J. P. (1990) "The Urban Informal Sector and the Labour Market in Sub-Saharan Africa" in D. Turnham, B. Salome, and A. Schwarz, eds, *The Informal Sector Revisited*, Paris: OCDE, 111–130.

Li, A. (2008) "China's New Policy toward Africa," in Robert Rotberg, ed., *China into Africa: Trade, Aid, and Influence*, Washington DC: Brookings Institution Press, 21–48.

Li, Z., L. Ma, and D. Xue (2009) "An African Enclave in China: The Making of a New Transnational Urban Space," *Eurasian Geography and Economics* 50(6): 699–719.

MacGaffey, J. and R. Bazenguissa-Ganga (2000) *Congo-Paris: Transnational Traders on the Margins of the Law*, Bloomington: Indiana University Press.

Mathews, G. (2007) "Chungking Mansions: A Center of 'Low-End Globalization'," *Ethnology* 46(2): 169–83.

——(2011) *Ghetto at the Center of the World: Chungking Mansions, Hong Kong*, Chicago: University of Chicago Press.

Mohan, G. and M. Power (2009) "Africa, China and the 'New' Economic Geography of Development," *Singapore Journal of Tropical Geography* 30: 24–28.

Morales, A. (2007) "Conclusion: Law, Deviance and Defining Vendors and Vending," in J. Cross and A. Morales, eds, *Street Entrepreneurs: People, Place, and Politics in Local and Global Perspective*, London: Routledge, 262–69.

Ogunsano, A. (2008) "A Tale of Two Giants: Nigeria and China," in S. Naidu and K. Ampiah, eds, *Crouching Tiger, Hidden Dragon? Africa and China*, Scottsville, South Africa: University of KwaZulu-Natal Press, 192–207.

Prah, K. K. (2007) "China and Africa: Defining a Relationship," *Development* 50(3): 69–75.

Ribeiro, G. L. (2009) "Non-Hegemonic Globalizations: Alter-native Transnational Process and Agents," *Anthropology Theory* 9(3): 297–329.

Rotberg, R. (2008) *China into Africa: Trade, Aid, and Influence*, Washington DC: Brookings Institution Press.

Schneider, F. and D. Enste (2003) *The Shadow Economy: An International Survey*, Cambridge: Cambridge University Press.

South China Morning Post (2009) "Guangzhou's African Bind" November 29.

Stoller, P. (2002). *Money Has No Smell: The Africanization of New York City*, Chicago: The University of Chicago Press.

Tull, D. (2006) "China's Engagement in Africa: Scope, Significance and Consequences," *Modern African Studies* 44(3): 459–79.

Waldron, A. (2008) *China in Africa*, Washington DC: Jamestown Foundation.

10

IN THE SHADOW OF THE MALL

Street hawking in global Calcutta

Ritajyoti Bandyopadhyay

"Globalization from below" has often been conceived as a conjuncture of grassroots politics across the globe struggling against the dominating might of contemporary neoliberal capitalism (see, for example, Appadurai 2002). The chapters of this book deal less with the political aspects than with the economic aspects of globalization from below; but these two forms are of course linked. Jeremy Brecher, Tim Costello, and Brendan Smith (2000) hold that economic, political, and cultural inter-connectedness augmented by globalization is irreversible and is not unquestionably beneficial for the elite and perilous for the poor, though it is not class neutral. They accept the fact that the rich and powerful have shaped globalization in their interest thus far, but point out that there is a counter-movement that seeks to reshape our interconnected world in the interests of people and the planet—which they call, as do the chapters of this book, "globalization from below." As Gustavo Lins Ribeiro has pointed out, the "globalization from below" school has thus far been "almost exclusively focused on political resistance movements" (2006: 233), refracting our eyes from the on-the-ground reality of the small-scale economics of the poor in their efforts to negotiate globalization. The economic "globalization from below" perspective seeks to confer recognition on the spaces of subaltern entrepreneurialism that often remains off the map in globalization studies.

The economic "globalization from below" perspective reveals the limits and fragilities of all forms of corporate capital. Those who have studied the lives of the poor in the last few decades (especially in the cities of the South) oscillate between apocalyptic visions and hope in the resiliency of the poor. Consider the contemporary debates on post-colonial cities in the neoliberal age. Mike Davis (2004) and AbdouMaliq Simone (2004) champion the two poles of apocalypse and hope in urban studies. Davis shows us how street vendors and garbage pickers are symbols among the global urban poor of the public service casualties of structural adjustment. But his work does not tell us how the poor can derive agency to negotiate with the structural inequalities inherent within global forces. Simone's work, on the other hand, presents the cocktail of contestations and negotiations that actually constitute the operation of the African city, while emphasizing the potential for change and transformation.

While being aware of the danger of portraying the poor as passive recipients of global forces (Davis) and of an overemphasis on radical openness and contingency (Simone), in my work I hold these two perspectives in tension to situate Calcutta within the global economy without obscuring the struggles of the poorer social groups on the streets of Calcutta.[1] This chapter seeks to show how street vendors work and negotiate with the incarnation of corporate retail, shopping malls. I show that street vendors are not replaced by malls, but rather regroup around them, catering to the needs of those who come to the mall to visit as a ritual, participating in the spectacle of the world-class city, but who cannot afford to purchase anything, and also to those who work in the malls.

The contemporary public opinion and scholarship on corporate retail across the globe fall in either of the two positions: a celebratory pro-liberalization approach in which corporate retail is seen to carry the message of "enhancing consumer choice," and a more apocalyptic view that corporate retail will eventually destroy small retail by introducing highly capital-intensive supply chains. However, both the proponents and opponents of corporate retail agree that it ushers in a watershed in contemporary rural–urban economy (Anjaria 2008). The debate on corporate retail in India started in the first half of the present decade, and has been rejuvenated very recently by the government's decision to open 100 percent of single-brand retail and 51 percent of multi-brand retail to foreign retail monsters like Walmart. The proponents of foreign direct investment (FDI) in retail have argued that the retail giants would eliminate various oppressive vertical and backward linkages in the commodity chains enabling the end user to access the commodity at a cheaper price. The army of primary producers would benefit from the retail giant's mediation because they would have a greater share in the profit even though the price of the commodities would decline. The opponents, on the other hand, argue that the opening of retail to global market forces would eliminate small retailers from the market, thereby destroying the lifeline of millions of Indians (Kalhan 2007). The opponents have gathered an impressive corpus of data to argue that the *Walmartization* of Indian retail will lead to serious unemployment in the sector and that, in the long run, profit-seeking corporate agencies would start increasing their profit margins by raising the prices of the commodities once their competitors make an exit from the market. However, both the proponents and the opponents, representing a wide spectrum of political affiliations ranging from extreme left to extreme right, have come to an agreement that something has gone wrong with Indian retail due to the "oppressive" nature of the wholesalers and commission agents who suck out the primary producers' rightful profit. Ultimately, the debate takes a liberal democratic form in which all the parties assign victimhood to the classless and placeless army of primary producers and consumers giving ultimate credence to the well-known Walmart formula of combining retail and wholesale into one agency and mediating between producers and consumers with emphasis on commodity chain efficiency. The more the coordination in the commodity chain increases, the more the wholesalers become obsolete. The giant retailer then begins to source directly from farmers through contracts. This debate has failed to appreciate the role of the intermediary (always a contentious figure in the literature) in the process of commodity circulation.

The current debate conceives corporatization of retail as a zero sum game—either corporate retail or non-corporate retail will give way, to exit from the market. The chapter seeks to complicate the opposition between corporate retail and non-corporate retail. Contrary to the view that the mall radically transforms retail aesthetics and consumption, serving as a panacea to unruly street practices, I show how there is a synergistic relationship between hawkers and the malls, both of which coexist in the same space. The chapter shows how the corporatization of retailing has not uniformly affected the hawkers. Their responses to global market forces depend on the type of trade they conduct and their location. To illustrate this point, I present case studies of two areas of Calcutta: a) an area where shopping malls are a relatively new phenomenon (Gariahat and Prince Anwar Shah Road in south Calcutta), and b) an area which has a long association with the global retail economy (Esplanade in central Calcutta). I also show how, through a critical engagement with the corporate economy, hawkers actively consent to market rules and discipline themselves according to such rules. Finally, I discuss the story of an individual hawker and show how the small economy of the hawkers survives in a fast neoliberalizing city. This chapter seeks to comprehend how, in a city that in many people's minds is emblematic of the developing world, hawkers, the preeminent figures of economic globalization from below, relate to the neoliberal world of malls and high-end capitalism that is springing up around them. In so doing, the chapter emphasizes the immanent relation of globalization from above and globalization from below.

The small economy of hawkers

Hawkers occupying public spaces such as sidewalks, parks, and thoroughfares and thereby denying access to "rightful" users have been, over the years, a highly contentious issue in major cities across the globe. There is an impressive corpus of literature on street hawking (for a review of the literature, see Anjaria 2008), one I have attempted to add to in my own work situating hawking in the life-world of Calcutta streets and sidewalks. Calcutta sidewalks have served as a modern architectural means of ordering circulation on the street, a commercial terrain for shopkeepers and sidewalk vendors, a place of leisure for strollers, a platform for people waiting for public transport, a place for everyday survival for beggars, a space for debate and protest for political activists, and a site for city beautification: these sidewalks are implicated in complex social, economic, and political uses. Thus, the sidewalk in Calcutta is integral to a contested democracy in which multiple claims, meanings, and group interests are enacted and negotiated (Bandyopadhyay 2011).

The hawkers I have studied are generally associated with small local producers and buyers belonging to low- and middle-income groups. In Indian cities, hawkers constitute the classic example of the informal economy in the sense that their economic activities do not figure in national accounts and that they are not subject to the rules of contract, licensing, wage relations, labor inspection, and taxation. The entry to the market does not presuppose institutionally acquired skill from the candidate (Dey and Dasgupta 2010). Their scope remains limited: labor intensiveness (low capital requirement per worker); unsophisticated technologies; and an unregulated and competitive market. The primary motivation of these business activities is survival rather than return on investment. Hawking provides subsistence existence. Returns tend to be low and intermittent, security and stability are minimal, and working conditions are poor.

Street hawking expanded in Calcutta in relation to the economic decline following the independence and the partition of the country, high unemployment even among the skilled labor force, and a lack of standardization of consumption patterns. The high unemployment among the skilled and unskilled combined with fresh waves of refugee influx and continued streams of rural–urban migration led to a severe dislocation of Calcutta's economy. Between 1966 and 1971, the number of stalls on the sidewalks increased spectacularly (Dasgupta 1992). By 1981, it had spread to all parts of the city, irrespective of functional land use, with little available space for subsequent spatial expansion (Dasgupta 1992).

The spatial expansion of street vending was accompanied by a qualitative change. Social maps of every area of Calcutta in which hawkers are clustered, organized by the era in which they arrived and the products they vend, reveal the interesting fact that in no part of the city except the B.T. Road (where manufacturing industries are clustered) does the population of hawkers significantly come from the erstwhile industrial working class. A majority of the hawkers in Calcutta came to the city as rural–urban migrants, and refugees from East Pakistan, with agricultural and artisanal backgrounds. This is what makes the hawkers and the politics of the hawkers in Calcutta different from those of other Indian cities.

In Calcutta, the relationship between the established retail and the informal street markets is complex. There are places where the two forms of retail have developed a symbiotic relationship. In such places, hawkers target the low-end market. They often sell recycled products and offer various types of cheap services. They may also work as commissioned agents to the established shops, selling at cheaper rates goods that have remained unsold in the established shops. The established shops and the hawkers may also engage in a credit relation. The shop owners provide weekly loans to the hawkers to purchase goods and the hawkers repay the loans once they are able to sell their wares. In other cases, the hawkers and the shop owners may engage in a competitive relationship. The hawkers divert the attention of the customer from the established shops, or they encroach upon the shop frontage and thereby irritate the shop owners. The probability of a police raid is less in areas where hawkers complement the interests of shop owners.

The hawkers are also important political actors in the city. Unlike the squatter groups or slum dwellers in Calcutta, the hawkers do not exist as a vote bank, as they commute from different parts of the city (this differs from Mexico City, as Vega explores in chapter 12). However, they do serve the local leaders and power brokers. They provide money for political campaigns and maintain order in the locality. In return, they receive protection and patronage from the leaders. Even the local-level state operators are complicit to such acts. The political leaders depend on hawkers to control streets and neighborhoods. The police constables and low-ranking municipal workers regularly come to the hawkers for cheap food and services and collect *hafta* (weekly bribes in cash and kind) from them. The relationship between constables and hawkers are often very cordial, as both parties understand petty corruption as a continuous performance. Even in moments of extreme state hostilities towards hawkers, the street-level state operators accept services from hawkers and provide warnings of police raids.

The hawker unions play an important role in fixing terms with other political and administrative actors. They maintain street order and impose restrictions on the"unruly" activities of the hawkers. These unions maintain a constant database on the activities of hawkers, updating and digitalizing their information. The unions mediate between the hawkers and high-level state actors, and organize regular campaigns and road shows, publish pamphlets justifying the importance of the street trade in the public domain, block the local police station if the hawkers' wares are confiscated, and vigorously participate in the Calcutta Municipal Corporation's planning endeavors. The Corporation finds it extremely difficult to conduct a street survey or implement a code of conduct for the hawkers without the active support of the unions. These unions are often large in terms of membership status and the volume of trade they cover may be substantial. To ensure that their members are able to eke out a living, the unions usually put a limit to the concentration of hawkers in a given area by preventing the entry of newcomers. On the other hand, there are many instances where, if the unions find that newcomers do not seriously jeopardize the existing equilibriums, they agree to allow new entrants.

Shadows of the mall

July 4, 2008. The Gariahat area (the commercial centre of south Calcutta) witnessed a severe roadblock by street hawkers under the banner of the National Movement for Retail Democracy (NMRD), an organization of petty traders, small retailers, and farmers that staged several protest movements against corporate retailing in different Indian cities over the past few years. The roadblock in Gariahat was erected by the hawkers affiliated to the largest union of hawkers—Calcutta Hawker Sangram [Struggle] Committee (HSC). The HSC is a loose conglomeration of more than 32 neighborhood-based hawker unions that came into existence in 1996, when the leftist state government declared its ambitious project of making the city congestion free by forming a "people's resistance" against hawkers. The HSC was remarkably successful in resisting this project. On July 4, 2008 the imagined dynamism of a world-class city came to be *gheraoed* or encircled by HSC's protest; HSC feared that corporate retail would destroy the small economies of hawkers, farmers, and small traders—its members. The HSC roadblock at the Gariahat intersection was protesting against the inauguration of a new hypermart, Spencer's, built by one of India's largest industrial conglomerates, the RPG Group. The RPG group vice chairman, Sanjeev Goenka, entered the mall with police protection and offered a completely different picture from that of the protesters:

Large format is currently driving modern retail in India. It promises to be a superior shopping experience for the current-day discerning shopper who values time and money and looks out for choice before making a purchase decision. The large formats, being essentially multi-category and multi-brand, successfully cater to this buying behavior, while being a family and entertainment hang-out as well.

(The Telegraph: 2008)

Note the comparison between large and small, modern and the past invoked here. The "large format" has been celebrated as "modern" and therefore a "superior shopping experience" selling the dream of consumer freedom to choose "brands," in relation to the "premodern," small and informal retail practices of the street. This freedom of choice is then merged with the "economy of time" and other forms of "family" leisure that come with shopping in the shopping mall.

The new mall fever has provoked much activism, protest, euphoria, and academic research in Indian cities in the last few years. As I have already mentioned, both the proponents and opponents of corporate retail converged in projecting the transformative potential of the mall. I frequently noticed how the mall loomed large in the perceptions of individual hawkers. Once I visited the Gariahat Spencer's store (near the South City Mall) with Jogen, a vegetable seller in the Gariahat bazaar. Jogen drew my attention to the vegetable and fruits corner, and tried his best to establish the fact that although costlier, the vegetables at Spencer's were of lesser quality than those sold in the bazaar. Jogen emphatically pointed out how even after packaging the vegetables looked dead.

The presence of the mall affects hawking in various ways. Vegetable and fruit sellers like Jogen did not welcome Spencer's selling of fruits and vegetables. They were negatively affected, as many of their customers preferred to buy fruits and vegetables inside the mall. Such a trend was also noticed by Anjaria (2008) when he studied hawkers at Mumbai in the middle of the last decade. Vegetable sellers in Calcutta retaliated politically by making the city mayor mediate between the corporate agency and them to arrive at the agreement that Spencer's "would not sell less than three kg of vegetables, six kg of potatoes and onions, less than one liter of oil and 500 gm of masala (spices) and only branded and packaged rice and pulses" (The Economic Times 2008).

There were also groups of hawkers who benefited from the mall. I noticed that malls generated a desire for luxury goods that ultimately promoted the counterfeit goods sold by many street hawkers. In addition to this, shopping malls create increased pedestrian traffic on the streets. This led to new demands for fast food in the neighborhood. It is interesting to note that before the advent of the South City Mall, where Spencer's is located, there were only a few low-cost eateries in the adjacent sidewalk, mostly selling staple food to transport workers. This was the site of a former factory,[2] and a few mini buses were garaged there. People used to defecate in the in-between spaces of the factory boundary wall and the stranded buses. Durga-di, who makes paratha-sabji (a type of bread fried on a griddle) during the day at this spot, told me that before the South City Mall was built, there were no hawkers on this street; everyone, including himself, came three years ago, when South City Mall opened. Now her business is closely tied to the cycle of the South City Mall; her best business comes in the early evening, when the mall crowd is at its peak. Durga-di's experience echoes those of hawkers who work outside the city center at Salt Lake, who like Durga-di target the mall visitors offering fast food, tea, and cigarettes. The workers of the malls are always their regular customers (*bandha khoriddar*) who usually display very strong "brand" loyalty to particular shops. Thus, Durga-di has 38 regular customers from the South City Mall who have their regular snacks and tea between 4pm and 8pm. Durga-di knows them by name. She maintains a register book for her regular customers as many of them have a subsidized monthly agreement of payment with her.

Thus, contrary to the extremist views on malls, my ethnographic experience in Gariahat and South City shows that, far from ushering in change in consumption practices, the mall has been incorporated in a host of already existing practices, and is well utilized by many of those working outside the mall. Bimal, for example, who runs a tea and cigarette shop outside the South City Mall, reported that he frequently used the "world-class" toilets of the mall and took a rest for a while in its air conditioned corridors before going back outside to his work. Similarly, Anjaria noticed in Mumbai how visiting the mall became a ritual practice for lower-middle-class and middle-class city youth who sought to participate in the world-class city making in the mediation of the dazzling mall. They used the mall, as Anjaria (2008) noticed, as a space of sociality. Thus, the mall corridors became an extension of the neighborhood park. The millennial metropolitan Indian public substantially "Indianized" the mall. They go to the mall, spend time there, and participate in the spectacles of global retail culture within a simulated environment. Then they come down to the streets, eat food on the streets, buy counterfeits and enter into the everyday realities of their lives. The footpath between the street and the mall serves as a transition in diverse mental and social processes. The street and the mall critically reference each other and co-evolve.

Esplanade and the banality of the mall

I have so far told the story of the mall and the street in an area of the city where the mall is a new experience. I will now move on to the area of central Calcutta called Esplanade, where modern and transnational retail have a history dating back to the late eighteenth century, when Calcutta was made the second capital of the British Empire. Until the 1860s, Esplanade hosted a large traditional Indian bazaar called the Dharmatolla, owned by the Seal family, a wealthy "merchant prince" family of the city (Goode 1916). This market, along with several such markets, was brought under vigorous municipal regulation in 1871 by the promulgation of the Calcutta Market Act. The Dharmatolla market was subsequently acquired by the municipality, paying a hefty compensation to the merchant family (Goode 1916). The market was kept open after acquisition and in 1891 the construction of a huge new building was completed, with much of the rest of the surrounding land auctioned off. The building hosted many of the old retailers of Dharmatolla Bazaar, but the fact of enclosure excluded many of the traders of the old bazaar. The market was named after a British Police Commissioner, Sir Stuart Hogg (Goode 1916).

The walled and roofed Hogg Market imported several new dimensions into the retail culture and market aesthetics of the city. As in the case of the shopping malls of the late twentieth century, this market was advertised and justified on the grounds that it represented an imposition of a "global trend" (Williamson 2005: 3) of market design to transform the nature of public consumption in the city (Goode 1916). The Hogg Market soon became an important retail node in the global commodity chains and of the aesthetics of retail organization. Even a cursory look at the advertisements in English newspapers in Calcutta such as *The Statesman* gives a sense of the nature of nineteenth- and early twentieth-century consumer culture in the city surrounding the Esplanade area in general and the Hogg Market in particular, revealing that the conspicuous consumption of expensive imported goods is not a phenomenon unique to the twentieth century. The famous Hamilton and Co. used to import tins of "Fern Leaf" biscuits from France (advertisement published in *The Statesman*, June 20, 1881). In 1935 the *Calcutta Municipal Gazette* reported that the Hogg Market had been stocked with a wide range of imported fruits, including oranges from Palestine, apples from the United Sates, and lemons from Italy (*Calcutta Municipal Gazette* 1935: 80–81). One of the first police records on the "hawker problem" comes from the Esplanade area, especially from the Hogg Market area. As early as in 1867, Sir Stuart Hogg reported the following in his Circular Order:

> The vendors of the Dharmatolla Bazaar have submitted a memorandum to me reporting several instances of encroachment of public spaces by the stationary hawkers in the vicinity of the bazaar diverting potential and regular clients of the bazaar vendors. There can be no doubt that the present machinery for dealing with hawkers and footpath sellers is quite inadequate. Their numbers are so enormous that the police can give them only partial attention and the results of prosecution in most cases hardly justify the time expended in arrest and putting up cases before magistrate.
>
> (*Annual Report on the Police in Calcutta, 1868*)

Even when Dharmatolla Bazaar was acquired, several senior municipal officials were skeptical about the future of the proposed market if the "hawker menace" was not curbed properly (Goode 1916). However, the colonial administration could not completely handle the hawker issue. In 1914, for example, K. Grear, the Administrator of Calcutta Municipal Corporation, wrote to the secretary of the Judicial Department that the norms of public space, as promulgated in the Indian Penal Code of 1902, had been entirely ignored by "pavement sellers" and that "in the vicinity of the Municipal Markets, serious obstruction persists, affecting public traffic and the fortunes of the legitimate markets" (Calcutta Municipal Corporation 1913–1914).

Esplanade today remains the commercial and political center of the city. Constituting the heart of the "white town" of the colonial era, this area at present houses

large commercial buildings, hotels, retail markets, malls, the largest market of electronic goods of Eastern India and a vast and variegated informal economy bordering
the administrative headquarters of the state of West Bengal, and the famous *maidan*
(the vast open fields for which Calcutta is well known). Like other Calcutta districts,
the Esplanade area juxtaposes the extremes of wealth represented by institutional
banking structures and middle- and upper-class office workers, and one of the major
five-star hotels (the Grand Hotel) with the beggars and hawkers who may live and
sleep in Calcutta's streets.

Like other major markets in the city, certain sections of the sidewalk are claimed
by more or less regular hawkers. An amazing variety of goods pass through the hands
of these hawkers: from fresh fruits and vegetables to adulterated baby food; from saris,
skirts, and shoes to hand printed leather bags and purses; from handloom cotton and
silk to glass and ceramic objects and brassware; from handmade wooden beads to
junk jewelry from China and Taiwan; pirated tapes, CDs, and DVDs, and secondhand books; glass bangles, kitchenware, and household essentials; herbs and spices,
cooked food, cigarettes, and cold drinks, and recycled and secondhand articles (Dasgupta 1992). This wide diversity of products has developed over the years as hawkers
have adapted themselves to greater competition and changing consumer demand.

Diverse commodities and services and billboards advertising new movies and political parties constitute the central part of the experience of street life in Esplanade.
Shopping in Esplanade, as in any other bazaar street, involves a series of micro man-
euverings from the part of buyers and sellers. Here, the degree of selling depends on
the particularities of display as well as the seller's ability to convince her customer.

How did the hawkers at Esplanade react to the recent emergence of malls? Unlike the
hawkers in Gariahat, the hawkers at Esplanade have been historically exposed to diverse
forms of retail practices. As we have seen in the colonial police record, the merchants at
the Hogg Market never happily accepted the presence of hawkers. The animosity
between established retail businesses and hawkers intensified over time in the Esplanade
area (unlike many other places in Calcutta, where the *mahajan* [moneylenders] and the
hawkers developed a complementary and symbiotic relation), resulting in several
eviction drives. Analyzing police records in the 1950s and 1990s, it seems apparent
that for Esplanade hawkers, anti-street-hawker drives are contingent on the operation
of local economies, and complex relationships between different economic and political
actors. These drives are often manifestations of factional rivalry between different
middle- to low-ranking government functionaries and their personalized calculations.
Street hawkers resist such operations by virtue of a complex patronage network
involving state functionaries, ruling political parties and the opposition; these relationships can hardly be reduced to electoral calculations, as street hawkers do not
form a clustered urban vote bank like slum dwellers and squatter groups. In many
cases, hawkers operate on a particular street based on mutual agreement between the
neighborhood political actors and commercial interest groups. These agreements are
often contextual and are not related to other sets of agreements on other streets.

Let me now portray two individual hawkers belonging to the same family to show
how hawkers work in the Esplanade.

Abdul's journey

I met Abdul in 2006. He was a middle-aged man with vast entrepreneurial experience in the informal economy. He had originally come from a rural district 200 kilometers northeast of Calcutta; his family had a garment shop in Murshidabad, a town known for illegal garment trafficking between India and Bangladesh. Some of Abdul's kin worked as semi-skilled assistants in Calcutta to *ostagar* units—traditional guilds of tailors. Abdul's father worked as a middleman in Murshidabad to traffic garments prepared in such units to East Pakistan (now Bangladesh). When Abdul was 12, he was sent to an *ostagar* unit along with his elder brother, Parvez. Ismail, who will appear shortly, was the son of Parvez.

When Abdul was 20, he was given an option by the head *ostagar* of his unit to open a retail garment stall on the Esplanade sidewalk; Abdul has been there ever since, selling his products, collecting orders from his clients and observing the changing market trends. He acquired a degree of freedom when his supervisor, the head *ostagor*, died, some time in the early 1970s. Abdul then began to search for new opportunities to expand his trade. This was also necessary for him because the *ostagor* units in the area were already in decline due to the coming of cheap garments of synthetic cotton produced large-scale in mills. Around this time, Abdul came in contact with a moneylender who agreed to give him a week-long loan at high interest—between 75 and 150 percent. The rate of interest would decrease and the duration of the loan would grow if the hawker had a good reputation in the credit market—a good credit history could act as collateral in the informal credit market, as eventually happened with Abdul. In the absence of the institutionalized banking system, for traders like him who had no initial collateral, this seemed to be the only viable option to continue and expand the business.

Towards the end of my field research, our friendship grew deeper, and I began to refer to Abdul as *Chacha* (uncle). The bond grew even more powerful when Chacha came to know that I came from the same village he used to visit frequently to see his maternal grandmother; he could even vaguely remember my father, who would be of his age. Chacha gave me a vivid account of the network that produces the cheap and often counterfeit garments that he sells. The cloth comes from Ludhiana in Punjab. The cutting, iron finishing and packing is done in Calcutta. The sewing is done at Guma and adjoining districts. Chacha holds that the recent spurt of "brand names" in the garment industry and the greater availability of high-end products through established retail chains have created a greater tendency of emulation by those who cannot afford those products. Showing me several Levi's jeans in his stock, Abdul confessed that he belonged to a network of counterfeiters who took part in producing and selling the copies of the branded garments. There are several middlemen in the business who supply the copied tags that are further processed in the *ostagor* units; a dying craft thus finds an avenue to survive.

Drawing a longer genealogy of the counterfeit garment trade, Chacha told me that when he was young, paralegal cross-border trades had already opened up a number of routes through which Indian manufacturers could access cheaper fabric from Korea and China (via Nepal and Darjeeling) and from Bangladesh through the land border of 24 Parganas, Nadia and Murshidabad and river borders with the rivers Padma and Jalangi. Further, Chacha claimed that yarn and saris were also part of the cross-border garment traffic (see Ganguly-Scrase 2006 for greater details of this garment trade network).

A fellow garment hawker informed me that Abdul owned another stall somewhere in Chandni Chawk (a huge electronics market adjacent to Esplanade). I returned to Chacha's stall and asked him to tell me something about his second stall. I found Chacha a bit embarrassed and reluctant to comment. Only after I convinced him that I would not write a newspaper article on the matter did Chacha reveal that the stall at Chandni Chawk was looked after by his nephew, Ismail, who produced and sold pirated music CDs. From my previous experience of trying to conduct ethnographic research on the production and circulation of pirated music at Chandni Chawk, I could understand why Chacha was not willing to share the secrets of the trade. My failure to generate a good amount of data on the subject back in 2004 taught me a lesson: "secrecy is the secret of survival."

With much hesitation, Chacha called Ismail to his shop and introduced me to him and began to talk about how he got into music piracy. Chacha said that the garment supply chains depended on a series of international as well as inter-border factors, making his clothing stall increasingly difficult to run. Moreover, it was getting increasingly difficult for him to keep pace with the changing fashions. Around 1990, Chacha became the local agent of T-series cassettes. By the late 1980s, as Peter Manuel (1993) and Ravi Sundaram's (2010) studies reveal, these new, readily available cassettes completely changed the rules of distribution of music in India by moving into neighborhood shops, grocery shops, *paanwalas* (traders selling betel leaf), and teashops to convert the cassette into a bazaar product.

When I asked Chacha how he justified copying as a livelihood option, he said:

> I never attempted to prosper in other people's wealth. I do mess with brands and not with men. Like you have your masters' degree, I have this […]. I never sold drugs, and poisoned people. I didn't put the gambling money into my pocket […]. But I do imitations and allow my family members to copy music. I'm a devout Muslim and copying is sanctioned in Islam.

Chacha does not have a high opinion of the act of making copy CDs though it brings him good money. He calls the production of CDs as simply a *machiner khela* ("game of the machine"). Contrary to this, what he himself does in his work requires a higher sense of art and technical skill, he says. An understanding of not harming people, not pouring gambling money into the business, an invocation of Islam and a celebration of personal skill constitute the moral universe in which Abdul and Ismail work. They have differences of opinion, but they violate the law of the state without a sense of guilt.

One day, I asked Chacha to take me to his home, to observe the CD production process. Ismail begins by getting the covers of the CDs he wanted to make. He would usually buy a master copy and then photocopy the cover in color. He has the blank CDs and cases delivered to his stall or his house by "runners" who go around the stalls of vendors offering their products. His sisters help him by folding the covers so that they are ready to be inserted in the CD cases at the final stage of packaging. Folding the cover can be done while watching a popular Bengali serial on Star Jalsha TV. "Encasing" (putting covers and inlay cards into the cases) involves a lot of skill and labor in the process. Abdul's daughters do this in the afternoons after the completion of household work. While encasing is going on, Ismail is unceasingly burning CDs, a process that takes a longer time. He burns six at a time on two machines, stacking up the copied CDs with slips of paper in between the different titles so that others would know where they belong.

Ismail described the business of copyright piracy as a slippery and risky game. He told me that whatever I had seen in his house had just been a part of a very complicated chain. He said that earlier, music piracy had been a very profitable business: "CDs that you could get from me for 20 rupees, five years ago, would cost 150 rupees in Music World. It was not something you eat; it was something you listen to […]."

Facing huge losses, the music companies decided to cut the prices of music CDs and DVDs. Today, they still cost more than what one gets from the pirates, but it may be a more difficult decision for the shopper to decide whether he would purchase a collection of Hemanta Mukherjee (a well-known singer) from a pirate paying INR 200 or an original version that cost INR 250. Ismail said that a slump in the profits of music piracy had led him to look for illegal collections of recently released films and, more importantly, pornography of different categories. Ismail rents out these CDs and charges customers depending on the demand and quality of the recording. Ismail does not know who copies these films and from where these products come. A group of runners comes every week to supply whatever the retailers want. The anonymity of the supplier makes it difficult for Ismail and other pirates to control the price of the product. Ismail and a few others had planned to do the work of copying themselves. They rented an apartment and established a high-speed broadband connection to download films; one of them even used his brother's visa card to purchase pornographic film online. Nevertheless, a raid by the police destroyed the project at its inception. Ismail has a hunch that the agents of the anonymous supplier might have informed the police about the workshop. Since then, Ismail depends on the runners for his supply of the latest Bollywood films and pornography.

As Ismail informed me, most pirates in Chandni Chawk are commissioned agents of big music and electronic stores. Due to the fear of a possible raid they cannot risk stocking pirated copies in their shops. They would rather outsource the risk by providing necessary infrastructure to the hawkers. The hawkers sell pirated goods competing with the retail stores, and get a daily commission on the sold product while the "owner" of the stall receives the rest.

Globalization from above/globalization from below

The continuing and in some cases invigorated presence of hawkers in the shadow of the mall shows how modernity and capital are irreducible to a particular theory of historical development (Sanyal 2007). The bazaar beneath the mall does not pertain to the moment of transition from pre-capital to capital. Nor is it an initial condition which capital transforms. Rather, post-colonial capitalism is a world of difference and heterogeneity in which the corporate economy lives in harmonious relation with other forms of capital. In cities like Calcutta, globalization is an ambiguous and indeterminate journey. While to the hawkers in the hinterland of the South City Mall, the corporatization of retail sales ("globalization from above") emerged as a new field of contestation, to the hawkers in Esplanade, there was historically very little that was new to them. Amidst this, corporate capital extends its hegemony over other forms of capital, and the consent to the neoliberal regime is produced and renewed.

In this context, it is important to question the view of globalization as two parallel forces: globalization from above and globalization from below. This is because the voices and choices from below do not reside in an autonomous field: economic globalization from below is caught in advance in the webs of power that it uses in order to survive. As many of the chapters of this book point out, analyzing the contemporary globalization of capital from the vantage point of the binary of above and below is fundamentally misleading, and may fall into the neoliberal euphoria of seeing the Third World as populated by "heroic entrepreneurs." The "people's economy" is the new site of this millennial hope—the much celebrated "bottom billion" (see Soto 2002) whose poverty-stricken collective entrepreneurship would produce and enliven corporate capital through the circuits of microfinance. In such a narrative the hawker economy is represented as a revolution from below. But of course this is not necessarily the case.

One institution that ties corporate capital to the non-corporate capital of the informal economy is microfinance. One should not miss the fact that the advocacy network of Mumbai that Appadurai celebrated as "globalization from below" (2002) also works to transform the slum and pavement dwellers to be entrepreneurial enough to earn a credit for housing. The poorest of the poor—the "bottom billion"— are thus made to serve as a frontier market opening up new horizons of capital accumulation. Globalization from below is then also a network of microfinance institutions, real-estate developers, and grassroots organizations manufacturing consent from the subjects for resettlement and rehabilitation in favor of a slum-free city and congestion-free street intersections, deciding the terms of inclusion and exclusion (Roy 2009). One should keep in mind the fact that microfinance institutions are not always non-profit organizations. They are often after profits, like commercial banks, investment vehicles, and money markets. The new accumulation economy mines the fortunes of the bottom billion by seeking to eradicate poverty through profit (Prahalad 2004).

If this is indeed the case, then what Ribeiro calls "globalization from below" (Ribeiro 2006) and Mathews calls "low-end globalization" (Mathews 2011) is far from being a sphere separate from the accumulation economy, as these two authors both realize. High-end globalization needs a quarantined low-end globalization to continuously provide for itself the conditions of its hegemony. Globalization from below and globalization from above are analytically inseparable, with the latter setting the terms under which the former must operate. This chapter, exploring the symbiosis of street hawkers and malls in Calcutta, has given one illustration of how exactly this is the case.

Notes

1 In 2001, Calcutta was officially renamed Kolkata to emphasize the Bengali origin of the city. The renaming involved the assertion of a new Bengali cultural identity over the cosmopolitan cityscape. Throughout the paper, I use the old official name of the city for two reasons. First, I do not subscribe to the provincial idea of the city. Second, this paper covers a period when Calcutta was the official name of the city.

2 The Usha factory, the first to make sewing machines in India in 1935, alongside other manufactured products like the electric fan, covered the area that has now been reclaimed by the South City Mall. In 1939, a large sum of British capital was put into the manufacturing of machinery and equipment for army vehicles and aircraft. In the wake of the 1947 Partition of India, the factory burgeoned, with many refugees being recruited in Usha; over the decades, many of the nearby refugee colonies were forged into middle-class residential areas. In the post-liberalization era, when the government sought to liberalize the land market by reclaiming public land, the Usha factory was demolished and the site became a lucrative spot for global capital (Ghosh 2011).

References

Anjaria, J. (2008) "Unruly Streets: Everyday Practices and Promises of Globality in Mumbai," PhD Dissertation, Department of Anthropology, University of California, Santa Cruz.

Annual Report on the Police in Calcutta (1868) Circular Order of the Commissioner of Police 97, Appendix, November 19, 1867.

Appadurai, A. (2002) "Deep Democracy: Urban Governmentality and the Horizon of Politics," *Public Culture* 14(1): 21–47.

Bandyopadhyay, R. (2011) "A Historian among Anthropologists," *Dialectical Anthropology* 35(3).

Brecher J., T. Costello, and B. Smith (2000) *Globalization from Below: The Power of Solidarity*, Cambridge, MA: South End Press.

Calcutta Municipal Corporation (1913–1914) West Bengal State Archives, Calcutta, Judicial Department, Abstract of Proceedings, K. Grear, Administrator to Secretary, JD, Calcutta Municipal Corporation, September 15, 1913, GOB, July 1914, A 44, p. 1205.

Calcutta Municipal Gazette (1935) "List of Goods Available at Municipal Markets," 80–81

Dasgupta, N. (1992) *Petty Trading in the Third World: The Case of Calcutta*, Bookfield, VT: Avebury.

Davis, M. (2004) "Planet of Slums: Urban Involution and the Informal Proletariat," *New Left Review* 26: 5–34.

Dey, D. and S. Dasgupta (2010) "Hawker Economy: Small Business, Big Role I", *Frontier*, 43(22).

Economic Times, The (2008) "Spencer's Second Hyper Mall opens in Kolkata," July 7.

Ganguly-Scrase, R. (2006) "Neoliberal Development and its Implications for the Garment Industry and its Workers in India: A Case Study of West Bengal," http://coombs.anu. edu.au/SpecialProj/ASAA/biennial-conference/2006/Ganguly-Scrase-Ruchira-ASAA2006.pdf (accessed November 3, 2009).

Ghosh, S. (2011) "Malling of a Factory: Apprehending a Chronicle of Change in Calcutta," http://www.inter-disciplinary.net/wp-content/uploads/2011/08/goshifapaper.pdf (accessed November 12, 2011.

Goode, S. W. (1916) *Municipal Calcutta, its Institutions in Their Origin and Growth*, Edinburgh: T. A. Constable.

Kalhan, A. (2007) "Impact of Malls on Small Shops and Hawkers," *Economic and Political Weekly* 42(22): 2063–66.

Manuel, P. (1993) *Cassette Culture: Popular Music and Technology in North India*, Chicago: University of Chicago Press.

Mathews, G. (2011) *Ghetto at the Center of the World: Chungking Mansions, Hong Kong*, Chicago: University of Chicago Press.

Prahalad, C. K. (2004) *The Fortune at the Bottom of the Pyramid: Eradicating Poverty through Profits*, Cambridge: Wharton School Publishing.

Roy, A. (2009) "Civic Governmentality: The Politics of Inclusion in Beirut and Mumbai," *Antipode* 41(1): 159–79.

Ribeiro, G. (2006) "Economic Globalization from Below," *Ethnographica* 10(2): 233–49.

Sanyal, K. (2007) *Rethinking Capitalist Development: Primitive Accumulation, Governmentality and Post-Colonial Capitalism*, Routledge: New Delhi.

Simone, A. (2004) *For the City Yet to Come: Changing Life in Four African Cities*, Durham: Duke University Press.

Soto, H. de (2002) *The Mystery of Capital: Why Capitalism Triumphs in the West and Fails Everywhere Else*, New York: Basic Books.

Statesman, The (1881) advertisement, June 20, p. 1.

Sundaram, R. (2010) *Pirate Modernity: Media Urbanism in Delhi*, London: Routledge.

Telegraph, The (2008) "Spencer's Opens Third Hyper Mart in Kolkata," August 9.

Williamson, D. (2005) "Order, Cleanliness, and 'A Building of Some Architectural Pretensions': Arthur Crawford and Market Reform in Victorian Bombay," MA Thesis, University of Virginia School of Architecture.

11

LOCALISM MEETS GLOBALIZATION AT AN AMERICAN STREET MARKET

Robert Shepherd

"Globalization," as Ribeiro (2009) notes, is not just an ideology but also for many a mantra. For proponents, "globalization" is a catch-all term to describe a revolutionary transformation of economic and social relations, one in which capital has been liberated, the state privatized, and trade expanded across the globe. For critics, this term describes not the privatization of the state but the gutting of state responsibilities, the erasure of cultural differences, and the hegemony of multinational corporations. As the editors of this volume have noted, much of the academic debate about globalization concentrates on transnational capital flows and actors from above or on the evidence of resistance to globalization from below (Ribeiro 2009: 298). Significant questions emerge from this limited perspective. A "top–down" perspective, whether by globalization advocates or critics, often glosses over the fact that alleged universal values and perspectives are more often than not the particular cultural values and norms of a transnational minority elite (Goodale 2009). On the other hand, a focus on supposed resistance to globalization mirrors debates among development critics about the possibilities for alternatives to development (see Esteva 1987, Korton 2006). And yet, as James Ferguson has argued, many development subjects do not desire freedom from development, but recognition as actors entitled to a "place in the world"—that is, recognition as members of an authentically global community (Ferguson 2006: 18–19).

This desire for a place in the world is what Ribeiro (2009) has termed "grassroots globalization" and Mathews (2007) "low-end globalization," and what this book labels "globalization from below." Rather than seeking to produce an alternative to a hegemonic global economic system, the actors at the low end of this system seek wealth, agency, and recognition as legitimate members of this system (Ribeiro 2006: 247). The "low end" of this global network of capital, goods, services, and people is not synonymous with either the "non-West" or with the "developing" world. Instead, it is found throughout the world, often among petty traders and street vendors.

Indeed, while street vending and other informal retail and trade practices may not be as common in New York City and Washington DC, as in Beijing, China or Lagos, Nigeria, they are nevertheless present.

This chapter analyzes what happens when "globalization from below" travels to and seeks a space within "globalization from above." I analyze how local vendors, community leaders, and city officials at an historic public market in Washington DC react to and seek to counter the presence of a diverse array of immigrant vendors. Far from embracing or celebrating this marketplace diversity, these hegemonic forces have actively sought to restrict the presence of both immigrant vendors and imported goods by using a discourse of authenticity and localism.

Informal markets in the United States

Street vending and public markets have for generations been economic entry points for immigrants to the United States. Operating in an ambiguous sphere between the formal and informal economies, requiring little capital outlay and no formal qualifications, street markets have enabled new immigrants to survive on the margins of the American economy until they have gained either legal status or accumulated sufficient social, financial, and cultural capital to succeed in the formal economy. In the last three decades, post-Cold War and post-Fordist political and economic shifts, new and cheaper forms of transportation and communication, along with reduced customs duties, have provided immigrants with certain comparative advantages against local citizens in these micro market import settings. These include built-in trade networks with friends, family members, and colleagues back home, a shared language with suppliers, and most importantly trust ties that enable long-distance global trade at the micro level.

These shifts have in turn provoked a response at the local level of public life, particularly in American urban settings. In response to the increased internationalization of public markets, an emerging coalition of anti-globalization critics, organic and natural food proponents, and urban planners advocate for a public market sphere protected from the standardization of global capitalism. Framed within a language of localism, authenticity, and an ambiguously defined "community," this process leads to a "cleaning up" of market diversity, ironically under the guise of promoting and protecting this very diversity.

This is an issue largely ignored among public market advocates in the United States. Instead, they point to the rapid growth of farmers' markets in the last two decades as evidence of a renewed public interest in local, quality food and artisan products. In 1970, there were approximately 340 such markets operating in the United States (Brown 2001: 655). Following passage of the Farmer-to-Consumer Direct Marketing Act by the US Congress in 1976, the number of such markets rose rapidly, reaching more than 3,700 in 2004 (Gillespie *et al.* 2007: 65). However, as Brown (2001) cautions, attributing the development of such markets to this law ignores a range of other factors, particular post-1960s American domestic politics, populist angst over the perceived dangers of chemical additives in foods, and a popular rhetoric of anti-globalization.

Classifying a vending market as a "farmer's market" as opposed to a flea market, public market, or festive marketplace is difficult, because very few pure farmers markets exist in the United States. Instead, most include not just farmers, but also middlemen and non-produce, meat and fish vendors (Pyle 1971: 167–169). Brown suggests that a farmer's market is best defined as a public market at which "some, if not all" vendors are farmers (2001: 658). US House Resolution 2458 (1975) defined farmers' market as "any marketplace where at least ten farmers congregate for the purpose of selling their agricultural commodities directly to consumers in a manner designed to lower the cost of food for the consumers while providing an increased income to the farmers" (quoted in Brown 2001). This utilitarian definition links neighborhood weekly farmers' markets with large urban public markets such as Philadelphia's Reading Terminal Market, Seattle's Pike Market, Chicago's Maxwell Street Market and the subject of this chapter, Washington's Eastern Market. Each of these public markets provides space for not just farmers but a wide range of vendors.

Situating a market

Eastern Market, a late nineteenth-century brick complex, is located two blocks off Pennsylvania Avenue in Washington's Capitol Hill neighborhood. When it opened in 1874, Eastern Market was one of four public markets designed to supply the food needs of a city that had expanded rapidly in the years after the American Civil War (1860–1865).

These markets were designed to provide a variety of fresh foods to a growing population by offering stalls to farmers and merchants at low rents. Public markets were supposed to eliminate middlemen in the urban food economy by providing a subsidized public space for food producers to deal directly with urban consumers. Besides this functional goal, public markets occupied a key role in the late-nineteenth-century "City Beautiful Movement" in the United States, which aimed to reshape urban public space, motivated in part by nativist concerns over the influx of new migrant communities from Eastern and Southern Europe (Tangires 2004: 189). With roots in the Progressive Movement, the City Beautiful Movement was based on a faith in the ability of urban planners to create social order and a shared moral foundation, thereby shaping immigrants into morally good Americans (Tehranian 1995: 83–87; Boyer 1995: 85–86).

After an initial period of prosperity, Eastern Market, like public markets in many American cities, gradually lost customers to supermarkets in the early twentieth century. This happened partly because these public markets had been established to aid food consumers, not local producers. Thus, when new forms of technology emerged such as refrigeration techniques and long-distance shipping, consumers no longer had to patronize public markets (Pyle 1971).

The post-World War II development of suburban communities further hurt city markets. In the District of Columbia, race riots and widespread "white flight" in the late 1960s, a sharp increase in street crime, and benign neglect by city officials, led to the near-closure of Eastern Market. By 1970 a handful of food merchants remained in the Market's South Hall, and the North Hall was used to store equipment for the District's Department of Public Works. In 1975 John Harrod, an arts promoter, was given a rent-free lease on the North Hall to create a community arts center. In 1979 Harrod began to sponsor weekend arts and crafts vendors on the sidewalk in front of the market complex and along what had become a largely abandoned farmers' line.

By the early 1990s this informal market was attracting not just thousands of weekend customers but also the ire of local residents, especially as Capitol Hill began to re-gentrify. Neighborhood activists, many of whom were quite recent to the area, waxed nostalgic about "their" market and what had become of it. They complained about noise, trash, and the abundance of vendors selling what they perceived as cheap imported products. These activists were supported by the dozen permanent food vendors located in the market's South Hall, who argued that street vendors harmed their businesses. For almost two decades renovations to the market needed to address building code problems were stalled while a range of community groups with titles such as "Concerned Citizens for Eastern Market," "Citizens' Committee for Eastern Market," and "Friends of Eastern Market" fought with city officials, street vendors, and often between themselves over market control (Wemple and Bauzá 1996).

An electrical fire in the spring of 2007 gutted the interior of the market building, spurring city officials to push forward on an ambitious renovation project. As part of this project the city's Department of Real Estate Services (DRES) took over management of outdoor vendors, ousting the vendors who had maintained this outdoor space for over two decades. This has resulted in competing street markets, the official Eastern Market in and around the historic market building managed by DRES officials, and "The Flea Market at Eastern Market," run by displaced vendors in the parking lot of a former middle school located across the street from the market building.

Reopened in June of 2009, Eastern Market attracts as many as 20,000 weekend visitors from the early spring through the Christmas holiday season. City officials aggressively promote this site as an historic food market and tourist destination. Indeed, the market has become the centerpiece of redevelopment plans for the area, as city officials have embraced the planning argument that a specific type of street market (a farmer's and artisan market) can help revitalize urban areas. "Eastern Market is far more than a market," the official website claims. "It is a community hub for the Capitol Hill neighborhood and a cultural destination for visitors from around the world" (District of Columbia, Department of Real Estate Services 2010).

But these plans also carry specific ideological assumptions about the status and worth of art and food, as opposed to retail objects, including what counts as market-worthy food, the intrinsic worth of "organic" and "natural" products, and who counts as a member of a community. Proponents typically argue that such markets stimulate new supply chains that in turn promote rural communities, provide health benefits to urban city residents, lower food transport costs and carbon emissions and strengthen social ties (Seyfang 2008; DuPuis and Goodman 2005). According to supporters of this perspective, a globalized food system separates economic acts from their social and environmental context, whereas local acts occur among socially embedded individuals (Seyfang 2008: 191; Gillespie *et al.* 2007: 69, 78). This bio-regionalism rests on the premise that emphasizing local place will link people to the natural world and, by implication, a more authentic life (Alkon 2008: 278–280).

Like the terms "wilderness" and "organic," the "local" in specific settings has become an unreflective good for Americans on the political left (DuPuis and Goodman 2005: 359). In terms of food and artisan production, the "local" symbolizes equity, fairness, environmental stewardship, and an ethics of care. It functions as the opposite of an ambiguous "global," vaguely defined as mono-cultural, inequitable, exploitative of both people and nature, and of dubious quality. This division mirrors one that divides eating into binary categories of "good" and "bad." Fast food is posited as gluttonous, unreflective, compulsive, and mindless, whereas a range of practices that together fall into the category of "ethical eating" are taken as calculated forms of opposition to industrial foods. These include vegetarianism, fair trade, farmer-to-consumer sales, organic foods, and the Slow Food movement (Guthman 2003: 46). In this context "organic," "natural," and above all "local," are valorized as moral alternatives to a host of assumed negativities, ranging from Third-World sweatshop exploitation and rights violations to personal health, concerns about environmental pollutants, and fossil fuel usage. But the production chains of organic food are seldom analyzed by those who advocate it. Instead, "the local" is taken as a good in and of itself, trumping "the global," which in this case is typecast as distanced, tasteless, banal, and uniform.

Just as a charismatic religious movement promises salvation through a ritualized rebirth, the Slow Food and "food with a face" movements promise a new life: changing food habits will not just make a person healthier, but also morally and spiritually better. In such a scenario, "localism becomes a counter-hegemony to this globalization thesis, a call to action under the claim that the counter to global power is local power. In other words, if global is domination then in the local we must find freedom" (DuPuis and Goodman 2005: 361). Yet in this marketplace, this counter-hegemony seeks to exclude not global capitalism or multinational corporations but rather "globalization from below"—those vendors who are not local but foreign.

This embrace of "the local" ignores the fact that it is as likely to be sectarian, bigoted, and dominated by elites as it is to be a meeting ground of rural and urban, black, white and other, across class, race, and gender lines (Alkon 2008; DuPuis and Goodman 2005). This is the case at Eastern Market, in particular its transformation into an official "local" space for fresh foods and artists. Farmers selling local foodstuffs are privileged, along with "local" artists. Inside the market building, a handful of "local" merchants sell "local" meats, fish, produce, breads, and other foodstuffs. Outside, market supervisors seek to shape a weekend market that combines organic farm products and artists, where visitors can buy a quart of berries from a local farmer, a loaf of bread from a neighborhood baker, or a print of the Eastern Market complex from a "local" artist. The actual economic feasibility of such a model appears to be beside the point: this is the sort of market neighborhood activists desire, and this is the sort of market city officials, understanding who votes, have decided to provide.

As part of this process, city bureaucrats in charge of the market require new vendors to submit an application to a committee of vendor-artists, who only approve either artists or crafters. Legislation passed in 1999 by the Washington City Council defined "artists" and "crafters" as creators of the objects they sell (Washington DC City Council 1999). This law in theory allows importers to also sell, but only if a vendor sells objects which are "ethno-specific and are designed, produced, and representative of the country of origin" (ibid, Section 2.20). Then-current vendors were given non-transferrable permits, guaranteeing them a fixed street or sidewalk space. These permits enable city tax administrators to collect more sales tax from vendors. More importantly, this formalization process will over time eliminate non-artist vendors, thus (in theory) creating a market space rooted in localism, individual creativity, and hence authenticity. According to promotional materials, Eastern Market includes a public space "where *locals* organize to hold meetings, wedding receptions, dance classes, and other events," a farmer's line "where *local* farmers sell fresh local produce year round," and an outdoor market "where *local* artists sell handmade arts and crafts and antiques" (District of Columbia, Department of Real Estate Services 2010, emphasis added).

Who vends?

Market realities are far more complex than this idealized image. Of 87 outdoor vendors observed in May 2010, just 11 sold produce or other food products. The remainder consisted of jewelry vendors (29), artists (27), importers (15), and second-hand goods sellers (5). Across the street, the 83 vendors at the adjoining flea market were importers (25), jewelry vendors (18), artists (14), furniture sellers (10), and an assortment of others (16), including a doughnut maker, several card sellers, and six second-hand household goods dealers. Combining all outdoor vendors (170), it is apparent that a majority are not farmers and artists (52 total) but jewelers and importers (87). Further-more, by not combining these numbers, the spatial division of the local and the global is clear: as city officials and neighborhood activists envision, Eastern Market proper is rapidly becoming a local market, whereas "The Flea Market at Eastern Market" has become the site of the global. This is true not just of what is sold but also in terms of who vends: the localization of Eastern Market has also been a process of flattening out diversity.

Of 84 vendors surveyed at the official Eastern Market in August 2005, before the market fire, renovation, and subsequent management takeover by city officials, 38 (45.3 percent) were white, 32 (38.1 percent) were African-American, 13 (15.4 percent) were Asian, and 1 (1.2 percent) was Latino. In May 2008, before renovations were com-plete, of 78 vendors observed, 33 (42.3 percent) were white, 32 (41 percent) were African-American, 12 (15.6 percent) were Asian, and 1 (1.1 percent) was Latino. Yet by September 2010, slightly more than a year after the market building reopened under city management, of 69 vendors, 40 (57.9 percent) were white, 20 (29 percent) were African-American, 8 (11.6 percent) were Asian, and 1 (1.5 percent) was Latino.

This erasure of diversity is not a conscious goal of local activists or city officials. Instead, it is a side effect of a vending policy that favors artists and farmers, both of whom are mainly white and male. In numerous surveys I have conducted of Eastern Market vendors, a clear pattern is evident. Artwork (including photography, sketches, and paintings) is largely the domain of white men, jewelry is overwhelmingly the domain of women, both white and African-American, and immigrant vendors sell imported goods. Yet despite these social facts, two very different narratives circulate at Eastern Market. The first, shared by (affluent, white) neighborhood activists and the small cohort of indoor merchants, portrays the market as a gathering place of local residents and vendors who constitute a century-old community. The fact that the large majority of market visitors are either tourists or live elsewhere in the metro region, or that, much like affluent Washington, Capitol Hill is a profoundly transient neighborhood, does not impact this narrative. The second narrative, one shared by many artists and jewelers, is that the market now suffers from an influx of "Chinese," who are blamed for a decline in prices and sales. Yet the market has almost no Chinese vendors and a relatively limited range of Chinese products for sale. Of the 170 total vendors surveyed in the summer of 2010, only 5 were Chinese. Of the 40 vendors selling imported products, 15 sold Chinese goods, slightly more than the 13 who sold Indian goods. Given these figures, what fuels these vendor complaints about "the Chinese"?

I suggest that what is happening in Eastern Market is a microcosm of feelings towards everyday globalization in the United States and perhaps other economically developed countries. Along with lower prices and a wider array of goods has come an ambiguous uncertainty and a feeling of loss. Management changes at the market have not only reorganized the market spatially but also have unintentionally transformed artisan vendors into both a colorful backdrop for a tourist destination/historic site and led to new forms of competition and price cuts. Hence, while "the Chinese" may be blamed by many vendors for their loss of business, the actual causes are far more complex.

The Chinese impact, both real and imagined, reflects the broader impact that Chinese products and people have had and continue to have on economic activities at both the macro and micro level across much of the world. Chinese investment across Africa has been matched by a flood of Chinese consumer goods and entrepreneurs and traders, while the tourist economies of Thailand, Indonesia, Cambodia, and Vietnam (not to mention Hawaii) are rapidly becoming dependent on Chinese tourist arrivals. In the United States, unease at the scope and presence of Chinese consumer goods has been heightened in recent years by media reports of food scares in China, questions about the safety of Chinese food products and toys, and activist complaints about human rights issues in the PRC.

These perceptions are present among vendors in Eastern Market, who believe themselves to be in direct competition with "the Chinese." This label does not describe Chinese merchants per se (given their low number) but instead functions as a signifier of a suspect global realm of commerce. Market management rules that emphasize the assumed authenticity of food merchants, farmers, and artists further marginalize retailers. Given this, how do vendors who either originate from the developing world or sell cheap products such as textiles, handbags, and handicrafts respond to their marginalization from vending space in what city officials promote as the "real" Eastern Market, and from local vendors who perceive them as unfair competitors?

For an economist, the origins of goods or people may be of little interest beyond whether these factors impact production, transportation, and labor costs. But it seems clear that how goods are marketed in this market is a question that encompasses more than supply and demand mediated by price.

Selling culture on the streets of Washington DC

As already noted, despite city marketing efforts to depict Eastern Market as a local farmer's market and neighborhood specialty-food mart, the majority of vendors in and around the site are not food vendors. Including merchants with permanent stalls inside the market's South Hall, just 14.4 percent (26 of 182) of vendors are engaged in the business of food. The majority of vendors (99 of 182) sell artwork and jewelry, but approximately 25 percent (40 of 182) sell imported goods, primarily products that carry not just a use function but also cultural value. These products range from Peruvian sweaters, flutes, and dolls to Tunisian pottery, Ethiopian religious objects, West African and Kenyan wood carvings, Indian textiles, and Chinese silk. Just over 50 percent (22 of 40) of these vendors are immigrants, the remainder primarily white Americans.

In observations and interviews, a divide was evident between white American vendors who retailed other people's culture and immigrant vendors who usually sold cultural objects linked to their own home countries. However, it was the Americans who insisted that they were not simply marketing culture for material gain and the immigrants who voiced little or no concern about making a living from marketing, in effect, themselves. Indeed, a common theme among white American cultural vendors was a personal link with what they sold. While some saw themselves as artists and others as activists, few labeled themselves as businesspeople.

Anna, who described herself as a textile artist, first traveled to India in 1998, to visit her sister, who was working with a rural income generating project. "I taught weaving for two months," she said. "Loved it, and wanted to be involved." Over the last decade, she has developed a successful textile business at the market, selling bags, tablecloths, blouses, and other items from a women's income-generation project in India as well as a company in Bali, which she described vaguely as "a Fair Trade workshop owned by Westerners."

Self-taught in the business of importing and selling, she started small, with visits to India, from where she would return with textiles in her suitcase. After a year she moved up to air parcels and then eventually sea shipments, at which time she confronted the maze of bureaucratic regulations around customs importation at the port of Baltimore. Unable to afford a customs broker, she initially spent several days working her way through forms and inspections, at times helped informally by sympathetic officials. Now she receives several shipments each year and is expanding to several other regional street markets.

Everything she sells is tagged and branded, highlighting the social nature of her marketing strategy: "I like to let my products sell themselves. […] when they see how the products were made, by people, it adds a lot […]. People are careful about where they spend their money. If their dollars can make a difference, they will make that choice." Indeed, she asserted that the production basis of her products was what made her different from other vendors, linking her practices with everything from her own spiritual wellbeing to women's rights issues and the plight of Tibet:

> It's really, really important to me that my stuff is fair trade, emotionally, psychologically, and spiritually [...]. There are many, many customers who feel the same way. With the China–Tibet thing, I really try not to buy stuff from China. If there was a fair trade group that was helping women [in China], I would consider it, but I feel like more businesses need to look at the social and spiritual impact of what they sell [...]. I support Free Tibet and I support the Dalai Lama. What's hard, though, is that a lot of my display stuff comes from China.

For Anna, selling Indian and Balinese textiles on the street was much more than a means of making a living. She explicitly rejected the label of street vendor. Instead, she saw herself as an artist and a socio-cultural mediator, enabling her customers to link themselves with the lives of rural Indian women, unnamed but presumably fairly paid Balinese, and the Tibetan independence movement. What was real and what was fake in this context had nothing to do with the tangible quality of her goods but their branding as cultural objects with social value.

Another American, Carson, also identified as an artist but had no interest in either fair trade or social entrepreneurship. He sold handmade Turkish carpets of his own design that cost hundreds and in some cases thousands of dollars. A few years after graduating from high school, he found a job with an airline as a ticketing agent. The most lucrative benefit was cheap air travel. "I would fly to London and Amsterdam for concerts," he said. "I hated the job, but the travel was great." In 1999 he flew to Turkey to see an eclipse, saw a business opportunity, and started making several trips each year. Each time he would return with trade goods. "I just traveled over there [Turkey] and started picking up small things. At first I carried things back on the plane with me, and then I started shipping them back." Beginning with wool scarves and jewelry, he later shifted into carpets—first with wholesalers in Istanbul, and eventually with villagers who were making the products. Unlike Anna, he professed no interest in using his vending work as a mediator of economic and social change. Instead he evoked a value relativism premised on trust:

> Look, I've been dealing with the same people for over seven years [...]. They might have values that are different than mine, but we both come to that endpoint that honesty is important. I'm honest with people because I think it's better for business. It depends on what you want to do. If you want to sell jewelry and get something different from a different supplier you are not looking to develop long-term relationships [...]. I'm more interested in finding people who can do quality work and can do that for me over a long period of time.

In other words, he sought to build social ties and reciprocal trust not as a means towards affecting a transformation of the social value or economic worth of the villagers with whom he did business but because this was in effect good for his business:

> It's different over there. It's not a contract society the way it is here, you don't necessarily deal in the same way you would here. A lot of it is just based on meeting people and determining if I trust them; there is trust on both ends. They have to know that I'm trustworthy and am going to send them money when they extend me credit.

Carson, like Anna, Tom (who vended Vietnamese handbags), and Lilly (Peruvian sweaters and textiles) insisted that traveling to the production site on a regular basis was crucial. While for Carson this had to do with quality control, for the others it was about social relationships or, as Lilly said, "recharging my batteries." Because they did not identify as either street vendors ("Vendors sell hot dogs and crap like that," explained one market vendor. "I sell art.") or as businesspeople, travel to these other cultural zones was crucial to their own identities as artists or social activists. This is in sharp contrast to immigrant vendors, as discussed below, who either cannot or do not want to spend their earnings on unnecessary travel.

Finally, most of these American cultural vendors distinguished between artistic cultural products and what one vendor dismissed as "container sales." He defined the latter as "stuff that has no connection with people or stuff that is mass produced." In his opinion the marketing of mass-produced cultural products was not just a threat to the culture of the places these objects came from, but just as importantly, to the "artistic community" of Eastern Market. "This could be a place for the people who are sick of Target," Monica, a jewelry artisan, explained. "The management just needs to be more selective. It's not a great market now but it could be." Gina, who sold textiles she advertised as the products of a women's collective in Peru, complained about what she referred to as a "Chinese takeover" of the market. This was a complaint also voiced by photographers and jewelers. These vendors meant not just an increase in Chinese vendors in all product areas but also an increase in Chinese products. They viewed this as not just a threat to their own sales, but also to the market's authenticity and purpose. Stories circulated among vendors about particularly egregious examples: Kevin, a Hong Kong man from New York who had appeared in the market two years before and started undercutting pearl sellers; Tony, a Chinese immigrant from Maryland who sold black-and-white prints of typical Washington tourist scenes at prices so low that he threatened long-established niche photographers; and the Chens, a local Chinese-American couple who sold an eclectic range of cheap Chinese purses, earrings, and other trinkets. But the most common stories recounted what had happened to the scarf and shawl market after "the Chinese arrived," as one vendor put it.

Whoever sells the real?

"Those people who sell the ten-dollar things, there's no natural materials. The ones I sold were pure fine wool, good quality. I had nice designs with flowers or Chinese things." Chun Mei Li pointed at me to emphasize her point. "Before [others] started to sell cheaper, I was okay. I could sell a piece for $30–$35, a complete color maybe $28 or $25, which is okay […] but when those others started to sell stuff for less, it really hurt me." Chun no longer sold at the market. After several years of making a living as a scarf and shawl vendor, she had been driven from business by a wave of other vendors (only two of whom were Chinese), who had undercut her prices. Between 2004 and 2009, the market price of a China-made "authentic" Pashmina scarf had dropped from $25–$35 to $10, and in some cases even $8. From the point of view of an economist, "the market" had worked, generating a realistic retail price, but from Chun's view, she had been destroyed.

Chun had not come to the United States to sell textiles in a street market but to study for a master's degree in public policy at a major state university in the Midwest. After graduating, she had taken advantage of visa regulations that allowed her to work for a year in the United States for training purposes. After this, like many in her position, she overstayed her visa in hopes of finding a professional job with a company that would sponsor her for a green card. Heightened scrutiny of would-be immigrants after 2001, combined with the economic downturn and her shaky English-language skills, had doomed her chances and led her to Eastern Market. A friend had introduced her to another Chinese woman who vended lacquer ware, and she had gone into business. When I asked her why she had chosen scarves to sell, her answer was straightforward: these were cheap to buy and ship and could bring a decent profit.

"I would spend a lot of time online, checking pictures, talking over the phone or on email, negotiating," she explained. "Then I would find a shipping company and have everything sent by air. Anything under fifty kilos can be labeled 'for personal use' and customs doesn't care." She knew precisely how much each scarf weighed (cheaper quality ones 180 grams per piece, better quality 240 grams, and lowest quality 120 grams) and thus knew how many pieces she could ship per each kilo. She said her shipping costs averaged around $1–$2 per scarf, depending on weight. When business was good, she could make as much as $25 profit on each scarf she sold, she said.

But no longer. "Chinese vendors ruin everything," she complained. However, her complaint was quite different than that of Anna, who believed that the increased availability of cheap Chinese imports in the market lowered the overall quality of the market experience. For Chun, market quality, cultural authenticity, or fair wages to production workers were irrelevant. As an outsider who knew little and appeared to care less about the history of Eastern Market or debates about its future direction, she viewed the Market as literally *a* market in the abstract economic sense (a place where strangers came together to buy and sell goods) and not as either a key aspect of her identity or as a social space. She had vended fake Pashmina scarves and silk scarves of dubious quality because this was a way for her to make a living (she made it clear that if she could find an office job with legal status, she would immediately take this). As for Americans who became vendors for reasons other than making a living, she found their actions perplexing:

> There was a black guy here before, he always was learning Chinese, so he decided to sell something from China. But he did something very stupid,

he tried to carry everything with him. But you cannot carry that much, two cases. You have to calculate—I don't care to pay the expensive shipping because I don't even need to go outside my door. I stay home and make the order online and pay with my checking account in China. In this way I don't even need to go to China.

Kumar, who had been a legal resident of the United States for more than a decade, was irritated with my questions about his occupation. What to me raised a range of questions (a South-Asian Hindu who made a living selling knock-off leather handbags he bought from a Colombian supplier) was to him just a business. Like the West African Muslims who sold pornographic tapes and other knock-off products on the streets of New York whom Paul Stoller describes (2002), money for Kumar "had no smell." He did not sell copies but what he termed "replicas." The fact that his bags were made of leather did not concern him ("I'm not killing the damn cow"), nor did any concerns about culture. In his view, he worked hard, not just at Eastern Market but on a yearly circuit to large trade shows in New York, Chicago, Las Vegas, and Nashville. Besides his Colombian supplier, he had recently become interested in China and was planning a trip to Shenzhen to investigate a lower-cost producer. As for fair trade, he summed up his view in a few words: "That's all bullshit, man. I'm worried about fair trade for me."

Selling Shangri-La

The romantic fantasy of Tibet that captivates many middle- and upper-class elites in North America and much of Europe has been well documented and analyzed by anthropologists and other scholars (Bishop 1989; Lopez 1998; Dodin and Rather 2001). Aided by astute public relations on the part of the Tibetan government in exile and sympathetic Hollywood film producers, the mythical land of Shangri-la continues to thrive, despite the fact that Tibet itself has in recent years become a popular tourist destination not for Europeans and Americans but for Han Chinese.

"Shangri-la" functions as a powerful marker of a particular world view that combines liberal humanism with a glossed-over form of Tibetan Buddhism attractive not to "The West" or "Westerners" at large, but to specific socio-economic classes (Frechette 2002). In other words, rather than being an elixir to the problems of the modern (Western) world, Shangri-la, in the form of Tibet, Tibetans, and Tibetan Buddhism, is the domain of a transnational class of like-minded liberal humanists who expect from it a perspective more at home on the Upper West Side of Manhattan than in a monastic community on the Tibetan plateau. Shangri-la also functions as a consumer marker, connoting just such a liberal humanist world view. Taking the form of jewelry, religious objects, Buddhist imagery, and clothing, this material marker of Tibet is bought and sold in markets such as the Eastern Market.

Jamyang had arrived in the United States from Nepal almost two decades earlier and had long held legal status in the US. After working as a shipping manager for a freight company for ten years, he had gone into business as an importer of all things

Tibetan. For the past eight years he had sold his wares at Eastern Market. He was not Tibetan but Newari, the dominant ethnic group in the Kathmandu valley of Nepal. His father had been a trader in Kathmandu, specializing in the gold ink used for Hindu and Buddhist religious paintings. Using his family contacts, Jamyang had built up his import business and now supplied almost 700 Tibet-themed retailers across the United States in addition to vending at Eastern Market. None of his products actually was made in Tibet; everything was made in Nepal.

Jamyang asserted that he did not buy wholesale in Kathmandu, as other importers did. "I always make the designs," he explained. "I know what Americans want." He had quickly learned that what sold best were the products (primarily textile prints, prayer flags, and jewelry) he designed based on what his non-Tibetan customers desired of "Tibet," not actual Tibetan religious or cultural objects. His success had led to a boom in business, and he usually imported between three and four metric tons of goods each year.

Jamyang had thought about importing directly from Tibet, but had never been able to secure a Chinese visa to investigate opportunities. As for buying products from India, he dismissed this on a quality and cost basis:

> Production is much cheaper in India [than in Kathmandu], but the handicraft work in Nepal is way better quality than in India. Most of the statues, the prayer wheels, these kinds of things are all made by Newaris. This is where I have my connections, too.

As for the social aspect of vending, he had no illusions. "Coming here every weekend, setting up, standing here all day, putting everything away at the end of the day, I get really sick of this," he said. "If I could find someone I could trust to take it over, I would."

Strategies of authenticity

For vendors selling imported goods, intentions differed between (white) American vendors and immigrant vendors. From the perspective of most American vendors, durability, sustainability, and fair trade practices (or, ideally, a combination of these qualities) marked the goods they sold as objects that carried a purpose beyond mere utility. A rug should not just cover a floor, it should be made with natural materials, last more than a lifetime, and be produced by hand by fairly paid artisans. A tablecloth should not just look nice and feel soft and be washable, it should also support women's rights, or the education of young girls, or the Tibetan independence movement. These vendors did not see themselves as just vendors, because they did not believe they merely sold imported products in a market. Instead, they identified as artists, educators, and activists. What they sold was a political position, one which championed social change as a key aspect of economic exchange and embraced the transformative rhetoric of neoliberal ideologies such as micro-credit. Their message was straightforward: through the right kind of consumption, people could support art and social movements, and be "good."

In contrast, many immigrant vendors focused on making a profit. How cheap could objects be bought, and what objects did Americans want? Kumar sold leather bags made in Colombia because he had contacts there and production costs were low. He voiced no concerns about worker rights, or the side effects of the productive process. Instead, he stressed his low prices, good quality, and the social status of his "replicas." Chun knew down to the gram the weight and shipping costs of different types of fake Pashmina products, while the Chen family sold small coin purses now, and no longer pearls or scarves of dubious quality because purses offered a better profit.

Some immigrant vendors enjoyed a comparative advantage over American vendors in their ability to effectively market themselves as part of their products. As Plattner (1982, 1996) explains, a price paradox exists in situations in which consumers lack sufficient expertise and information to judge the value of objects. Given this lack of information, price becomes a common method for determining quality, which means that lowering prices can potentially harm sales, not increase them. At Eastern Market, a jeweler's dilemma existed for precisely this reason. As the number of vendors selling jewelry increased in the years leading up to the 2007 fire, prices declined. This affected the sales of higher quality jewelry vendors, since many customers were not skilled at determining real silver from white metal or plated metal and therefore had to rely on price as an indicator of authenticity and quality. Nakhon, originally from the Thai beach resort of Phuket, managed to protect his market share by marketing himself as a simulacrum of a generalized Thai "hill-tribe" member (which he was not), much like Jamyang strategically performed as a Tibetan. The irony is that, from the perspective of many middle-class Thais, he undoubtedly did not look Thai at all but, with his long hair, tattoos, and Bob Marley T-shirt, more like a foreign beach boy of dubious moral standards. But this did not prevent his American customers at the market from buying from him, because he was "the Thai jewelry guy."

This placed some consumers in a dilemma. Does one buy an imported tablecloth from an American vendor who promises social justice and the promotion of creativity? Or does one make a purchase from a "real" Indian or Thai or Javanese vendor, who offers a different form of authenticity, one linking the material object to the vendor and his or her purported home?

In summary, when faced with a management plan designed to remove non-artists and non-farmer vendors from this market, retail vendors responded in several ways. Some American importers sought to transform commercial transactions into a signifier of moral worth, while others repositioned themselves as not retailers but artists. Immigrant vendors, on the other hand, strategically embraced the cultural roles cast for them by their customer base, whether Tibetan exile, Third-World Rastafarian, or indigenous Peruvian, a performance of self that helped sell products.

Conclusion

As Judith Butler (1997) has shown, identity emerges from performance. In other words, people perform, in a productive sense, their identities by drawing from a range of scripted frames that constitute both dominant normative and implicitly sanctioned non-normative practices. Butler argues this demonstrates that no original, fully developed or pure identity exists beneath the surface; what we perform is not "the real" but an always emerging and contingent self.

Street markets function much the same way. The "character" and "color" of a site such as Eastern Market noted in guidebooks and by visitors does not exist independent of the vending community that forms each weekend morning. Indeed, the market as a separate entity does not exist beyond its physical manifestation. It is useful to distinguish between *this* Eastern Market (the physical building, outdoor farmers' line, north plaza, and streetscape) and *the* Eastern Market (a weekend social event). This social event is increasingly linked to bureaucratic plans that seek to manage how the market functions and what counts as a legitimate product, and hence what sorts of customers frequent this space. Local farmers, artists, and artisans are welcome in this reworked public space, while retail vendors, particularly those selling goods that originate through the supply chains of globalization from below, are not.

This transformation of a largely unregulated marketplace filled with vendors selling everything from artwork and jewelry to used furniture, vintage clothing, and a wide array of cheap imports into a supposedly local community-centered market has been welcomed by affluent neighborhood activists who claim ownership over Eastern Market. But their vision of a restored neighborhood market of quality local foods and artwork is at best a convenient fiction, a desire for something that historically never has existed. It is also an ambivalent reaction to a process of globalization from the street level, led not by a nativist conservative movement but instead emanating from an urban, highly cosmopolitan and privileged group of elites. This case illustrates the underlying tensions within a supposedly global anti-globalization movement, particularly the different goals of privileged people located at the center of the global trade system and citizens of more marginal areas. If for the former, resisting global forces means protecting and privileging an abstract "local," for the latter, particularly for global traders "from below," a place in this world is the goal; the rest is, to quote Kumar, "all bullshit."

Ironically, the reinvention of Eastern Market as a cleaned-up space of properly credentialed artists, farmers, and neighborhood merchants has not led to the erasure of what this market until 2008 was—a chaotic, thinly regulated street market with little government presence. The latter market has traveled across the street from Eastern Market, to the parking lot of a closed middle school. It is in this alternative public space, that the vendors who managed and sustained Eastern Market for most of the past three decades have survived by eluding the oversight of the city's Division of Real Estate Services (DRES). Instead, their landlord is the city's Department of Education, custodians of the shuttered middle school.

Rather than a counter-hegemonic space, this satellite market is more aptly characterized as a non-hegemonic space, one in which vendors go about dealing in the everyday realities of globalization (Ribeiro 2009). It is also a very crowded marketplace, primarily because many of the people who visit Eastern Market on weekends are not Capitol Hill residents buying fresh vegetables and fine art but tourists and others browsing an eclectic assortment of products from around the world, vended by people to match.

Far from proclaiming their localness, managers of this market foreground the global basis of this site, asserting they have vendors from five continents. "Though not the largest," they proclaim on their website, "it is arguably one of the most diverse in the nation. The Flea Market features arts, crafts, antiques, collectibles, and imports from around the world" (The Flea Market at Eastern Market 2010).

While this contingent market space has flourished since 2008, vendors at the "authentic" Eastern Market complain about a decline in sales. This is not a result of a sudden influx of Chinese vendors but rather because the management plan for this site aims to eliminate imports and products that do not qualify as either fine art or "local" foods. Contrary to the market model shared by community activists and market managers, "authenticity" cannot be reduced to either an unreflective naturalism as expressed in "local" foods or to aesthetic judgments about high versus low or "art" versus "junk."

How long this satellite market can survive is unclear, since the organizers' lease expires in 2012. After this, depending on the extent to which the local real estate market has recovered from the current recession, the former school parking lot that hosts this flea market might well be sold to private developers, thus perhaps ending the story of an organic Eastern Market and leaving a carefully staged historic marketplace in its wake—one suitable to the privileged elites of Washington's Capitol Hill.

References

Alkon, A. (2008) "Paradise or Pavement: The Social Constructions of the Environment in Two Urban Farmers' Markets and their Implications for Environmental Justice and Sustainability," *Local Environment* 13(3): 271–89.

Bishop, P. (1989) *The Myth of Shangri-la: Tibet, Travel Writing, and the Western Creation of Sacred Landscape*, Berkeley: University of California Press.

Boyer, M. (1995) "The Great Frame-Up: Fantastic Appearance in Contemporary Spatial Politics," in H. Liggett and D. Perry, eds, *Spatial Practices*, London: Sage, 81–109.

Brown, A. (2001) "Counting Farmers Markets," *Geographical Review* 91(4): 655–74.

Butler, J. (1997) *The Psychic Life of Power: Theories in Subjection*, Stanford: Stanford University Press.

District of Columbia, Department of Real Estate Services (2010) "Eastern Market: Food, Flowers, Arts & Crafts": http://www.easternmarket-dc.org/default.asp?ContentID=3 (accessed September 17, 2010).

Dodin, T. and H. Rather (eds) (2001) *Imagining Tibet: Perceptions, Projections, and Fantasies*, Boston: Wisdom Publications.

DuPuis, E. M. and D. Goodman (2005) "Should We Go 'Home' to Eat? Toward a Reflexive Politics of Localism," *Journal of Rural Studies* 21: 359–71.

Esteva, G. (1987) "Regenerating People's Space," *Alternatives* 12(1): 125–52.

Ferguson, J. (2006) *Global Shadows: Africa in the Neoliberal World Order*, Durham and London: Duke University Press.

Frechette, A. (2002) *Tibetans in Nepal: The Dynamics of International Assistance among a Community in Exile*, New York: Berghahn Books.

Gillespie, G., D. Hilchey, C. Hinrichs, and G. Freensta (2007) "Farmers' Markets as Keystones in Rebuilding Local and Regional Food Systems," in C. Hinrichs and T. Lyson, eds, *Remaking the North American Food System*, Lincoln: University of Nebraska Press, 65–83.

Goodale, M. (2009) *Surrendering to Utopia: An Anthropology of Human Rights*, Stanford, CA: Stanford University Press.

Guthman, J. (2003) "Fast Food/Organic Food: Reflexive Tastes and the Making of 'Yuppie Chow,'" *Social & Cultural Geography* 4(1): 45–58.

Korton, D. (2006) *Getting to the 21st Century: Voluntary Action and the Global Agenda*, Kumarian Press.

Lopez, D. (1998) *Prisoners of Shangri-La: Tibetan Buddhism and the West*, Chicago: University of Chicago Press.

Mathews, G. (2007) "Chungking Mansions: A Center of 'Low-End Globalization,'" *Ethnology* XLVI (2): 169–83.

Plattner, S. (1982) "Economic Decision-Making in a Public Marketplace," *American Ethnologist* 9(2): 399–420.

——(1996) *High Art Down Home: An Economic Ethnography of a Local Art Market*, Chicago: University of Chicago Press.

Pyle, J. (1971) "Farmers' Markets in the United States: Functional Anachronisms," *Geographical Review* 61(2): 167–97.

Ribeiro, G. L. (2006) "Economic Globalization from Below," *Etnografica* X(2): 233–49.

——(2009) "Non-Hegemonic Globalizations: Alter-native Transnational Processes and Agents," *Anthropological Theory* 9(3): 297–329.

Seyfang, G. (2008) "Avoiding Asda? Exploring Consumer Motivations in Local Organic Food Networks," *Local Environment* 13(3): 87–101.

Stoller, P. (2002) *Money Has No Smell: The Africanization of New York City*, Chicago: University of Chicago Press.

Tangires, H. (2004) *Public Markets and Civic Culture in Nineteenth Century America*, Baltimore: Johns Hopkins University Press.

Tehranian, K. (1995) *Modernity, Space and Power: The American City in Discourse and Practice*, Cresskill, NJ: Hampton Press.

The Flea Market at Eastern Market (2010) http://www.easternmarket.net (accessed September 17, 2010).

Washington DC City Council (1999) "Eastern Market Real Property Asset Management and Outdoor Vending Act of 1998," approved April 16, DC Law 12-228), Section 2.3-9.

Wemple, E. and V. Bauzá (1996) "Food Fight: The Battle over Eastern Market has Capitol Hill Preservationists Running on Autopilot," *Washington City Paper*, 28 June, http://www.washingtoncitypaper.com/articles/10637/food-fight-the-battle-over-eastern-market-has-capitol-hill-preservationists-running-on-autopilot (accessed September 11, 2010).

12

LOCAL POLITICS AND GLOBALIZATION FROM BELOW

The peddler leaders of Mexico City's historic center streets

Carlos Alba Vega

Introduction

On September 6, 1996, the *New York Times* reported on the death of Guillermina Rico, aged 63, a street vendor of lemons in Mexico City. But she was no ordinary vendor:

> "[she] bargained her way to wealth and power as the head of a political machine she forged from the ranks of Mexico City's itinerant vendors […] In a 40-year career, Mrs Rico led thousands of market peddlers through cycles of street war and peace with successive Mexico City mayors, who have repeatedly sought to clear the streets of the informal merchants who block sidewalks in front of tax-paying businesses."
>
> *(Dillon 1996)*

The obituary discusses the outpourings of grief following her death, with 2,000 people walking three miles with her coffin from the city center to her burial site. It also mentions how Mrs Rico's office was replete with photos of her meetings with mayors, police chiefs, senators, and the Mexican president. Indeed, she was an immensely powerful woman by the time of her death, as the head of the Civic Union of Street Vendors of Old Merced. "Today Mexico City's central market," which Mrs Rico organized and represented, "is among the largest outlets in the world for contraband" (Dillon 1996). The area once represented by Mrs Rico is the focus of my investigation in this chapter.

Mexico City has one of the highest peddler concentrations in the world (Monnet and Bonnafé 2005). No one knows exactly how many there are; estimates range between 350,000 and 500,000. There are at least 20,000 peddlers in downtown Mexico City—who during certain periods of the year can double in number—and most of them were represented by Mrs Rico. These merchants sell the formal economy's

FIGURE 12.1 The most important leader of street peddlers, Guillermina Rico, with her daughter Silvia Sánchez Rico. Photo from the Sánchez Rico Family Archive. Reproduced with permission

products such as Telmex cell phone cards, made by a company owned by Carlos Slim, the Mexican businessman who is the richest man in the world, and products from big food companies in Mexico like BIMBO. They also sell smuggled and pirated products, many of which now come from China: CDs, DVDs, clothing, and shoes.

Located in the symbolic heart of the capital, every day these peddlers contravene many laws (Cámara Nacional de Comercio 1987; Austin 1994). They block vehicle circulation on the streets and curbs; they prepare and sell food in the street without permits from the health department; they don't pay most taxes; they sell contraband and pirated merchandise; and they are not covered by the Federal Labor Law, meaning that their employees are not guaranteed minimum wage or social security. In many cases they draw electricity from the power mains without paying for it; in other cases they adversely affect public and historical buildings. Since 1993 there has been a legal statute in the Federal District that prohibits peddling in what has been denominated the historic center's "Perimeter A." How can these merchants sell in prohibited places and contravene laws in plain sight? In this chapter I explore this in terms of the political dimension of the existence and development of globalization from below. What are the social and political conditions that make it possible for street merchants to sell legal and illegal goods coming into Mexico City's historic center?

Globalization from below has been ethnographically and theoretically examined by a number of scholars (Tarrius 2002; Portes, Guarnizo and Landolt 2003; Ribeiro 2007; Mathews 2011), but its political organization within the various locales in which it takes place has not often been considered. Behind the informal economy's apparently unruly front and reduced state intervention, there are systems of political, cultural, and social regulations that sustain and make possible commercial activities (Tokman 2007). In this chapter, based on 100 in-depth interviews with street peddler leaders and their advisors, and shopkeepers and peddlers, and two surveys of 750 peddlers in all, I focus on the different forms of political organization that Mexico City's historic center peddlers have developed in order to get, use and distribute public space—the central element of disputes among them—and global merchandise of both legal and illegal origin (Escobedo: 2006).

Street commerce in Mexico City's historic center is a shifting century-old phenomenon that since the end of the twentieth century has achieved economic significance, social importance, and political interest. Because of their numbers and characteristics, street peddlers have become relevant economic and political actors.

Unlike dispersed and fragmented informal industrial producers, who usually have no political representation (Alba and Kruijt 1994), street peddlers in Mexico's Federal District need a high degree of organization in order to defend their interests and carry out their trade. In this chapter I focus on street peddler organization leaders. Who are they, and how do they rise and develop? What functions do street peddler organization leaders fulfill in the economics and politics of informality? I also examine the organizations' inner workings: the changes and continuities they have experienced in the context of the political transition Mexico underwent in the 1980s.

Street peddlers in Mexico City

One of the main characteristics of street peddlers is their versatility and flexibility in adapting to product change. A single merchant might change products ten times a year, depending on the season and fashion. These products' origins also change over time. Peddlers generally sell three categories of products: those produced in Mexico's "formal" and "informal" economies, those legally imported, and those imported through contraband and piracy, involving a major proportion of these goods. The Director of the American Chamber of Commerce of Mexico, Larry Rubin, considers that smuggling and piracy characterize "80% of movies sales, 70% of music CDs sales, 65% of software, 50% of the clothing market, 30% of books […]. 33% of retail alcoholic drink sales and 30% of jewels" (Posada García 2007).

As my fieldwork has shown, most of the commodities sold in the street belong to the informal economic circuit, some produced in Mexico, but even more smuggled from overseas. Street peddling in Mexico flourished well before economic liberalization (Barbosa Cruz 2008). However, the opening up of Mexico to foreign merchandise since the mid 1980s has coincided with the distribution of pirated and smuggled goods in Mexico's internal market (Esquivel 2008). Before that time, many of these products were manufactured in Mexico. Up until 2000, smuggled goods came almost exclusively from the United States, as much from small-scale smuggling—concealing goods in suitcases or luggage, referred to as *fayuca* in Mexico (see Gauthier's chapter 8)—as from large-scale container contraband, which necessarily relied on police and customs employees' connivance. *Fayuqueros* used to get their supplies in many cities in the Southern United States, in the case of textiles, from LA's "Fashion District" in California (Alarcón 2008: 94–102). At first peddlers traveled frequently by bus to the US to buy *fayuca* products; but over time, wholesale intermediaries that delivered merchandise to peddlers in Mexico City appeared—notably in Tepito, a neighborhood that serves as a major distribution node (Alba Villalever 2008). Progressively, suitcase *fayuca* turned into container contraband.

Historically, clandestine importers have prospered in Mexico because they provide a wider variety of products, better prices, and better quality in comparison to Mexico's own protected goods. However, the twenty-first century has changed the nature of the goods transiting in the lower circuits of the economy. On the one hand, the onset of NAFTA in 1994 progressively eliminated taxation on a wide variety of products made in the USA; hence, foreign product prices in Mexico dropped and as a consequence smuggling—especially suitcase *fayuca*—became largely obsolete. On the other hand, economic reform in China and the country's inclusion in the World Trade Organization in 2001 has led to products from China holding an ever-growing importance not just in "globalization from above" but also in "globalization from below," informal trade down semi-legal or illegal channels. The distribution networks which transited overland on a north–south axis prevailing in Mexico throughout the twentieth century begin to be complemented by trans-Pacific contraband commercial networks through Mexican docks or through the intermediary of Southern United States' Pacific docks.

Some of the main operators of this new form of contraband commerce are the same as in earlier eras: Mexican "formal merchants," "informal merchants" with experience in international commerce (many of them from Tepito), and Mexican customs functionaries and employees. Other operators were weakened: especially Mexican migrants who had become intermediaries in the United States. New actors have appeared, especially Asian merchants: Koreans started arriving after the Argentinian crisis at the beginning of the 1990s, sometimes with previous commercial experience in that country, and Chinese started arriving during the later 1990s. Both ethnic groups have rented or bought businesses in areas of dense popular commerce in Mexico City's center as well as in Tepito; however, they generally do not directly retail goods on the street. They started in their businesses while speaking practically no Spanish, assisted by street peddler leaders in exchange for a fee. In Mexico City's historic center, there are nearly 100 Chinese importers, some 70 percent of them women; they bring products from China and distribute them among street peddlers or sell them directly to established businesses.

These Chinese importers give short-term credit to small street merchants, something that Mexican providers do not do. Furthermore, they have established several Chinese import business schemes in association with Tepito's merchants. Tepito's most important street merchant leader, who runs the Popular Organizations' Metropolitan

FIGURE 12.2 Tepito's street vendors' leader, María Rosete, associated with Anne Lang for Chinese products importation. Photo by Carlos Alba Vega. Reproduced with permission

Front (Frente Metropolitano de Organizaciones Populares (FMOP)), which has 28 organizations with some 5,000 merchants in all, is associated with a Chinese female doctor, who arrived 17 years ago in Mexico and, after being unable to work as a physician, decided to go into commerce. She now has six Chinese imported goods shops specializing in women's bags. Her project is carried out with the support of Chinese entrepreneurs and its goal is to become an import business for inexpensive, legal products from China, retailed by the peddler organization's affiliates.

Today, Tepito's merchant leaders' business cards are often written in Mandarin as well as Spanish. There are several dozen merchants in Tepito who travel several times a year to China in order to buy merchandise, and one of their favorite spots is Yiwu, as discussed in Pliez's chapter. Some of them charge other Tepito merchants a fee to teach them their know-how of the Chinese import business and to accompany them to China. For several years now, a "Tepiteño" community has settled in Beijing to facilitate this "international commerce from below." The main commodities smuggled from China are textiles and low-quality clothing, plastic footwear, toys, glass and pottery products, appliances and electronics, perfumes, accessories (bags, watches, sunglasses, etc.), and blank and recorded CDs/DVDs, as discussed in Aguiar's chapter.

Contraband expansion in the context of market liberalization and the dismantling of import barriers is at first sight paradoxical. In reality, contraband consists of merchandise that is still highly taxed or subject to compensatory fees, when it is proven that they have been introduced under conditions of price discrimination (dumping) (Nadima 2004), which is the case for textiles, clothing, and shoes coming from China. One of the main characteristics of contemporary contraband is its extreme diversity of actors, circuits, and provision techniques (Tarrius 2002). In Mexico, the sale of smuggled goods in street commerce is just one kind of distribution among others, even if it is the best known because of its visibility. Some large distribution groups, supermarkets, and specialized warehouse chains, representing some 55 percent of the national clothing market, have resorted to illegal imports (Salmon 2002). Some cases are those of Gigante, Liverpool, and Zara-Inditex, just to mention companies that have been subject to penalties.

Triangulation—moving Asian products with elevated fees through third countries such as the US in order to re-export them after tampering with their associated legal documents and labels in order to benefit from free trade agreements—is the most common procedure to introduce large quantities of smuggled merchandise. The financial power of those distribution groups and companies and the support they receive from the governments who harbor their headquarters make them almost invulnerable to customs investigations. A part of the exporting of what are known as *maquilas*[1] also takes place in contraband circuits, especially for fabrics. Once the fabrics have been transformed by the industries or by their subcontractors, the products are transferred to formal commercial establishments, or to small street merchants through wholesalers. It is inaccurate to characterize illegal commerce as a specialized segment of informal trade. In fact, in many cases it is the large, registered companies who are the origin of contraband flows, a part of which is redistributed through thousands of street peddlers. Non-hegemonic globalization isn't always an independent circuit from the hegemonic: often they are in a symbiotic relationship.

Peddler organizations and their leaders

According to official records issued by authorities from *Delegación Cuauhtémoc* who handle the historic center's administration, on the eve of the third massive relocation of street merchants in Mexico City's contemporary history in October 2007,[2] in Mexico City's historic center there were 18,973 peddlers grouped in 69 organizations. On average each organization had 275 merchants. However, this average hid great heterogeneity. Some organizations have had only a few peddlers while others have thousands.

It is important to note that, unlike peddler organizations in other Latin American cities, women play an important role in street leadership. Just over half of the organizations, including some of the biggest, are run by women, such as Guillermina Rico (until her death in 1996), Alejandra Barrios in Mexico City's historic center, and María Rosete in Tepito.

Almost half of Centro Histórico and Tepito small vendors' business belongs to women (46 percent), a higher proportion of participation when compared with other business women in the Mexican economy, where gender segregation is large. Women make up 23 percent of the Mexican labor force, but only 16 percent in the business sector are women. Among the most important reasons explaining the place of women as street vendors is the need to support themselves and their children when they become widows, are divorced, or are abandoned by their husbands. Half of these women working in downtown Mexico City are married or living in free union, while the other half are single, divorced, separated, or widowed. A third of women are single and most of them are single mothers with children under their care. Informal commerce is a very important option for these women, who couldn't work in a formal enterprise even if they could find this type of job, as they need flexible hours in order to balance their work at home and the care of children. Working in the streets as merchants is also important for divorced and widowed women (one in five in our sample) who need to support their dependants.

Leaders, like the peddlers they represent, are the result of three major transformations that occurred in Mexico during the second half of the twentieth century: a demographic shift, an economic crisis and its aftermath, and a political transition. The Mexican population radically transformed during the last century, from being primarily rural to mainly urban. In 1900, Mexico's capital had some 500,000 inhabitants, representing 14 percent of its 13 million people; by 2000, Mexico City had 17 million inhabitants— about 18 percent of the country's 100 million people—turning it into one of the world's largest cities. Like other Latin American countries, the exhaustion of the import substitution model,[3] the public debt crisis that arose in 1982, and the installation of liberal policies for "adjustment" and free trade provoked a decrease in job creation in the traditional industrial sector (textile, clothing, shoes), which were now highly exposed to outside competition. Street peddlers have had powerful organizations linked to political parties, whose members, in exchange for tolerance and connivance, are mobilized by politicians and leaders throughout electoral competition (Alba and Labazée 2007).

Leaders, as well as merchants, were born for the most part in Mexico City and its surroundings. They are the children of street peddlers or small merchants; most of their parents were also born in the capital and its surroundings. Most leaders experienced family issues, parental abandonment, or were orphans. Leaders and many peddlers from the capital's historic center, the Merced market, and Tepito commonly inhabited *vecindades*, precarious two-story buildings where many large families lived in overcrowded conditions, each in a single room with kitchen but no sanitary facilities.

Peddler leaders started working from a very young age. Some remember being in the street since their early childhood, next to their parents, usually accompanying their mother every day at work. Many of them undertook their first jobs at six or seven; others started even earlier. These leaders sold products of the informal economy like pirated CDs and DVDs; they also traded clothing made in clandestine workshops in the city's historic center until the earthquake in 1985, when they were displaced to neighborhoods on the periphery of the megalopolis or its surrounding towns. Leaders have also sold products issued by the formal economy: candy and chocolate, packaged food, paper, cosmetics, and school supplies. Most of these leaders only completed elementary school, with some not even finishing that, while a few managed to complete junior high school. Many of the leaders, like many of the women who peddle in the street, got pregnant in their adolescence, and either formally married or lived with their significant other, but in many cases they were unable to sustain the relationship. They have also been exposed to the abuse of colleagues, police, and government personnel. Most wish for their children not to have to be peddlers, which they consider stigmatized and dangerous work. Sometimes they have to assume punishment for transgressions of traditional roles in Mexican homes for their husbands to accept their roles not just as wife and mother, but also as peddler, and as peddler leader.

In street peddling, as in other spheres, political capital is a crucial factor in wielding power. During their lives, leaders accumulate experience, relationships, contacts, and know-how that can be transferred to their successors. Knowledge of bureaucratic proceedings in government offices, access to government employees, knowledge of how to deal with the police, and facility in finding political consultants, are all "intangible valuables" that can be taken advantage of by their successors. They are, however, no guarantee of success for new generations. Structural economic, social, and political conditions, as well as personal qualities belonging to the new leaders are also needed in order for them to foster the political capital they inherited.

In downtown Mexico City, one can distinguish between two generations of contemporary peddler leaders. The first generation is made up of pioneers. Some of them started trading during the 1950s and 1960s, and their leadership predates the Mexican financial crisis of 1982, after which street commerce became a mass phenomenon. This first generation of peddler leaders suffered persecution and imprisonment at the hands of the Federal District's market authorities. They were the first women to show true and formal leadership functions in the context of street peddling. Even though they were poorly educated, some have managed to control thousands of street merchants.

In earlier eras, peddlers were a marginal sector from a political point of view. It was the time during which the import substitution scheme spiraled towards its crisis, and Mexico's youth started migrating massively to the United States. The economic crisis and the change in the production model, along with a shift in the District Federales' governing political party in 1997, from the PRI, the political party that governed Mexico without interruption from 1929 until 2000, to the PRD, a left-wing party created in 1989, transformed street peddlers into important economic and political agents. If, at first, they were rejected and repressed, later on they became tolerated and politically channeled.

A second generation of leaders was born after the 1982 financial crisis and subsequent economic reforms and adjustments (adoption of free trade, abandonment of regulations, privatization) that led to the rise of informal commerce. A significant number of these second-generation leaders worked as delegates in Guillermina Rico's organization. They took advantage of three situations in order to leave their original group: the death of "la Jefa," "the female boss" on September 4, 1996, as mentioned in the quotation at the start of this chapter; the organization's crisis during the leadership's succession process, when la Jefa's daughter Silvia Sánchez Rico took possession of the organization with a different governing style and new ground rules that weren't easily accepted by many of the delegates; and finally the violent conflicts and confrontations over the control of retail locations in the streets, provoked by the disappearance of the discipline that had been established by the actions of that historical leader, which led in July 1999 to the imprisonment of Silvia Sánchez Rico and her son Julio. With them behind bars, many of these delegates were able to establish their own leadership.

Before the early 1980s, street peddler leadership was very concentrated. A few leaders represented all the street merchants from downtown Mexico City. At first, leaders didn't belong to any party organization; it wasn't until the PRI, the governing political party at that time, and the street merchants both saw the convenience of political mediation through peddler organizations' incorporation into the party that they became political. This allowed them to move from street confrontation and bribery of local authorities to higher-level negotiations enabling benefits for both the government and for peddlers.

When the PRD took office in Mexico City in 1997 there were 13 street peddler organizations in its historic center. Ten years later, on October 12, 2007, when Marcelo Ebrard's administration undertook the third massive street peddler relocation action in downtown Mexico City there were nearly 70 organizations. Political motives can help explain this phenomenon. With the appointment of PRD militant Dolores Padierna to head *Delegación Cuauhtémoc*, street peddling expanded notably, from 12,000 in 2000 to 20,000 in 2003.

Peddler organizations and their political structure

Almost all street peddler organizations were formally registered after the 1982 economic crisis; Guillermina Rico's association had operated without official papers from the 1960s onwards, and was the first to register in the early 1970s. Seen from the inside, merchant organizations present formal structures with few hierarchical levels and a strong concentration of power on leaders. However, there is a difference between the formal organization legally required to constitute a nonprofit organization and the real structure of power. The biggest and most complex street peddler organizations have a *"líder"* (the leader), *"delegados"* (their delegates), and other positions such as *"chalanes"* (handymen with multiple functions), and *"charoleros"* (collectors of organization fees, whose name comes from the *"charola,"* a tray where peddlers pay their money).

The organization's top position is that of the leader, even though many of them prefer to be called "representatives" instead, out of respect to Guillermina Rico, the one and only true leader. The leader works as a hinge between two worlds: that of the ruling class, the political, economic, and religious authorities, and the subaltern class of those who become peddlers. Leaders arise from the necessity to organize and regulate informal commerce in urban public spaces. They are social agents that street peddlers see as actors capable of getting, defending, and providing, or taking away retail spots in the streets. Whoever wants to trade in the street has to go through them or their delegates to obtain a retailing spot. The leader will decide whether or not to grant this, and will assign the specific location and territorial spread (usually 2 meters by 1 meter) where the peddler can sell goods. They will also decide on the weekly fee the peddler will have to pay to the organization in order to keep the informal commerce system lubricated and running.

One of the leaders' main functions is to exert control over the urban space under their dominion. Such spaces can range from 50 meters on a single street, in the case of the smallest organizations, to ten downtown streets and other locations with high demographic concentrations such as public transportation systems, especially the subway.

In those spaces leaders negotiate and mediate potential conflict between peddlers. For example, they will not allow two retailing spots selling the same merchandise to be located next to one another. They watch over the interests and relationships among merchants and clients, and make sure that peddlers aren't overly aggressive towards pedestrians and customers.

Líderes also carry out social and welfare functions. The most powerful among them provide social benefits to their informal commerce associates, such as establishing nurseries for mothers to be able to leave their children while they work. Even though small organizations lack the resources to offer these benefits, they are guided by the influence of bigger organizations and aspire to provide sport fields, gyms, or schools. It is common for leaders to give some help and protection to the neighborhood beggars and the unemployed, such as breakfasts or hot coffee on cold mornings. Less commonly, retailing spots are offered to ex-convicts who have difficulty finding jobs. Every week, Tarín, one of the leaders, visits ex-convicts and helps them through their process of reintegration. An ex-convict himself, he was helped in the same way by Guillermina Rico.

Líderes must be rooted to the space they control. One way to be rooted is that of having been born near the neighborhood one controls, as is often the case. Socialization at the *barrio*'s school also counts, because this institution provides a sense of belonging that unites a leader with other members of the community. Persistence is another important trait: leaders' survival capacities grow through time, in the face of adversity and the challenges they must overcome in the streets. Ability to re-establish contacts with new local authorities every term, maintaining power over their *delegados*, and preventing the peddler base from taking radical action and engaging in violence, are all necessary traits. Time is usually a factor that plays in favor of leaders; it allows them to accumulate experience, contacts, prudence, and political capital. However, it can also be a risk: if they stay away too long from their peddler base, leaders may come to be seen as "fat cats" living off the earnings of their peddlers, who can easily be shoved out of the way. It is common for downtown leaders to maintain peddlers' support for years and even decades, but in order to succeed, they have to be useful to their relations at both the top and the bottom of the community. In Mexico City's historic center and in Tepito as well, leadership is often held for life, and may be passed on to one's descendants.

For peddlers, one of the most appreciated qualities in a leader is their "capacity for struggle" in terms of defending and expanding retail territory in opposition to other groups as well as local authorities. At times, leaders take matters into their own hands to settle situations against adversaries or the police. They round up their followers and defend their territory armed with what they can find at hand: stones, sticks, and a few firearms. However, there are no recorded confrontations involving high-caliber guns, a common choice for organized crime groups. I have no records of street peddler organizations infiltrated by criminal organizations. Nevertheless, since 2008 I have observed new pressure from criminal groups attempting to engage in the sale of pirated and smuggled goods and to control peddler organizations to whom they try to sell protection. On the other hand, some peddler organizations themselves engage in the selling of stolen goods like clothing and food.

Speech is a resource leaders must commonly employ, as much to convince and negotiate with their organization during periodic assemblies as to motivate and spur hundreds or thousands of followers during demonstrations, meetings, and protests against or in support of authorities or politicians during their campaigns. Not all leaders are good speakers. Some of the leaders' descendants have been to oratory workshops to become clearer and more effective when communicating their messages; sometimes they even have image consultants. In some cases they use their assistants' help to write speeches to be read to the organization, such as Mazahua, Triqui, and Zapoteco Indians leaders who do not have a full grip on Spanish.

Líderes may also be businessmen. They have been peddlers and may continue to be so. In some cases, their relationships both inside and outside the organization enable them to distribute national and international merchandise from the formal or

FIGURE 12.3 Merchants of used clothes protesting in front of the National Palace in Mexico City. Photo by Ingeborg Denissen. Reproduced with permission

the informal economy to the merchants in their organization. Sometimes they even import the merchandise; they travel to the United States, and now China, to order custom-manufactured goods, including original brand names like Rosete, or they buy goods directly from wholesalers and import agencies.

Leaders bring together the world of formality and the world of informality. Some formal shopkeepers in Mexico City's historic center need leaders to help them distribute their merchandise, legal and illegal. Leaders also help them find occupants for their commercial plazas, in which case they receive a commission. If a leader has a great number of followers and political power from below, she can enjoy considerable independence from state and party authorities. However, it is common for a leader to enjoy support from above and outside the organization, whether from a political party or from some city official. Their main support comes from congressmen, the heads of political party factions, a state secretary, or a representative of the *Delegación*. Many leaders do not hide their wish to run for office in formal political posts; however, up until now very few leaders have managed to be elected to official posts, among them Celia Torres, with a seat in congress, and Sergio Jiménez Barrios. Guillermina Rico, with all her power, never went beyond being a substitute congresswoman. She said she didn't want any political positions because she could not write or speak well.

Most of the leaders support the PRD. Nevertheless, the biggest and most powerful peddler organizations have been led by PRI supporters. The fact that the PRD came into office in the capital in 1997 posed a crucial problem. How should the peddler leaders engage a new government? Should they keep their political affiliation or switch parties? Since then, confrontations between opposing peddler groups, and against Mexico City's authorities, have pushed leaders to adopt pragmatic and politically ambiguous postures in order to adapt and survive. Many of them have turned to the PRD, currently in City Hall, and the *Delegación* chieftaincies where their organizations trade. Others stayed with the PRI. Leaders have deployed adaptation strategies, such as simultaneously "betting" for the PRI and the PRD through their children, who are also leaders. Another alternative is to foster and promote smaller leaders with a political affiliation different than theirs. For that reason it's not unusual for a PRI-affiliated leader to protect a smaller PRD-affiliated group.

Most peddler organization leaders have at least one *consejero* (advisor) or several in some cases. While leaders develop an ability to perceive challenges, opportunities, and risks unseen and unheard by others, advisors watch and listen for what is invisible or inaudible to leaders. Advisors tend to have fewer direct relations with heads of office and with peddlers than the leader. However, they tend to have more time at their disposal and the right connections to give and receive information from the press about the political atmosphere. The distance they keep from peddlers' positions allows them to interpret what they see without anybody interfering through pressure or public demands; this helps leaders to get the lay of the land before advising between, for example, moderate or more radical actions. In most cases, having worked in the city's administration at some point, advisors are familiar with the problems of street peddling and have direct access to certain government employees in middle positions in the local administration. This allows them to get useful information and access to audiences when they need to raise issues. Because of their higher level of schooling and wider reading—some advisors have some college education majoring in law, political science, communication, or philosophy—they can also help leaders to wrap their actions in certain theories or authorities in order to interpret events or justify them before their members, the authorities, or public opinion. That is why every leader tries to keep advisors with experience as city officials, road administration deputies, journalists, TV reporters, or intellectuals.

Even though all members with a place in the power structure of the organization earn their support through trust, for *delegados* this is particularly the case. They are responsible for carrying out political functions like the delimitation of spaces for the peddlers to set out their merchandise, especially along the territorial borders of other organizations. They administer the internal security of the spread of territory in their charge; they keep loyalty among peddlers, and maintain loyalty towards the leader in the event of another delegate's effort at secession from the group. In addition, they take part alongside the leader in dealings with road administration deputies and the police. They are also responsible for collecting dues and quotas from peddlers, although they do not carry this out themselves. The organization collects quotas weekly in exchange for various services: a retailing spot, security, waste management, protection from police, contacts at the *Delegación*'s office, legal counsel when facing problems and, in the case of powerful organizations, the right to loans and lodging. It is difficult to know how much money is surrendered to the leader through delegates, and where exactly the money goes. This money pays the wages of the organization's employees (advisors, watchmen, chauffeurs, bodyguards, office boys, secretaries), as well as the police, the *Delegación*'s road administration deputies, and even political parties in order to pay for campaigns.

"*Chalanes*" are handymen who carry out specific tasks for leaders and delegates. They are everybody's surrogate. In some cases they transport and deliver the leader's merchandises for retail to the merchants. They pass messages on. They set canvases up as roofs and then dismantle them after use, run errands, and pay attention to whatever might be needed. *Chalanes* fill up the ranks at demonstrations and protests, and may become part of the leader's security teams.

"Tax collectors" have the responsibility of picking up quotas for the right of space. Weekly quotas for each peddler vary from one to the other depending on the size of the space they occupy and its location. The most expensive locations are those with the highest police intervention probabilities—those with the most dense pedestrian concentration, near government offices like *Palacio Nacional*, which houses part of the Mexican Income Revenue Service, the office charged with controlling smuggling activities. These retailing spots, in close proximity to Mexico City's main square (the *Zócalo*, or *Plaza de la Constitución*), flanked by *Palacio Nacional*, the city's government building, are the most expensive locations, along with spots on major avenues and much pedestrian circulation. In 2007, six blocks from the *Zócalo*, peddlers had to pay 60 pesos (US$5.50) as weekly quota for a 1.20 by 2 meter curb space. Payments can multiply several times over as the peddler's location approaches the *Zócalo*.

There are many peddlers from indigenous ethnic groups who wander the streets offering fresh drinks; they pay 10 or 20 pesos (US$1–2) per week as quota. They are the peddlers with the lowest income, 500 pesos (US$45) per week as of summer 2007. Leaders charge variable fees to peddlers, ranging from 10 to 60 pesos (US$1–6) and also ranging from daily to weekly payments in 2007, depending on where they are located. In return for payment, peddlers get to sell their products on the street. Quotas can rise notably for spots in corners, where more pedestrians cross and business is best, a reason for the leaders to often save corner spots to set up their own food, clothing, CDs/DVDs, or costume jewelry stands.

In the streets with the most pedestrian traffic, quotas can reach up to 50 pesos (US$5) a day or more. In the densest commercial zones, street space is seen almost as private property; peddlers keep it under their control for many years. Street peddlers even affirm that the right to occupy such spaces can even be sold for several hundred thousand pesos. One street peddler, for example, sold her spot on the street, and the money she received was enough to buy her own downtown apartment.

Finally, struggle for territory between rival organizations, defense of sales space against thieves, and protecting merchandise from possible confiscation by the police have led some merchant organizations to develop different surveillance and security teams referred to as *grupos de choque,* or "strike forces" in the street's jargon. They are some organizations' strong arm; they specialize in the exercise of violence. Large organizations have made use of these organized units to protect their zones borders from rival organizations' advances.

Relations with police and government

Peddlers and their organizations must pay off those who work for the government. Policemen receive money from peddlers and their leaders so as not to distinguish between legal and illegal activities. Other policemen receive money from leaders in exchange for enhanced security. Furthermore, leaders may demand of the authorities that the police leave their handguns behind and take up assault weapons to better inhibit robbers. Road administration deputies (*jefe de vía pública*)—government employees working for the *Delegación*'s administration—generally receive more money than policemen, because of their authority over the streets. Their main function is to regulate peddler sales space. Many of these deputies practice extortion; they "make agreements" with small organizations while in bigger peddler groups it is the leader who charges himself with administering the money. Deputies rely on helpers to collect the money thus avoiding being "burnt" by its touch.

The relationship between peddlers and the Federal District's government swings from tension to collaboration depending on the party and the authorities and their shifting policies. After the 1982 crisis, the legitimacy the PRI had managed to achieve through employment growth and social mobility started to erode. Downtown streets began filling with vendors, who in just two decades went from food to *fayuca* retail and finally to smuggling and pirating goods from China. During those years the leaders' power and defense of peddlers against removal by the police grew considerably.

Guillermina Rico never witnessed the triumph of the PRD in the Federal District, dying a year earlier. The operators of the new party tried to dismantle the earlier corporate networks, raising serious problems for PRI militant organizations. The two most important organizations—Guillermina Rico's, now in her daughter's and grandson's hands, and Alejandra Barrios'—began suffering pressure and persecution. Political operatives encouraged the emancipation of the *delegados* from big peddler organizations and maneuvered conflicts between them to take the main leaders out of the picture. Silvia Sánchez Rico lost a big part of the space controlled by her mother due to the secession of many of her *delegados*, and to Alejandra Barrios' territorial expansion. Later, she was put in jail for two years; she was freed with help from the PRI's leaders.

Conflict and confrontation between organizations have their source in the struggle for space, and happen mainly in their territory's borders or during competition for new locations—strategically located plots and buildings and plazas—assigned by the *Distrito Federal* (DF) authorities. Confrontations and power struggles may happen among leaders and organizations belonging to the same party. However, the most violent conflicts and confrontations are the ones that combine the struggle for space and power with political struggle against groups rival in space occupation and party affiliation. This confrontation is over disputed trading spaces. It was also a dispute between two opposing parties fighting, more generally, over the control of the street.

Repression against street peddlers has changed shape. Every peddler in the business for long can describe in detail police and anti-riot squad raids. They have had to run with their merchandise or leave it behind and lose it to the police in exchange for their freedom. When captured, peddlers may be held for 24 to 36 hours or even for weeks if they are known offenders. Mazahuas have particularly suffered violence, because added to the discrimination they undergo at school, hospitals, and the subway,[4] they are prosecuted for selling fruit in the street. Because of that legal offense they have been threatened, beaten, and incarcerated. The problem is worsened when they have small children with them and must defend family and merchandise. On some occasions police try to help them solve the problem; at other times police threaten them by telling them that their children will be taken away to orphanages.

Conclusion

Street peddling in Mexico City's historic center is the result of what is happening in a global and national context characterized by demographic, economic, social, technological, and political transformation. Some of those transformations are structural in nature while others relate to demographic changes and their impact on the labor market, which in turn depends on the capacity of an open-door economic model to create jobs. Thus, the informal sector, especially small-scale commerce, and migration to the United States remain as two sturdy levers for the model's "adjustment from below." Since the 1982 economic crisis, these changes have brought tension to the city center, where commercial, political, and cultural interests converge as it once was the economic heart of the country, and it still has an important symbolic significance.

Street commerce is a fundamental mechanism of globalization from below. In downtown Mexico City, like many other places in Mexico, street peddlers sell legal and illegal products as well as pirated and smuggled goods. In order to be able to do this in the symbolic heart of the Mexican capital, peddling needs thorough organization. While in the midst of the import substitution model all the merchants were grouped and disciplined through a few organizations, since the PRD's arrival in City Hall, the number of peddlers has grown and organizations and leadership have become fragmented. Half of the peddler organizations, including the bigger ones, are run by women. This shows their importance in such activities and indicates the family and social conditions they are under, with a strong single mother presence, adaptability when facing law enforcement, and organizations run through structures of matriarchy.

The rise of leaders and the peddlers they represent occurs in the context of three grand transformations: demographic shifts, crisis and abandonment of an economic model, and political transition. The country's and the capital's great demographic expansion and internal migration led thousands of families to search for employment alternatives through street commerce. The external debt crisis in 1982, switching the economic model to a neoliberal one, led to a significant increase of unemployment and underemployment. These factors increased the number of street peddlers in the cities. In addition, the PRD's mayoral victory in 1988 to an office having been held by the PRI for many decades, divided peddlers into different groups, and fragmented their organizations.

Street peddling has long been a part of Mexico City's history, but did not become a massive phenomenon until recently. Merchant groups are solidly organized and their formal structure has only limited hierarchical levels and a strong concentration of power in the leader. The leader is a hinge that links political, economic, and religious authorities with the poorer mass sectors of society: migrants, the unemployed, the underemployed, and anybody who may go into informal commerce. The leader arises from the necessity to organize and regulate urban space, and serves as a social agent defined by peddlers as capable of giving and taking retail spots on the street. Leaders perform social and welfare functions. Those from the biggest organizations open daycare centers, manage housing credits, use funds to create social help programs, and maintain child daycare centers with health and food services. Even leaders from small organizations aspire to building sport fields, gyms or schools.

There are several important attributes leaders must have in order for them to build power. First, they must have roots in the space they control in order to know its specificities, to be able to handle the weave and warp of the neighborhood's social fabric. They must be persistent, pitting their basic survival skills against adversity and the challenges common to street trade. Leaders must be capable of struggle—both symbolic and material—in order to defend their territory against rival organizations or local authorities. They must have a way with words, a resource they often turn to in order to negotiate and persuade members of their organization as well as to rouse followers. Leaders must also have highly developed entrepreneurial skills. In short, leaders must have the power to bind and regulate the world of "formality" with the world of "informality."

Leaders are at the top of the organization, but they rely on diverse forms of support from within: *consejeros* (advisors), *delegados* (delegates), *chalanes* (handymen), *charoleros* (fee collectors), and security personnel. They also benefit from outside support, primarily police and road administration deputies. Interaction between street peddlers and the officials from *Delegación Cuauhtémoc* shifts from tension to collaboration and back depending on the party and the authorities in power. It is incontrovertible that street commerce has to be regulated by the state; merchants themselves ask for regulation due to the implacable competition brought by more and more merchants to the streets. But for any regulatory measures to succeed, they must be supported by peddlers, the fundamental local actors of globalization from below.

Notes

1 *Maquila* refers to an industrial subcontracting system transnationally divided. The capital-intensive part is produced in the United States and the labor-intensive part is in Mexico because of the low cost of the labor force. The most important *maquila* activities are in producing garments, auto parts, and electronics.
2 See Cross (1998) for a discussion of the first massive street merchant relocation in the twentieth century, during Ernesto P. Uruchurtu's terms as city mayor (1952–1966), during which he tried to eradicate street peddling. The second merchant relocation was carried out by Manuel Camacho Solís during Carlos Salinas de Gortari's term as president (1988–1994). The last relocation program, which removed all street merchants from "Perimeter A" of Mexico City's historic center, was on October 12, 2007.
3 The import substitution model, also referred to as "development from within," was the dominant policy in Mexico from the end of World War II until the external debt crisis in 1982. It consisted of protecting the nation's industries from outside competition through tax barriers and import permits. After 1982, it was replaced by a policy more open to outside competition and external trade.
4 The indigenous group, the Mazahuas, are the biggest ethnic minority in the State of Mexico, one of Mexico City's neighboring states. Many of them migrated in search of work as fruit or handcrafts merchants in the streets, or work as bricklayers or as domestic servants. They suffer from much discrimination. For example, at school, some kids mock Mazahua children because they speak another language and sometimes do not speak Spanish correctly. In administrative offices, whites are often served before Mazahuas. In the subway, it is common practice for young people to yield their seat to the elderly, or for men to yield their seat to women but this rarely happens when the ones standing are indigenous Mexicans.

References

Alarcón, S. (2008) *El tianguis global* [The Global Street Market], México: Universidad Iberoamericana.

Alba, C. and P. Labazée (2007) "Acteurs économiques et enjeux politiques dans le centre historique de Mexico. Entrepreneurs et ambulants dans la controverse post-électorale" [Economic Actors and Political Challenges in Mexico City's Historic Center: Entrepreneurs and Street Vendors in the Post-Electoral Controversy], *Problèmes d'Amérique Latine* 64: 33–49.

Alba Vega, C. and D. Kruijt (eds) (1994) *The Convenience of the Minuscule: Informality and Micro-enterprise in Latin America*, Latin America Series 3: Amsterdam: Thela Publishers.

Alba Villalever, C. E. (2008) "Piratería: la economía política en Tepito, México" [Piracy: The Political Economy of Tepito, Mexico], Bachelor's Degree Thesis in History, Faculty of Philosophy and Letters, National Autonomous University of Mexico.

Austin, R. (1994) "'An Honest Living': Street Vendors, Municipal Regulation, and the Black Public Sphere," *The Yale Law Journal*, 103(8): 2119–31.

Barbosa Cruz, M. (2008) *El trabajo en las calles: subsistencia y negociación política en la ciudad de México a comienzos del siglo XX* [Work in the Streets: Subsistence and Political Negotiation in Mexico City in the Beginning of the 20th Century], México, DF: El Colegio de México, Centro de Estudios Históricos/Universidad Autónoma Metropolitana, Unidad Cuajimalpa.

Cámara Nacional de Comercio México (1987) *El comercio ambulante en la ciudad de México* [Street Peddling in Mexico City], Mexico: National Chamber of Commerce.

Cross, J. (1998) *Informal Politics: Street Vendors and the State in Mexico City*, Stanford: Stanford University Press.

Dillon, S. (1996) "Guillermina Rico, Boss of Mexico Vendors, 63," *The New York Times,* September, 6.

Escobedo Lastiri, A. (2006) *Economía y política ambulantes: el comercio popular en las calles del centro histórico de la ciudad de México* [Street Economy and Politics: People's Commerce in Mexico City's Center Streets], Bachelor's Degree Thesis in International Relations, El Colegio de México, Centro de Estudios Internacionales.

Esquivel, E. (ed.) (2008) *La república informal: el ambulantaje en la Ciudad de México* [The Informal Republic: Street Vendors in Mexico City], Mexico, DF: Tecnológico de Monterrey/M.A. Porrúa.

Mathews, G. (2011) *Ghetto at the Center of the World: Chungking Mansions, Hong Kong*, Chicago: University of Chicago Press.

Monnet, J. and J. Bonnafé (eds) (2005). Seminario "El Ambulantaje en la Ciudad de México: investigaciones recientes" [Seminar: Street vendors in Mexico City], Mexico DF: Universidad Nacional Autónoma de México, Coordinación de Humanidades, Programa Universitario de Estudios sobre la Ciudad/Centro Francés de Estudios Mexicanos y Centroamericanos.

Nadima, S. (2004). "Prácticas desleales e ilegales de comercio internacional en las industrias de textiles y prendas de vestir en México" [Fraudalent practices and illegal international commerce in textiles and garments in Mexico], in I. Rueda Peiros, N. Simón, M. L. González, eds, *La industria de la confección en México y China ante la globalización* [The Garment Industry in Mexico and China confronts globalization] Mexico: UNAM-Porrúa.

Portes, A., L. Guarnizo, and P. Landolt (eds) (2003) *La globalización desde abajo: Transnacionalismo inmigrante y desarrollo, la experiencia de Estados Unidos y América Latina, México* [Globalization from Below: Immigrant Transnationalism and Development, the Experience of the United States and Latin America], Mexico: FLACSO/Miguel Ángel Porrúa.

Posada García, M. (2007) "México, cuarto lugar mundial en venta de piratería y contrabando" [Mexico, fourth place worldwide in piracy and smuggling], *La Jornada*, July 4.

Ribeiro, G. L. (2007) "El sistema mundial no hegemónico y la globalización popular" [The Non-Hegemonic World System and Economic Globalization from Below], *Série Antropología* 410.

Salmon, Kurt y Asociados (KSA) (2002) *El mercado mexicano de ropa* [The Mexican Clothing Market], Mexico: KSA-Canainvest.

Tarrius, A. (2002) *La mondialisation par le bas. Les nouveaux nomades de l'économie souterraine* [Globalization from Below: The New Nomads and the Underground Economy], Paris: Éditions Baland.

Tokman, V. E. (2007) *Informalidad, inseguridad y cohesión social en América Latina* [Informality, Insecurity and Social Cohesion in Latin America], Santiago, Chile, Naciones Unidas, Comisión Económica para América Latina y el Caribe, División de Desarrollo Social, Serie Políticas sociales 130.

CONCLUSION

Globalization from below and the non-hegemonic world-system

Gustavo Lins Ribeiro

Copies, illegality, and globalization from below

All kinds of gadgets, unauthorized copies of global brands, and copyrighted material may be seen for sale in stalls in street markets or offered by hawkers on sidewalks almost anywhere. Entrepreneurs, lawyers, development agencies, and law enforcement agents blame "piracy" for some of the worst current social and economic evils. Intellectual property rights and the capacity of tax enforcement are major preoccupations of private and state institutions eager to control the wealth generated by systems of commodity production and distribution. It is impossible to think of our times without considering these issues. This book goes to the heart of one of the world's most contemporary pressing problems.

There are millions of people, all over the globe, who are directly or indirectly involved with the activities that we discuss in this volume as globalization from below.[1] They are producers, sellers or consumers of commodities that flow within the circuits of this kind of global economy. The markets, flows, and trade networks that are part of globalization from below make up what I call the non-hegemonic world-system, simply because it is not the dominant form of globalization seeking to mold us all in its image, but rather an alternative to this, following different patterns and rules. Its activities are usually considered to be illegal; much of the merchandise sold there is called "pirate goods," counterfeits by the establishment. From the point of view of the powerful, such activities are illegitimate and must be confronted in the name of legality. Some scholars (Naím 2005, for instance) stigmatize the actors involved in this kind of global trade as if all were criminal. Views such as these tend to obliterate the visible presence of men and women who are workers on the fringes of the legal and illegal worlds, stretching the limits between them and taking advantage of the prevailing ambiguous positions and viewpoints about globalization from below and the non-hegemonic world-system. More often than not, the capacity to classify such activities as illegal is based on power differences between the actors involved. In the end, there is no moral monopoly of honesty by any social segment, and relationships between what is legal and illegal are complex and often blurred as Heyman and Smart (1999) show and many chapters of this book illustrate.

The centrality of the protection of intellectual property rights to contemporary capitalist reproduction has turned it into a major point of contention. Globalization has meant the increase of fragmented global production spaces, of global commodity chains and of global trade, deepening old international economic conflicts and creating new ones. However, nation-states are where laws are made and, more importantly, enforced. To deal with an increasingly intertwined and complicated international situation, different kinds of multilateral institutions and new regulations have emerged; thus the creation, for instance, of the World Trade Organization in 1994 and its growing importance in global governance. Concurrently, the hegemony of electronic/computer capitalism, in the last three decades, has unleashed new forces and capacities, and generated crucial demands on economic actors. The internet and other digital technologies brought about new capabilities and challenges to normative systems, especially regarding the control of copyrights and the ability that individuals almost everywhere have to produce copies that are increasingly perfect, veritable simulacra. In such context, it is not surprising that the unauthorized reproduction of any product has become a major issue and linked to what has been called "illicit global trade" (Naím 2005).

Copying desired commodities is not a new historical phenomenon. Coins, for instance, have been falsified since ancient times. Copying luxury foreign goods has been central to the Chinese economy at least since the nineteenth century (Pinheiro-Machado 2011). There certainly are many reasons for the current usage of the term "piracy" to classify and stigmatize the production and distribution of unauthorized copies, but I would like to stress the ambiguity associated with the term. Pirates are part of the Western imaginary as legendary historic figures, sometimes seen in a romantic, adventurous vein, other times in a cloud of violence, cruelty, and lawlessness. Piracy can trigger meanings that place all contemporary social agents involved in the matter (producers, traders, consumers, private and state agents) in a semantic field full of ambiguities since, although these goods are viewed by the authorities as illegal, they are sold in open public spaces. Is this kind of trade good or bad? Is it licit or illicit?

To deal with this ambiguity, Abraham and Schendel (2005) coined the notion "(il)licit" after tackling the difficulties of finding universal solutions for the contradictions existing between the terms "legal/illegal" and "licit/illicit." These authors are interested in the interrelations between the licit and the illegal that create a "third space" in which the (il)licit means activities that are "legally banned but socially sanctioned and protected" (Abraham and Schendel 2005: 22). The (il)licit characterizes globalization from below. This is the reason why unauthorized copies can be sold in the open air during daytime in busy streets and in crowded street markets while drugs cannot.

The activities involved in the non-hegemonic world-system are usually considered as destructive and dangerous to national and global developmental goals and policies (Naím 2005). They represent to the economic and political establishment a great challenge. Shepherd and Bandyopadhyay describe in their chapters some of the conflicting relations between actors operating within the circuits of the non-hegemonic world-system and the political and economic establishment of Washington DC and Calcutta. In the next section, I further explore the non-hegemonic world-system and its relation to globalization from below.

Globalization from below and the non-hegemonic world-system

Globalization from below provides access to flows of global wealth that otherwise would not reach the more vulnerable ranks of any society. It may open an avenue for upward mobility or offer the possibility of survival in national and global economies that are not capable of providing full employment for all citizens. Globalization from below is structured by flows of people, goods, information, and capital among different production centers and marketplaces which, in turn, are the nodes of the non-hegemonic world-system.

This volume is based on field research conducted in some of the central cities in the world: Cairo, Calcutta, Hong Kong, Mexico City, São Paulo, Shenzhen, Washington. It also covers some of the busiest border zones of the globe such as El Paso (US)/Ciudad Juárez (Mexico), Ciudad del Este (Paraguay)/Foz do Iguaçu (Brazil), Hong Kong/Shenzhen (China) and the Bedouin village of Salloum on the Egyptian/Libyan border. The authors provide a broad and detailed vision of a kind of globalization that traditionally has been seen through negative lenses such as those implied by labels such as "the shadow economy" and "the underground economy." This volume could well be thought of as a set of studies of the "global informal economy," an option that would certainly be in tune with an established and theoretically sophisticated body of literature. But the term "the global informal economy" obscures an essential distinction that the expression "from below" allows us to make clear: the main difference between globalization "from below" and "from above" is a power difference.

In saying that we are studying globalization from below, we are stating that there is a standpoint that is privileged in our analysis. In the social sciences, we know that perspective is crucial for the understanding of social reality and its different implications. Below and above are metaphors of unequal relationships that exist in mutual relations of conflict, cooperation, and contradiction. In consequence, globalization from below cannot be seen as separate from any other kind of globalization, just as the idea of a "non-hegemonic world-system" cannot be seen as separate from the idea of a "hegemonic world-system." The research and theoretical challenge is to understand the characteristics of each of these analytical categories, in all their entanglements, reciprocal reinforcements, and contradictions. The fact that this volume is dedicated to the analysis of globalization from below does not mean that its authors ignore the structuring power of globalization from above; indeed, every chapter in this book portrays the overwhelming power of globalization from above. Globalization "from below" provides a perspectival gaze, a subject position, while "non-hegemonic" provides a clear relational and systemic frame of reference. These double lenses are not innocuous, they have political implications since they openly refer to subaltern positions in social and political systems.

The notion of a "non-hegemonic world-system" calls attention to the fact that globalization from below needs to be understood as a system of global reach, as an interconnected whole. I am appropriating here some of the connotations of Wallerstein's (1974) world-system concept. But I am not so much interested in the discussion on the relationships between centers and peripheries, perhaps the most criticized angle of the Wallersteinean approach. I am much more interested in his consideration (Wallerstein 2006: 16–17) that the world-system is not a system of the entire world but a system that is a world, a space–time zone that traverses several political and cultural units, an integrated zone of activities and institutions ruled by certain systemic rules. Abraham and Schendel's (2005: 15–17) discussion of commodity chains (paths traveled by goods, from production to consumption) and regulatory spaces (zones within which specific state or social norms or rules are dominant) is equally central to understanding this systemic transnational quality. Commodity production, circulation, and consumption may occur in circumscribed spaces or traverse different regulatory spaces. In this way, some commodities that flow within the circuitries of economic globalization from below traverse certain regulatory spaces and change from legal to illegal status or vice-versa. For instance, bottles of Scotch may be legally produced, legally exported to a country and illegally imported into another. For Abraham and Schendel (2005: 17) "what determines legality and illegality at different points of the commodity chain is the particular regulatory scale the object finds itself in." This is why it is important to identify "the origin of regulatory authority" and, in consequence, "to distinguish between political (legal and illegal) and social (licit and illicit) origins of regulatory authority."

The "non-hegemonic world-system" contrasts with the hegemonic world-system which reflects the rationales and interests of the economic and political establishment.[2] I use "non-hegemonic" as an adjective to call the attention to the main difference between the two systems: the unequal access to economic, fiscal, and political state controlling power. As we know, states and major corporations everywhere view activities within the non-hegemonic world-system as illegal, a danger to national and global economies. These activities are often treated as a police matter. However, the two systems keep complex and deep relationships of complementarity. As Bandyopadhyay indicates in chapter 10, these are not parallel universes but a relationship whose borderlines are multifarious and imprecise. They may have contradictory interests but are not necessarily antagonistic to each other. In reality, those who operate within the non-hegemonic world-system do not intend to destroy capitalism (this is why I call it non-hegemonic instead of counter- or anti-hegemonic); quite the contrary, they want to benefit from it. The same can be said of many who operate within the hegemonic system, who really do not want to destroy the non-hegemonic system, since many of their transactions may be made through it in order to avoid taxation, to launder money, to practice illegal capital flight or primitive accumulation, for instance. The hegemonic system reflects the institutional logics of power holders operating within state apparatuses and private firms. In recent decades, the hegemonic world-system has been dominated by the interests of neoliberal capitalist globalization. Agents in the hegemonic system keep close relations to state power and manage to generate and keep the appearance, to society as a whole, that they hold a monopoly of legality and legitimacy in economic transactions, even when they are involved in illegal activities. Ports illustrate perfectly this last contention. As noted in the introduction, in the most organized and operationally capable harbors, only 5 percent of the containers are really inspected (Nordstrom 2007: 118). As Nordstrom notes:

> The media and popular culture focus on shadowy criminal organizations as the primary smugglers, but in fact legitimate businesses and multinational corporations are the biggest offenders. Underdeclaring and misrepresenting the goods they ship are basic tools of the trade.
>
> *(Nordstrom 2007: 119–20)*

The non-hegemonic world-system is structured by diverse segments and networks that congeal in a pyramidal fashion. At the top there are money-laundering schemes, mafia-like activities, all sorts of corruption. Indeed, the higher one goes in the pyramid, the more likely one will find fully criminal activities rather than (il)licit ones, as discussed above. In the circuits of globalization from below wholesalers are usually involved in illegal activities, as Aguiar, Milgram, and Telles have shown in their chapters. However powerful and elitist many of the agents involved in the parallel global economy may be, they cannot act on their own. There is a massive and differentiated involvement of poor people in the lower segments of this pyramidal structure. Networking and brokerage cement this global system. The activities at the bottom of the pyramid are what make up real economic globalization from below. This book is more interested in this segment of the non-hegemonic economic globalization than in its upper echelons.

Two basic globalization processes make up the non-hegemonic world-system. First, there is the "global illegal economy," coinciding with what is called global organized crime. Second, there is the "global (il)licit economy," coinciding with what this volume studies as globalization from below. Their frontiers are not clear. In reality, they are processes that may intertwine, feed on each other, and keep hierarchical relations. For instance, in spite of the fact that globalization from below is, from the perspective of the state, characterized as contraband, it is quite different if we consider the so-called "ant contraband" on the border of Argentina and Paraguay (Schiavoni 1993), between Hong Kong and the Philippines (Milgram, chapter 7) and between the US and Mexico (Gauthier, chapter 8) or great smuggling schemes controlled by organized gangs. Rather than using general and indistinct categories, it is more productive to see that one set of social processes belongs to the global (il)licit economy, another to the global illegal economy—these are clearly not the same.

The importance of social networks and networking in this world is widely presented in this book's chapters. Heyman and Smart (1999: 17) provide a definition of "illegal network" useful to think about in terms of the global illegal economy: "an ordered web of people centered on an illegal activity." Such networks imply but not necessarily require "an alternative social world to the formal, legal state." They are vital for illegal practices since they rest on "the human capacity for mutuality, trust and exchange in relationships." Illegal social networks engage in their illegal practices within a hierarchical structure in which central planning, private plotting, and the use of illegitimate violence prevail as fundamental factors of economic regulation (see Sousa 2004 on the importance of violence in illegal economic activities). On the other hand, within the global (il)licit economy, there are social networks operating in a decentralized horizontal way based on trust; these networks are often made up of domestic groups in search of economic niches where they can explore commercial activities that are seen as (il)licit. Violence is not the primary means of controlling this economic activity. These social networks engage in practices within informal systems previously constructed by diasporas and migratory networks (Lyra 2005) or typical grassroots economic forms (such as street fairs and their associated market systems). Not surprisingly, some of the largest diasporas—the Chinese and Lebanese ones, for instance—are greatly involved in the flows of people, commodities, and information within the non-hegemonic world-system (see Shepherd's and Rabossi's chapters for their discussions of the Chinese diaspora).

Several chapters of the book show that retailers, peddlers, hawkers and "ant traders" largely ignore the origins of the merchandise they sell; they either do not know or do not want to know who is involved in the networks that make available the goods they sell. Ignorance of their activities' criminal ramifications is important to reinforce these social actor's self-perception as workers and as citizens (as opposed to criminals), struggling for the survival and hope of prosperity for their families.

The many circuits of globalization from below are animated by thousands of social networks that are in pendular movements of variable scale among different nodes of the non-hegemonic world-system (see the chapters by Mathews, Pliez, and Shepherd describing, using their own metaphors, some of these pendulums). In Brazil, "trader-tourists" who make these connections are called *sacoleiros*, literally "baggers," a reference to the many huge shopping bags they carry back to their hometowns, full of gadgets and unauthorized copies which they buy in major nodes of the non-hegemonic world-system in South America, such as Ciudad del Este in Paraguay, or the 25th of March street in São Paulo (see Rabossi and Telles' chapters in this book). This area of São Paulo plays a central role in the redistribution of goods to thousands of Brazilian trader-tourists, and has functioned as an alternative marketplace whenever control on the Brazilian/Paraguayan border intensifies. There are other nodes of the non-hegemonic world-system in major Brazilian cities such as Rio de Janeiro, Belo Horizonte, Brasília and Porto Alegre. Street fairs and vendors can be found in many other cities and towns, making up a system of distribution that may reach even small localities. In Mexico, "baggers" are called *fayuqueros*, people who trade with *fayuca*, contraband in Mexican Spanish, in such key nodes of the non-hegemonic world-system as Tepito, in downtown Mexico (see Alba's chapter and Alarcón 2008), in Guadalajara or in Ciudad Juárez (see Aguiar's and Gauthier's chapters).

Other important marketplaces in Latin America include, in different Colombian cities, the so-called San Andresito markets (a reference to the Caribbean island and free port of San Andres). In the US, New York's Chinatown is a major node of the non-hegemonic world-system and Chinese migrants of the Los Angeles Fashion District are widely responsible for supplying Tepito in Mexico City with all kinds of imports (Alarcón 2008).

Beyond the Americas, Dubai is certainly a major node of the system in the Middle East. There are also the African and Muslim traders described by Yang in the marketplaces of Giangzhou, as well as the Filipina women Milgram presents in Hong Kong, and Chungking Mansions as described by Mathews. Pliez vividly describes markets in Egypt, and Bandyopadhyay describes, in passing, those in Calcutta; and there are other major market nodes not described in this book, such as the major trading center of Onitsha in southern Nigeria. These nodes and the people in them provide examples of economic practices that are prevalent worldwide (on Bulgarian trader-tourists see Konstantinov 1996; on African–European connections see MacGaffey and Bazenguissa-Ganga 2000; on the importance of this global industry, especially in East Asia, see Chang 2004; on the flows of unauthorized copies between China, Paraguay, and Brazil, see Pinheiro-Machado 2011; see also Peraldi 2002, Tarrius 2002, and Schendel and Abraham 2005).

The relationships between the non-hegemonic world-system and the hegemonic world-system can also be considered by looking at the production side. The main production centers of the system are located in Asia, in Korea, Thailand, Singapore, and Taiwan, but especially today in southern China, as was emphasized in the introduction, in the province of Guangdong that has been for centuries a gateway to world trade and to the Chinese diaspora. This does not mean that other areas in China are unimportant for the non-hegemonic system. Pliez explores in his chapter the pivotal role played by Yiwu as another node located in the province of Zhejiang, two hours south of Shanghai. But Guangdong and its capital, Guangzhou (Canton), has long been a point of contact with the West. The Portuguese colonized Macao from 1557 to 1999 and, in 1841, also on the Pearl River delta, Hong Kong was founded as an entrepôt of the British Empire, and returned to China in 1997. Today, Macao and Hong Kong are Special Administrative Regions of the People's Republic of China in accordance with the model "one country, two systems." As a consequence of its intermediate role between Western and Eastern trade, there developed in Guangdong, at least since the nineteenth century, a sophisticated industry of copying dedicated to replicating Chinese luxury goods and imported Western commodities (Pinheiro-Machado 2011). But more important in understanding the role of this area as the manufacturing core of the non-hegemonic world-system has been the extraordinary development, in mainland China, of Shenzhen which, in 1980, became the first Special Economic Zone. Located a few kilometers from Hong Kong, in China's most dynamic economic region, the Pearl River delta, Shenzhen has become, over the past 15 years, the heart of the system of production of the commodities that flow within the circuits of grassroots globalization. Currently, the production of these commodities is based on the exploitation of a large migrant labor force, largely made up of recently proletarized peasant women, who live and work in the many small factories in Guangdong, many of them owned by former workers who, with the help of *guanxi* (relations), experienced upward social mobility (Pinheiro-Machado 2011; Lee 1998; Pun 2005).

Hong Kong and Guangdong have developed complementary relations over time. Smart and Smart in chapter 6 explore this complementarity, focusing on how economic globalization from below is entangled with the Chinese petty capitalists entrepreneurship and the investments they made at different junctures both in Guangdong and in Hong Kong. The former British colony is also a doorway for the entrance of traders from all over the world, especially from Asia, Africa, and the Middle East. Many of these traders can shop in what may be the most globalized building of the non-hegemonic world-system, Chungking Mansions, in Hong Kong, as Mathews describes in chapter 4. They increasingly go to mainland China, to Shenzhen and Guangzhou, with Chinese visas acquired in Hong Kong; they also fly directly into Guangzhou. The African presence in Guangzhou is the subject of Yang's chapter 9. Little Africa is an ethnic enclave created by the flows of economic globalization from below. In many African shops, African trader-tourists may engage in commercial transactions in Igbo, French, and Arabic, as well as in Mandarin Chinese. Indeed, economic globalization from below is heavily impacting the ethnic segmentation of different Chinese cities and creating new heterodox diasporas. Pliez describes in chapter 1 an Arab community in Yiwu with Algerian, Egyptian, Iraqi, and Lebanese restaurants where Arab trader-tourists can find halal food conforming to Muslim precepts. The Arab presence strengthens the links with Chinese Muslims.

But it is the Chinese diaspora, the largest in the world, that plays the most fundamental role in globalization from below, and, to a large extent, is its mainstay. It is not a coincidence that Chinese migrants, mostly Cantonese migrants, are increasingly associated with the non-hegemonic world-system. Their presence is highly visible in Ciudad del Este, as Rabossi shows in chapter 3, and on the 25th of March street in São Paulo, as discussed by Telles in chapter 5. In fact, the history of this area in São Paulo illustrates some central dynamics of the system as a whole. The 25th of March street neighborhood has been, since the last decades of the nineteenth century, characterized by the presence of Lebanese and Syrian migrants (Nascimento 2006). In the last years of the twentieth century, they started to be displaced by Koreans and especially by Chinese. The Syrian-Lebanese diaspora may be the second most important network of social actors for the non-hegemonic world-system (although Indians have also been important in Africa and elsewhere). Generations of migrants have been weaving this social fabric tightly, based on networks of kin and friends. The Syrian-Lebanese have been central to the growth of the 25th of March street in São Paulo where they were responsible for the establishment of many international trading practices and connections as well as for the transformation of the area into an ethnic urban territory (Nascimento 2006).

The same is true for the downtown area of Rio de Janeiro known as Saara (Cunha 2005). Since the late 1950s, thousands of people of Arab descent have also become main actors of the Ciudad del Este/Foz do Iguaçu transfrontier (Arruda 2007). They were equally crucial for the establishment of a network of San Andrecitos, the nodes of the non-hegemonic world-system in Colombia. In some situations, such as on the

25th of March street, in Ciudad del Este/Foz do Iguaçu and in the Saara area in Rio, recent Chinese arrivals are displacing Lebanese migrants, a fact that generates new ethnic segmentations and creates new potential interethnic conflicts. In other situations, such as those in the so-called Paraguayan Fairs in Brasilia (Rocha 2007) and in Caruaru (the latter in the state of Pernambuco, Brazil; see Silva 2008) or in Tepito, Mexico City, a growing Chinese presence is noticeable. In fact, globalization from below may have become the strongest stimulus to Chinese migration in Brazil and in other Latin American countries such as Argentina and Mexico, as well as on other continents, such as Africa (Alden 2007). Diasporas of the scope of the Chinese, Lebanese, and Indian ones provide a highly organic basis for the development of transnational activities. In a world where there is a weak capacity of law enforcement, migratory networks may provide trust and predictability (see, among other chapters in this volume, Smart and Smart's chapter 6), implicit, for instance, in the Chinese notion of *guanxi,* or social connections (Pinheiro-Machado 2011; Kipnis 1997).

Theoretical considerations

As previously stated, different labels could be used to name what we study here. However, "globalization from below," albeit still having the hierarchical connotation of above/below, is meant to highlight the uncharted economic dynamics of globalization rather than the political dynamics of the anti/alter-globalization movement (see Ribeiro 2009), which, as has been noted in several chapters of this book, is the focus of most studies on globalization from below. However, it does not follow that politics is unimportant in understanding these economic phenomena, as the chapters by Alba and Telles indicate.

The study of the nodes of the non-hegemonic world-system can be subdivided into two major areas, those of transfrontier areas and of street markets. Both are well described in this book. Some of the most complex transfrontier social spaces (Jiménez Marcano 1996) and their flows are the subject of several chapters (by Gauthier, Rabossi, and Yang). Other chapter writers depict a few of the largest and most interesting markets of economic globalization from below (Alba, Bandyopadhyay, Mathews, and Telles). There are also the routes linking nodes on a global scale. Almost all the chapters in this volume consider their strategic importance. When Aguiar studies the market in Guadalajara (Mexico) in chapter 2, he must take into account the routes from the US and Mexican harbors that reach as far as South America. Pliez in chapter 1 is explicitly interested in the new Silk Road and Milgram in Philippine–Hong Kong flows. This work shows how important these routes are, how traders take advantage of previous migratory and commodity paths, how the latter can change over time in accordance with complex geopolitical and economic factors as well as according to the action of different controlling state actors. Corruption is endemic in the nodes and routes of the non-hegemonic world-system.

Research on the non-hegemonic world-system clearly shows that it is inseparable from the hegemonic system. Non-hegemonic and hegemonic processes thrive on each other. Indeed, non-hegemonic systems presuppose the existence of hegemonic ones. Such systems also entail the existence of brokerage practices that I call "connecting mechanisms." The latter are the processes through which these systems communicate with one another. In many examples in this book, politics is shown to be the channel most capable of creating flows between agents engaged in globalization from below and those representing long-established local, national, and global interests. There are other connecting mechanisms that clearly relate to economic interests. One example is the money laundering that occurs in transfrontier social spaces such as that of Foz do Iguaçu/Ciudad del Este, among other borders; another is the formal transnational financial instruments such as the many credit cards with which a shopper can buy anything in the largest nodes of the non-hegemonic world-system. The differences between hegemonic and non-hegemonic systems are blurred in the liminal situations where connecting mechanisms allow for the articulation of common political or economic interests of agents and brokers from both systems. Corruption is also a social practice that fosters interaction between both systems.

Non-hegemonic economic globalization processes are power fields that exist in relation to other established power fields that have the prerogative to normalize the activities involved, by setting the standards of what is and what is not legitimate. Alternative economic agents seek access to wealth and to the social, cultural, and political benefits arising from wealth. Since struggles between non-hegemonic agents and the hegemonic establishment are mainly power struggles, they often are mediated by state agents of various sorts. Police or city officials are clearly involved when activities occur in public spaces such as those of street vendors and markets (see the chapters by Aguiar, Alba, Bandyopadhyay, and Shepherd in this volume).

The convergence of large numbers of people is another characteristic of grassroots globalization. Here the more the merrier prevails. The multitudes involved in open air operations reveal the vast numbers of people who participate in this segment of globalization, and sometimes overwhelm the state structures deployed to manage the situation.

As we discussed in the introduction, the agents of globalization from below are not really aiming at constructing another world from that of globalization from above; they aim at becoming rich and powerful, just like those who consider them illegal smugglers or pirates. It is the rich and powerful who, through the control of state apparatuses and wider political structures, create a transgressive image of the workers and entrepreneurs of the non-hegemonic system. Without such an image, it would be impossible to control the activities of globalization from below, and they would proliferate far more than they actually do.

The construction of translocal systems, translocal cultures, and networking (such as those described in the chapters by Gauthier, Smart and Smart, and Yang, among others) is also a common characteristic of globalization from below. This reveals how "alter-native" transnational agents may disregard or bypass the normative and regulating power of nation-states and create ever more complex political and cultural units. Translocal political links are often studied under the rubric of transnational activism and global civil society. Transnational political cultures still need to be studied in more depth ethnographically. Several existing studies are on transnational elites, for instance, Hannerz's (2004) work on foreign correspondents or my own on World Bank ethnic diversity (Ribeiro 2002). Studies on transmigrants, such as those by Basch, Schiller, and Blanc (1994) reveal transnational agents' political and economic practices. Other works on migration and transnationalism also show how migrants upset existing boundaries and power structures creating translocal networks and cultures (Kearney 1996, and Sahlins 1997, for instance). But we still need a stronger focus on the transnational politics of globalization from below for this involves processes through which migratory labor and/or contemporary global nomads become involved as alternative transnational agents in order to get their share of global flows of wealth. Is their realpolitik the grassroot vision of global citizenship and of a truly borderless world?

Pirating capitalism: originals and copies

The literature on the informal economy has pointed out several motivations under-lying the competitive force of the economic activities we have discussed in this volume: tax evasion; the absence of controlling mechanisms in commercial transactions and services; the vulnerability of the workers involved in production and trade, and so on. But instead of these, I will now explore two major forces that currently boost globalization from below: the existence of global brands, and the capacity of making copies that are so close to the original in quality that it is increasingly difficult or irrelevant to identify differences between fake products and original ones. Of course it is not only copies of well-known luxury brands that are produced and traded within the non-hegemonic world-system. All kinds of regular goods and sometimes useless global gadgets are also copied. However, unauthorized copies of luxury products reveal, like no other commodities, what is behind the global craze for what is sometimes called "the China price."

To a large extent, the enormous profitability of "pirate" products is based on the copying of what Chang (2004) has called superlogos, i.e. brands that are highly desired and celebrated and which have become global symbols of privileged status (Gucci, Chanel, Calvin Klein, Louis Vuitton, Christian Dior, Versace, Armani, Ralph Lauren, Prada, Yves Saint Laurent, Fendi, Victor Hugo, LaCoste, Nike, Adidas, Rolex, Ray-Ban, Sony, and many others). The competitive edge of the production and distribution systems of fake superlogos is based on the exploitation of cheap labor (see Smart and Smart in this volume) as well as on the absence of an economy of excess associated with luxury goods. This economy of excess is apparent in fashion shows and parties, fancy stores, expensive publicity, and highly paid staff, all of which aim to create an atmosphere of opulence, with its extravagant display of luxury, which supposedly informs today's identity politics of distinction and status. Unauthorized copies are the cheapest gateway to a symbolic economy of appearance that is perceived by social actors as useful for identity manipulation. At the same time that copies allow millions to save money and consume goods they otherwise would not have access to, copies also enhance social actors' ability to manipulate their identity on their own behalf, and feel that they are in tune with globalized modern consumption canons.

The superlogo generates an exceptional surplus based on its symbolic value, on what it means as a status symbol for consumers. This exceptional surplus is added to a commodity through the maintenance of a monopoly, as incarnated in the superlogo. The largest corporations attempt to create and then manage superlogos in order to own exclusive niches in the market of global symbols of status, and to greatly increase their profits. The difference between the real value of a specific object and its symbolic surplus value is what creates the market for unauthorized superlogo copies, always sold at much cheaper prices than "the original." In sum, superlogos, fake or real, play a central role in today's symbolic economy of luxury, at a time when status distinction is confused with the capacity to purchase certain objects and with manipulating images that impart to consumers differentiated social identities.

The industry of unauthorized copies triggers a competition for the control of the extraordinary value superlogos add to commodities. However, the impact that copies have on the corporations who own the superlogos is not necessarily negative, as we saw in the introduction. Brazilian writer Mário de Andrade used to say that copies valorize the original. The more that consumers seek to buy copies of a product, the more valued will be the original, especially for a segment increasingly made up of *connaisseurs* who are capable of ascribing authenticity to objects/symbols that should be considered genuine and, therefore, the bearers of the most desired markers of social distinction.

In reality, copy quality is subdivided into at least three different categories. Third-rate copies are coarse imitations. They have, for instance, gross spelling mistakes of the names of the superlogos, often not in order to seek dubious legal protection by not being exactly like the original, but from incompetence. Second-rate copies are reasonable replicas; first-rate copies may be true simulacra, fakes that sometimes can only be detected by experts. The prices of these products vary according to the quality of the copies. It is commonly said that in Shenzhen there are factories that produce original goods during the daytime and unauthorized copies at night. It is true that many of the factories involved in the production of copies may also be subcontracted by corporations that own superlogos to manufacture genuine goods (Pinheiro-Machado 2011). In these cases, the only difference between the original and unauthorized copies would be the superlogo label. The increased quality of copies may well be what has attracted middle-class consumers to different marketplaces of the non-hegemonic world-system.

Copies of superlogos are losing market share as the main source of profits of the non-hegemonic world-system to pirated DVDs and software (see Karaganis 2011). This is linked to the current hegemony of electronic and computer capitalism and its internal flexibility, especially with its capacity to reproduce perfect copies. In the digital age, it is increasingly easy to copy music, movies, images, texts, and other copyright-protected material from the internet or from other sources. The changes that were introduced in recent years by the new technologies of reproduction are rapidly appropriated not only by teenagers in their bedrooms but also by people who are interested in making money in the streets and markets of the non-hegemonic world-system. The normative system that regulates the intellectual property rights of global superlogos and particularly of cultural goods is out of tune with current technological innovations that strengthen the capacities of individuals and networks to make copies. Since it cannot keep pace with this new dynamic nor with the multiple and often inventive appropriations made by millions of people throughout the world, the current normative system criminalizes and stigmatizes the vast creative and entrepreneurial energy located in different fragmented global spaces. It became, in short, a hindrance for the innovative and entrepreneurial forces it can neither control nor absorb. The non-hegemonic world-system thus becomes the outlet, no pun intended, for this repressed energy, the umbrella under which many of its forbidden operations may occur.

The term "piracy" reveals the extreme nature of the surplus added to a commodity by the ownership of a superlogo. Since capitalism is based on socially sanctioned appropriations of surpluses, by making this extraordinary surplus evident, "piracy" has a subversive potential that puts in danger a major force underneath capitalist reproduction. At the same time, piracy is positively related to contemporary capitalist growth since it is organic to its wider production and consumption needs, as well as to the fetishized (re)production of social identities and of distinction under the edge of electronic and computer capitalism.

The structural impulse given by current copying technologies as well as by today's communication and traveling capacities makes me think that globalization from below will continue to consolidate itself and to shrink the distances between the many nodes of the non-hegemonic world-system. In short, globalization from below will remain as a heterodox force creating alternative economic experiences. Economic and development experts will continue to classify it as the underground, obscure side of economy, but as all the chapters of this book have shown, it is indeed far more than that.

Notes

1 I have also called it "grassroots globalization" (Ribeiro 2006) and "non-hegemonic globalization" (2009). Mathews (2007, 2011) has called it "low-end globalization."
2 The concept of the non-hegemonic world-system fuses two concepts of Marxist political economy. I have already referred to the first, the capitalist world-system. The second is hegemony, inspired by Gramsci's work. I understand hegemony as the naturalized and silent exercise of power, the naturalization by different social groups and classes of the sanctioned modes of the reproduction of social life.

References

Abraham, I. and W. van Schendel (2005) "Introduction: The Making of Illicitness," in W. van Schendel and I. Abraham, eds, *Illicit Flows and Criminal Things*, Bloomington: Indiana University Press, 1–37.

Alarcón, S. (2008) *El tianguis global* [The Global Street Market], Mexico City: Universidad Iberoamericana.

Alden, C. (2007) *China in Africa*, London: Zed Books.

Arruda, A. M. T. (2007) *A presença Libanesa em Foz do Iguaçu (Brasil) e Ciudad del Este (Paraguai)* [The Lebanese Presence in Foz do Iguaçu, Brazil, and in Ciudad del Este, Paraguay], MA Thesis, Centro de Pesquisas e Pós-Graduação sobre as Américas, Universidade de Brasília.

Basch, L., N. G. Schiller, and C. S. Blanc (1994) *Nations Unbound: Transnational Projects, Postcolonial Predicaments and Deterritorialized Nation-States*, London: Routledge.

Chang, H. (2004) "Fake Logos, Fake Theory, Fake Globalization," *Inter-Asia Cultural Studies* (5)2: 222–36.

Cunha, N. V. (2005) *Libaneses & Chineses: Sucessão, conflito e disputa numa rua de comércio do Rio de Janeiro* [Lebanese and Chinese: Succession, Conflict and Disputes in a Trading Street in Rio de Janeiro], Paper presented at "Anthropology of the Mercosur," Montevideo, November 16–18.

Hannerz, U. (2004) *Foreign News: Exploring the World of Foreign Correspondents*, Chicago: University of Chicago Press.

Heyman, J. and A. Smart (1999) "States and Illegal Practices: An Overview," in J. Heyman, ed., *States and Illegal Practices*, Oxford: Berg, 1–24.

Jiménez Marcano, E. (1996) *La construcción de espacios sociales transfronterizos entre Santa Elena de Uairen (Venezuela) y Villa Pacaraima (Brasil)* [The Construction of Transfrontier Social Spaces between Santa Elena de Uairen, Venezuela, and Villa Pacaraima, Brazil], Doctoral Dissertation, joint PhD Program FLACSO/University of Brasilia in Comparative Latin American and Caribbean Studies.

Karaganis, J. (ed.) (2011) *Media Piracy in Emerging Economies*, New York: Social Science Research Council.

Kearney, M. (1996) *Reconceptualizing the Peasantry: Anthropology in Global Perspective*, Boulder: Westview Press.

Kipnis, A. (1997) *Producing Guanxi: Sentiment, Self, and Subculture in a North China Village*, Durham: Duke University Press.

Konstantinov, Y. (1996) "Patterns of Reinterpretation: Trader Tourism in the Balkans (Bulgaria) as a Picaresque Metaphorical Enactment of Post-Totalitarianism," *American Ethnologist* (23)4: 762–82.

Lee, C. K. (1998) *Gender and the South China Miracle: Two Worlds of Factory Women*, Berkeley: University of California Press.

Lyra, M. R. S. B. (2005) "Sulanca x muamba. Rede social que alimenta a migração de retorno" [Sulanca vs. Smuggled Goods. Social Networks that Feed Return Migration], *São Paulo em Perspectiva* (19)4: 144–54.

MacGaffey, J. and R. Bazenguissa-Ganga (2000) *Congo-Paris: Transnational Traders on the Margins of the Law*, Bloomington IN: International African Institute/James Currey/Indiana University Press.

Mathews, G. (2007) "Chungking Mansions: A Center of 'Low-End Globalization,'" *Ethnology* XLVI(2): 169–83.

——(2011) *Ghetto at the Center of the World: Chungking Mansions, Hong Kong*, Chicago: University of Chicago Press.

Naím, M. (2005) *Illicit: How Smugglers, Traffickers, and Copycats are Hijacking the Global Economy*, New York: Doubleday.

Nascimento, M. (2006) *A Rua 25 de Março e a imigração Sírio-Libanesa para São Paulo* [The 25th of March Street and Syrian-Lebanese Immigration to São Paulo], Undergraduate paper, Department of Anthropology, University of Brasilia.

Nordstrom, C. (2007) *Global Outlaws: Crime, Money, and Power in the Contemporary World*, Berkeley: University of California Press.

Peraldi, M. (2002) *Cabas et containers: Activités marchandes informelles et réseaux migrants transfrontaliers* [Shopping Bags and Containers: Informal Trade and Networks of Transfrontier Migrants], Marseille: Maisonneuve et Larose.

Pinheiro-Machado, R. (2011) *Made in China. (In)formalidade, pirataria e redes sociais na rota China-Paraguai-Brasil* [Made in China: (In)formality, Piracy and Social Networks in the China–Paraguai–Brazil Route], São Paulo: Hucitec/ANPOCS.

Pun, N. (2005) *Made in China: Women Factory Workers in a Global Workplace*, Durham: Duke University Press.

Ribeiro, G. L. (2002) "Diversidad étnica en el Planeta Banco: Cosmopolitismo y transnacionalismo en el Banco Mundial" [Ethnic Diversity within the Planet Bank: Cosmopolitanism and Transnationalism within the World Bank], *Nueva Sociedad* 178: 70–88.

——(2006) "Economic Globalization from Below," *Etnográfica* X(2): 233–49.

——(2009) "Non-Hegemonic Globalizations. Alter-native Transnational Processes and Agents," *Anthropological Theory* 9(3): 1–33.

Rocha, R. D. M. (2007) *Nem daqui, nem da China. Um estudo antropológico sobre identidades multifacetadas dos migrantes chineses na Feira dos Importados, Brasília, D.F.* ["You're not from Here, You're not from China": An Anthropological Study of the Multifaceted Identities of Chinese Migrants in the Imported Goods Market, Brasilia, DF]. Undergraduate paper, Department of Anthropology, University of Brasilia.

Sahlins, M. (1997) "O 'pessimismo sentimental' e a experiência etnográfica: porque a cultura não é um 'objeto' em via de extinção" ["Sentimental Pessimism"and the Ethnographic Experience: Why Culture is not an "Object" Facing Extinction], *Mana* 3(2): 103–50.

Schendel, W. van and I. Abraham (eds) (2005) *Illicit Flows and Criminal Things*, Bloomington: Indiana University Press.

Schiavoni, L. (1993) *Frágiles pasos, pesadas cargas. Las comerciantes fronterizas de Posadas-Encarnación* [Fragile Steps, Heavy Loads: The Border Traders of Posadas-Encarnación], Asunción/Posadas: Centro Paraguayo de Estudios Sociológicos/Editorial Universitaria Universidad Nacional de Misiones.

Silva, M. A. (2008) *Guanxi nos trópicos: um estudo sobre a diáspora Chinesa em Pernambuco* [Guanxi in the Tropics: A Study of the Chinese Diaspora in Pernambuco], MA Thesis, Federal University of Pernambuco, Recife.

Sousa, R. S. (2004) "Narcotráfico y economía ilícita: las redes del crimen organizado en Río de Janeiro" [Drug Traficking and Illicit Economy: The Organized Crime Networks in Rio de Janeiro], *Revista Mexicana de Sociologia* 66(1): 141–92.

Tarrius, A. (2002) *La mondialisation par le bas. Les nouveaux nomades de l'économie souterraine* [Globalization from Below: The New Nomads of the Underground Economy], Paris: Baland.

Wallerstein, I. (1974) *The Modern World-System. Vol. 1: Capitalist Agriculture and the Origins of the European World-Economy in the Sixteenth Century*, New York/London: Academic Press.

——(2006) *World-Systems Analysis*, Durham: Duke University Press.

INDEX

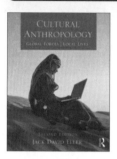